Xmas - '15

D0005711

The Unlikely Governor

Other Books by Robert Heller

International Trade, Prentice Hall, 1968, 2nd ed. 1973
Japanese ed. 1969 and 1973; German ed. 1975, 1992 and 1997;
Spanish ed. 1970 and 1983; Portuguese ed. 1978; Malay ed. 1982;

The Economic System, The Macmillan Co., 1972
Portuguese ed. 1977

International Monetary Economics, Prentice Hall, 1974
Japanese ed. 1974, Malay ed. 1982

Japanese Investments in the United States, 1974
With Emily E. Heller, Praeger Publishers

The Unlikely Governor

An American Immigrant's Journey
From the Ruins of Wartime Germany
To the Federal Reserve Board

Robert Heller

MAYBRIDGE PRESS

The Unlikely Governor
Copyright © Robert Heller 2015
Contact: www.robertheller.info

All rights reserved. Printed in the United States of America.
No part of this book may be reproduced or transmitted in any
form or by any means, electronic or mechanical, including
photocopying, recording, or by any information storage and
retrieval systems, except in brief extracts for the purpose of
review, without the written permission of the author.
All photos © Robert Heller, except as noted.

CATALOGING DATA:
The Unlikely Governor
By Robert Heller

Publisher's Cataloging-in-Publication data

Heller, Robert (Heinz Robert), 1940-.
    The Unlikely Governor : An American Immigrant's
Journey From the Ruins of Wartime Germany To the Federal
Reserve Board / Robert Heller.
    pages cm
    ISBN 978-0-9964390-2-2

1. Heller, Robert (Heinz Robert), 1940-. 2. Immigrants --
United States. 3. German Americans --Biography. 4. Board of
Governors of the Federal Reserve System (U.S.) --Biography.
5. Economists --Biography. 6. Corporate governance --United
States. I. Title.

HG2563 .H45 2015
332.1/1/092273 --dc23   pcngoeshere

Cover, interior design: Jim Shubin, www.bookalchemist.net

Cover photograph: My mother, Karoline Heller, took this
picture secretly from the second floor of our house in
Cologne. During the war, it was strictly prohibited to take
pictures of ruins or corpses. The Nazis called this "defeatism"
and the potential penalty was death.

Library of Congress Control Number: 2015910708
Printed in the United States of America

To My Children
Kimberly and Christopher
And Their Children

Contents

About this Book

These are my memoirs. It is the story of my life as I recall it. It contains the good, the bad and the ugly.

Readers may find different parts of this book of interest. The chapters on my childhood in Germany and World War II history offer a perspective different from many other books on that period in history. The experiences in coming to America and my college years at "Flunk Out U" and at Berkeley during the heyday of the "Free Speech Movement" were somewhat crazy and turbulent. Federal Reserve buffs will find the chapters on what went on behind closed doors at the Federal Reserve during the banking crisis and the battle against inflation revealing. The days at the helm of VISA, the "Chaordic Organization," were full of corporate intrigue and individual challenges. Finally, there are a few chapters on management, leadership and corporate boards that distill a lifetime of experiences. Readers may want to begin by reading the chapters most interesting to them personally. Hopefully, they will then be enticed to read the rest of the story as well.

This book recounts numerous episodes and events that occurred many decades ago. My memory of these sometimes traumatic events is still vivid and lucid. This is in contrast to my short-term memory, when I sometimes have trouble recalling what I ate for lunch last week. It has been said that memories are like Swiss cheese: there are many holes in the cheese, but the rest is delicious!

I am very indebted to the over one hundred friends and colleagues that reviewed various events and episodes described in this book. They offered encouragement and validation, as well as numerous suggestions for improvement. To preserve their anonymity and to respect their privacy, I have decided not to mention their names. They know who they are and I am most grateful to them.

Particular gratitude goes to my loyal wife Emily, who read the entire manuscript and eliminated any inappropriate and offensive observations, exhortations and comments.

Jim Shubin expertly designed the book cover and saw the book through production.

Like all memories, mine is flawed at times. Other participants in the episodes described in this book may have different recollections. I am sorry for any inaccuracies, but welcome comments and corrections, so that I will be able to report the events more accurately in future editions. I am hopeful that I will be blessed with a long life, so that there will be further chapters to come as well as new and improved editions of this book!

Robert Heller
Belvedere, California

PART I

Wartime in Germany

Disasters have followed me around for all my life. Fortunately, there was always a moment of redemption as well. I was able to achieve unexpected successes in academia, business and governmental service.

I was born a few months after the beginning of World War II, the greatest disaster in world history. Over 60 million people perished in that global conflict that left most of Europe and much of Asia in ruins.

My family lived in Cologne, Germany, one of the most heavily bombed cities in the entire war. At the end of the war, only about 5 percent of the original population was still living in the city and 95 percent of all buildings were damaged or totally destroyed.

The following chapters chronicle what life was like in the cellars of Cologne and in the small towns to which we moved to escape the bombings. At the end of the war, we even lived in an old cave.

In contrast, my father, who served throughout the war in the German army, had a much more pleasant life. He lived usually in safe and peaceful surroundings, was frequently on home leave and — as far as I can tell — never fired a single shot, until he was taken prisoner towards the end of the war.

Unfortunately, my mother passed away just after the end of the war at the age of 35 as a result of one of the epidemics that raged in Germany at that time.

In the immediate post-war period I attended pretty chaotic schools and almost flunked out of high school, but eventually made it and graduated near the top of my class, garnering a prize for editing the best school newspaper along the way.

Surviving in the Cellar

Chairman Paul Volcker adjourned the official meeting of the Federal Open Market Committee of the Federal Reserve Board. It was August 19, 1986 and it was my inaugural meeting as a Governor of the Federal Reserve. I had taken the Oath of Office in the adjoining private office of the Chairman just before the actual meeting started.

It was my first time in the ornate boardroom of the Federal Reserve. I stood up from my elegantly upholstered chair at the large oval conference table and strolled over to the head of the table, where Volcker was seated. At that moment, I noticed a metal plaque mounted next to the enormous fireplace dominating the end of the boardroom.

I stepped closer and deciphered the embossed metal inscription. Under a depiction of the American and British flags, the plaque read:

"The Combined Chiefs of Staff held meetings in this Board Room during May of 1943. These meetings were during the TRIDENT Conference between President Roosevelt and Prime Minister Churchill.

The decisions reached in the Board Room of the Federal Reserve Building during 1942 and 1943 set the pattern for allied collaboration and the successful prosecution of World War II."

I started to think back in time. 1943? I was a small child in Germany and that was the year that my mother and I spent many days and nights in the cellar of my grandparents' house hiding from the bombers that targeted Cologne on a regular basis.

What had life been like for me over forty years ago, when I was living in Germany, an enemy country to the United States? And what had happened in the intervening years after I experienced the end of the war while hiding with my mother in a limestone cave? It had been an unusual journey from wartime Germany to my present position as a Governor of the Federal Reserve Board — one of the highest and most prestigious positions in the land.

The Cat Overhead

The earliest childhood memory I have is sitting with my mother in the *Luftschutzkeller*, the air-raid shelter under my grandparents' house at the Chlodwigplatz in Cologne, Germany. It was 1943. After the sirens howled, we would all run down into the cellar under my grandparents' house and wait for the bombs to drop. The explosions followed one-by-one: boom-boom-boom while the ground shook and the lights started to flicker.

All of us in the cellar were sitting on wooden benches along the sides of the small room with rough concrete walls. As the adults moved a bit closer together for comfort and support, our dog Barry howled miserably every time a bomb came whistling down — like all dogs are prone to do when they hear a fire truck siren.

As the bombs exploded overhead, I kept thinking of the *Gestiefelte Kater* or the "Puss in Boots" story that my mother had told me many times. I imagined a gigantic tomcat in his huge boots marching overhead: boom-boom-boom. As a result I was not all that frightened as the ground shook. I knew that the big cat in his giant boots and the feathered hat would eventually pass and the boom-boom-boom would stop.

Tree Trunks in the Cellar

In the middle of our cellar stood six white tree trunks. They were arranged in two rows comprised of three trunks each and were painted with a white phosphorous material that made them glow in the dark. Wedged between the floor and ceiling of our cellar, the trunks helped support the weight of the building above. Sometimes, when a bomb exploded nearby, the tree trunks would bulge a bit in the middle. They seemed to become wider as the air pressure from the overhead explosions pushed the ceiling of the cellar down and compressed the trunks holding up the ceiling.

Our cellar measured about twenty-by-twenty feet and we reached it via a steep staircase that descended from our house below ground. At first, you had to pass through a series of anterooms that were part of my grandparents' cellar. Then, you opened two heavy iron latches that secured a heavy steel door protecting the entrance to the bunker. Four wooden benches lining the perimeter of the room offered enough space for the dozen inhabitants of our five-story house. It was not a very comfortable room and probably looked more like the inside of a tomb.

All the walls of the cellar consisted of raw concrete. On the wall to the left of the steel entrance door was a large map of Western Europe on which someone would plot the advancing bomber squadrons. Next to the map was a radio that stood on a small wooden shelf mounted on the wall. The radio was a *Volksempfänger* or a "People's Receiver" and had a simple rotary dial to tune in the different stations. When the door was securely latched, we would sometimes secretly listen to the British enemy broadcasts although that was strictly prohibited. But not many policemen came by to check when the bombs were falling.

Decades later, I am standing in front of the heavy steel door that protected the entrance to our air-raid shelter in the basement of our house.

The Inhabitants

Whenever the air raid sirens started to blare, we assembled in the cellar: my mother Karin, my grandparents Oma Lisa and Opa Toni Hermann and my unmarried aunt Tante Li. My other aunt, Tante Mia, lived with her small son Toni in Neunkirchen at the Saar. My dad and my two uncles all served in the German army and they were stationed far away: My dad was with General Rommel's troops in Africa, Onkel Heini was somewhere in the Ukraine or Romania, and Onkel Aedi was at the Russian front — or maybe he was already in a hospital in Eastern Germany after having been shot through his elbow.

We shared our cellar with the other families that also lived in our house. There was Karl Fackenthal and his wife Käte, who lived on the third floor. From the fourth floor came the Jahn and the Kreisel families, as well as Herr Friedrich, a business manager. The retired Herr Horbeck also lived in our house. Every now and then, some of the employees who worked in my grandfather's distillery and restaurant would also shelter with us in the cellar. And then there was Barry, our German shepherd dog, who was very distressed when the bombs exploded above.

The Bombers Above

I can still hear the scratchy radio voice announcing: *"Schwere Fliegerverbände befinden sich im Anflug auf Köln!"* That was the standard announcement that heavy bomber formations were approaching Cologne. This was the reason why we were sheltering in the bunker underneath our house.

During the daytime, these were American bombers and during nighttime, they were British. The Germans thought of the Brits as being somewhat cowardly as they would attack mainly under cover of darkness, while the Americans were willing to attack during the day, when it was easier for the defensive Flak to identify and target the incoming bombers. The British generally engaged in "strategic" bombing of residential neighborhoods — and that meant us. The

Americans typically targeted industrial or "tactical" targets. But that made little difference for us as an important railroad bridge across the Rhine was only a few blocks away from our house and a factory was even closer. Little did the Allies know that it was just an abandoned Stollwerck chocolate factory — they would bomb it anyhow!

Escape Routes

But what struck me with great fear was the sight of a small steel door at the far end of the cellar. This door was similar in design to the heavy steel entry door, but it measured only about two by two feet. It also had a strong metal door with a latch and handle. It was an escape hatch through which we would have to crawl in case that there was a direct hit on our house and the main entry way to the cellar was blocked by fire or rubble.

Every now and then we practiced how to escape through the steel hatch. The hatch opened towards a narrow vertical shaft with iron prongs embedded in the far side of the wall. After climbing some eight or nine feet upward in this narrow shaft, one would reach another steel hatch — this one leading to the outside world and our backyard. This shaft was designed to provide an unobstructed escape route in case we were entombed in the cellar. But for a four-year-old child, climbing through that dark and narrow vertical shaft was too scary to contemplate — at least it was for me. Sitting in the cellar and waiting until the puss in his boots overhead had passed was something much easier to comprehend and to tolerate. The mere thought of having to crawl though that narrow escape hatch was something much more terrifying for me.

In addition, there was another escape route for us. We could go back out through the iron entry door into the main cellar. Because my granddad earned his living as a distiller of liquor, a wine merchant and a restaurant and bar owner, we had a very large cellar that stretched under the entire house. That cellar was full of liquor, wine and beer kegs. Given the wartime shortages, most of the kegs were probably empty, but the actual barrels were still there.

Our house was built in 1879 after the medieval city walls had been razed. But the foundations of the city wall had remained and the huge granite boulders now constituted the northern side of our cellar wall. On the southern side of the cellar, where our neighbor's shoe store — *Schuhhaus Schoentgen* — stood overhead, there was a hole in the cellar wall. The hole was just large enough for an adult person to creep through. The stones that had been taken out of the wall were again carefully piled up in the hole, but without any mortar holding them together. Such *Durchbruchs*, or break-troughs, existed in all of the cellars of Cologne. They allowed the inhabitants to reach the neighbor's cellar in case that their own house had collapsed or was on fire and thereby prevented an escape to the outside. In that case, the people trapped in the cellar would simply knock down the loose bricks and make their escape from the inferno through the neighbor's cellar. Of course, anybody attempting to climb through the Durchbruch to burglarize the neighbor's house would be shot on the spot by the block warden or the police — even children knew that.

Eventually, the radio would give an all-clear signal and I would return with my mother and grandparents to our rooms upstairs to continue our interrupted sleep.

These days, when I hear young parents complaining that they cannot get a good night's sleep because the baby wakes them up in the middle of the night, I cannot help but wonder how the mothers in those days did it. They had to bundle up their infants and toddlers in the middle of the night, rush them into the cellar or to an air raid shelter down the block. Then they would sit there for a few hours, while fearing for their lives. When the bombers had passed, they had to put the little ones back to sleep. That is, if they and their babies were lucky enough to be still alive.

Our House Gets Bombed

The family home at the Chlodwigplatz had been hit by numerous firebombs in the early years of the war, but my granddad as well as some of the other inhabitants had stood *Brandwache*, or fire watch, during these early attacks. That meant standing on the roof of the house during the bombing raids and throwing the small incendiary devices that landed on the roof with a long-handed shovel into a sandbox on the roof of the house. The sandbox allowed the firebombs to burn out harmlessly. But in the later years of the war, the bombers would drop a mixture of detonation bombs and firebombs. The detonation bombs would rip open the roofs of the houses and then the firebombs would set the buildings ablaze. No Brandwache could defend against this tactic!

In early 1945, the Battle of the Bulge was raging 40 miles east of Cologne. The Germans were making one last desperate attempt to throw back the Allied troops invading Germany. The railroad bridges across the Rhine River were still standing and endless German troop and munitions trains were crossing the Rhine River bridges in Cologne to resupply the troops fighting against the Allies.

January 6 was *Dreikönigstag*, or Three Kings Day, when all Catholics celebrated a holiday in honor of the Three Wise Men. The Three Magi, as they are also called, are buried in the Cologne cathedral that was erected in their honor starting in 1248. In English speaking countries, the holiday is also known as "Epiphany" because that was the day when the Three Wise Men allegedly worshipped the baby Jesus twelve days after his birth.

On that holiday, Allied bombers launched a large daytime raid aimed at the bridges of Cologne. A big detonation bomb hit our house, but it did not explode right away. Instead, it descended through the five floors of the building and then blew up. Regular detonation bombs would explode on contact, so that they would rip open the roof structure to allow the firebombs dropped by following aircrafts to find the best possible flammable material. In contrast, "our" bomb detonated only after making it through the entire house and then blew the foundation apart, causing a good part of the house to collapse. The bomb ripped a huge gash into the side of our house. Two rooms on each floor were destroyed, but the other four rooms were still standing. While part of our house had been destroyed, a large part of our house was still intact. But the staircase was damaged and the house was no longer habitable unless you did not mind having a gaping abyss next to your room.

The shattered building looked more like a carcass than a house. The bomb also killed one of our workers, who happened to be near the staircase at the wrong time. Maybe he was trying to seek shelter in the cellar, but it was too late!

My grandparents' house at the Chlodwigplatz in Cologne. The restaurant and bar are on the ground floor. The distillery is in the building to the left.

The delayed fuse denotation bomb that hit our house was probably destined for the *Südbrücke*, or South Bridge, an important

Our house after it was hit by a bomb on January 6, 1945. Note the persons in the front who are climbing over large piles of rubble.

The view from our house at the Chlodwigplatz towards the destroyed houses across the plaza. Note the column of men carrying shovels in the foreground. These were probably foreign prisoners doing forced labor. During the war it was strictly prohibited to take pictures of ruins or dead bodies. It was considered "defeatism" and could be punishable by death.

three-span railroad bridge over the Rhine River, which was only five blocks away. In fact, during that bombing attack several bombs did hit the targeted bridge and destroyed both the eastern and the middle spans. This vital railroad bridge across the Rhine tumbled into the river, thereby keeping the trains from crossing the river towards the western front, where the Battle of the Bulge was raging. The collapsed bridge also blocked the entire shipping traffic on the Rhine River, and further disrupted the war effort. That day was a great triumph for the Allied bombers and a devastating blow to Germany and to our family.

Towards the end of the war, virtually all the houses in our neighborhood were gone. Our distillery next door, where my granddad used to produce the fine liqueurs and schnapps concoctions for which he was famous, was totally destroyed as well. The rubble from the demolished houses covered the street with four to six foot high mountains and we had to walk up and down over these small hills that were now where the regular street once used to be. Cologne was reduced at that time to some 100,000 inhabitants, down from the 750,000 people who lived there at the beginning of the war.

The Survivors

What happened to all the people sheltering in our cellar? All members of our immediate family members luckily survived the war.

Herr and Frau Meyer also survived. Paul Meyer apparently had been a staunch Nazi. He had served as a "Blockwart" or a block warden, as the Nazis called the persons that were supposed to keep an eye on the other persons residing in the neighborhood.

Sometime towards the end of the war, the police picked up Herr und Frau Kreisel. Kreisel means Dreidl in Yiddish and as far as our family knew, they were Jewish. I remember the old couple, which had lived in our house for many years, walking down the street away from our house. They both carried a small suitcases and a policeman accompanied them. My grandmother and I watched from our window as they disappeared towards an uncertain future.

Karl and Käte Fackental survived the war and she worked for many years thereafter faithfully as our cleaning lady. Her husband Karl was a stout Communist, who worked as a bricklayer. He resumed his profession after the war. The pious Magdalena Jahn also continued to live in our house after the war. I do not know what happened to Mr. Jahn, Mr. Friedrich and Mr. Horbeck.

As I already mentioned, one of our distillery workers was killed in the entryway to our house when a bomb hit our building in early 1945. The explosion ripped away one side of our house and he could not reach the safety of the cellar in time. He was the only known casualty.

Our German shepherd dog Barry, who howled pitifully when the sirens sounded and the bombs came whistling down, had to be put to sleep as the cellar inhabitants complained about his constant howling in the crowded shelter. Maybe this was better for Barry himself as well.

SAGE ADVICE:
When the Bombs are Falling — Find a Good Hiding Place

2 Wartime in Germany

My parents were avid photographers and as a result, I own several old picture albums that chronicle and document in detail what happened to our family during the years of World War II.

There are two major albums: one covers my dad from the day that he was drafted into basic training in August 1939. During the war, he was first stationed in Holland and France. Then he was posted with General Rommel in Africa. He experienced the end of the war in Italy, where he was taken prisoner by the Allies towards the end of the war.

A second album covers the war years at home in Germany. Throughout the war, Cologne was the target of frequent air raids. Therefore, my mother and I spent as much time as possible in the countryside away from the city. One of our favorite near-by destinations was the *Drachenfels* near Königswinter, a steep mountaintop crowned by an old ruin about 30 miles south of Cologne. We usually stayed with family friends who owned a small hotel halfway up the mountain.

Another frequent destination was the *Gasthaus Bachmaier* in Rottach Egern at the Tegernsee in Bavaria, where we could row in heavy rowboats on the lake. When the bombings in Cologne became very intense, the government evacuated my mother and me to the Eastern border to shelter us from the bombing raids in the

West. Our destination was Bad Gottleuba, a small village near Dresden, and only two miles from the Czech border.

The three locations, Cologne and Königswinter in the West, Bad Gottleuba in the East and Tegernsee in the South of Germany effectively form a large equilateral triangle. The distance between each corner of the triangle is about 600 kilometers or 400 miles. In modern times, it may take 5 or 6 hours by car or train to travel from one location to the other, but during the war years it could take an entire day to make the trip.

Map of Germany in its current borders
Map by John Swain

Wartime Travels

My mother and I travelled frequently to these far-flung destinations. We managed to do this in spite of the bombings and the shortages created by the war. In the rural areas that were not targeted by the bombers, life was fairly normal — even as the bombs rained down in the large cities nearby.

But the travel itself was pretty dangerous. During the war, trains and railroad lines were among the favorite targets of the allied bombing campaigns. The goal of the bombers was to hinder German troop movements and to destroy the supply lines of the German army, which was fighting both on the western and eastern fronts. But the pilots had no idea whether civilians or soldiers were in the trains, and consequently every train was a target. In spite of the airplanes overhead, we continued our travels.

Here is the war chronology for our family as best as I can piece it together from the various picture albums and other sources.

I was born on January 8, 1940 in Cologne, just four months after the invasion of Poland by the German army in September of 1939. Soon thereafter, Britain and France declared war against Germany, but not much happened in the following months on the western front. That changed in May 1940, when German troops invaded Holland, Belgium and France and achieved a quick victory. But at the same time, Cologne became the target of almost daily bombing attacks. These were generally fairly light attacks, with just a few bombs falling each day. Life was not greatly disrupted in those early years of the war.

My dad was with the occupation troops in Holland, but he was able to visit us frequently in Cologne, as he was stationed only 150 miles away. After France surrendered in June, my father was stationed in Paris and he continued to visit us every few months. There probably was not much need for an English translator in France.

In early 1941, my mother, grandmother and I visited with family friends in Königswinter — and my dad was there as well. I got to ride on a giant turtle in the local zoo.

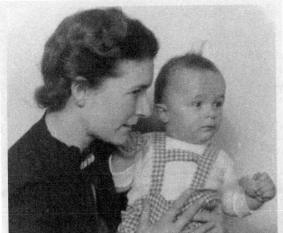

My mother Karoline Hermann Heller and me as a baby.

My father was frequently on home leave and carried me around.

A few weeks later, our entire family traveled for an extended vacation to the Tegernsee, a scenic Bavarian lake some 100 kilometers south of Munich in the foothills of the Alps. Of course, my dad joined us there to teach me how to row on the lake and we watched the cows on the Alpine meadows. Our family stayed at the Hotel Bachmair, a wonderful resort hotel in Rottach Egern. The Hotel Bachmair is nowadays the training headquarters for Germany's most famous soccer team: Bayern München. Was there a war going on? It did not seem so as everything was pretty peaceful at the Tegernsee in Bavaria.

My dad teaches me how to row on the Tegernsee in Bavaria.

At the end of 1941, we were all back in Cologne for Christmas. My dad was on leave from Rommel's army, which just had been beaten back by the British near Tobruk. For my second birthday, my dad gave me three coconuts with faces painted on them. He himself had obtained them in Africa, while he was stationed with Rommel's troops.

Soon, we were back in Königswinter riding on donkeys to the top of the Drachenfels, like all good tourists on vacation would do. April also brought my dad back on another visit and all of us went to the Cologne zoo. Together with my dad we looked at the African elephants and lions, while in Northern Africa the second and decisive Battle of Tobruk raged — again without my dad.

But in the following year, the bombings became heavier as the war was intensifying. On May 30, 1942, Cologne became the target of the famous 1,000-bomber attack — the largest air raid of the war so far. I am not sure whether we were there and experienced the devastation or whether we were still at the Drachenfels near Königswinter. I hope that the latter was the case.

As Cologne was largely devastated, the government evacuated my mother and me to eastern Germany. Our assigned destination was Bad Gottleuba, a small village right on the Czech border. It is about as far as one can go east and still be in Germany. Our move was part of the *Kinderlandverschickung* that resulted in enormous train caravans carrying mothers and their children to the eastern part of the country in order to escape the increasingly devastating bombing raids on the large industrial cities in the western part of Germany.

My mother must not have liked it too much there. In letters to my dad, she bemoans the fact that she is very lonely, not knowing any people in the East. So it is no surprise that we were back in Cologne in July, and my dad is visiting there as well. Together with my dad in his army uniform and our German shepherd dog Barry, we play on the banks of the Rhine River.

My mother and I try to dissuade Barry, our German Shepherd dog, from swimming in the Rhine.

In early December 1942 my dad was again on home leave and together we traveled to Königswinter. He stayed on to celebrate Christmas with us in Cologne under a nicely decorated Christmas tree. At the same time, the battle for Stalingrad, the most decisive battle of World War II, was raging in Russia. Together with my dad, we were singing *"Stille Nacht — Heilige Nacht!"* or "Silent night — holy night" while sitting under a small Christmas tree in my grandparents' house.

Even as a small child, I got to help my grandfather in the cellar with his wine and liquor business. I rolled kegs to their proper locations and helped to bottle wine or glue labels onto the bottles.

As a three year old, I am helping to roll small wine barrels in my grandfather's wine cellar.

It was fun for a little kid to be able to play with big toys!

Soon thereafter, my mother and I took another trip along our triangle: first we went eastward to Bad Gottleuba, then south to the Tegernsee in Bavaria, and finally back to Cologne — a round trip of some 1,200 miles.

In the fall of 1943, my dad was back on home leave from Italy and we visited nearby Königswinter yet one more time. In January 1944 we celebrated my fourth birthday in Cologne — but all the houses on our street were now in total ruins. Our own house at the Chlodwigplatz was still standing, but a year later, in January 1945, a large bomb ripped a deep gash into the side of the four-story building.

Soon, we are on another train back to Bad Gottleuba. While there, we also attended the wedding of my uncle Aedi and his bride Emma in Sternberg, a small town that is now in the Czech Republic. Onkel Aedi had served on the Russian front and a bullet hit him through his right elbow. As a result, he was evacuated back to Germany. Onkel Aedi was lying flat on his back in his hospital bed. A huge plaster cast that pointed straight to the ceiling forced him to remain in this prone position in his hospital bed. A while later, nurse Emma got pregnant and the two got married in

The view from our house towards the ruins across the street. See also the title page of the book.

Sternberg, which is now called Sternberk and is part of the Czech Republic. I had the honor to be the ring bearer at their wedding.

Two things stand out from these experiences: One, my mother and I were able to crisscross wartime Germany by train numerous times. To do so was a very dangerous endeavor. There were Allied bombers overhead that targeted the entire transportation system. Moving trains were prime targets for strafing and bombing attacks. Two, my dad was on home leave at least fourteen times during the war. Several times, he even came back from Libya and Tunisia in Africa, a travel distance of over 2,000 miles. For the German army to devote substantial resources for home leave by its soldiers was certainly not an inexpensive proposition.

The Bombings in Cologne

When the Allies invaded Normandy on June 6, 1944, my mother and I were back in Cologne, which was by now almost totally in ruins. Most of the houses in our neighborhood were destroyed and our house was slightly damaged. But most of it was still standing, although the roof was gone. With the winter approaching and the Russians closing in from the East, we moved back to Königswinter in September 1944 and stayed there until the end of the war.

A total of 67,000 tons of bombs were dropped during the war on Berlin, a city of 4.3 million people. Cologne, with only 750,000 people received 44,000 tons of bombs. In comparison, the famous Dresden bombings entailed only 7,000 tons of explosives for a similarly sized city of 642,000 inhabitants. On a *per-capita basis*, Cologne residents received the most bombs of any major German city.

Cologne was probably also the most *frequently* bombed city in Germany. According to the official records, there were some 262 air raids on Cologne during the war. That included several very large scale bombing raids, including the gigantic attack by over 1,000 bombers on May 30, 1942 code-named *Operation Millennium*. This was one of the largest air raids of the entire war. During that attack, a total of 1.5 million bombs descended on Cologne, or two bombs per person. The Allies hoped that after that devastating attack, Germany might surrender — but Adolf Hitler was not about to give up until the entire country was in ruins!

At the beginning of World War II, Cologne's population of three-quarters of a million people was about equal to the number of people living in San Francisco right now. At the end of the war, when the Americans took over the city, they found only 30,000 persons living in the ruins of the city. That meant that only five percent of the original population was still living there. Ninety-five percent of all houses were turned into ruins.

Of course, not all the people perished. Most men served far away in the army and many women with small children had been evacuated to the eastern part of the country. Much of the rest of the population had fled to rural areas that were unlikely to be bombed. And the rest hunkered down in bunkers or cellars that enabled them to survive. Approximately 20,000 inhabitants of Cologne perished in the city during the war, although no one has a precise count.

This picture was taken by an American bomber as it was passing exactly over our house in 1945 at the end of the war. It shows the totally ruined city of Cologne. The cathedral is still standing, but all the bridges across the Rhine have been destroyed.
(Source: U.S. Department of Defense. Dept. of the Army. Office of the Chief Signal Officer)

While there were 1,122 air raid alarms recorded in the city of Cologne that sent the inhabitants into their cellars, there were only 262 actual air raids with bombs falling. Why the large discrepancy?

There were several reasons why Cologne was a favorite target for the Allied bombing raids. First of all, it was the westernmost large industrial city in Germany and was one of the first cities that could be reached from air bases in England. Obviously, spending as little time as possible over enemy territory was also a significant advantage for the bombers.

Second, Cologne was an important industrial city in the German war effort. It was the home of the *Deutz* engine factories that built Diesel engines for German submarines and tanks. Cologne was also home to essential chemical factories that were significant to the war effort. The huge American-owned Ford car factory was also located in the northern suburbs of Cologne. Amazingly enough, the Ford complex was bombed only sparingly until the very end of the war although it produced numerous vehicles for the German army.

Third, Cologne had five important railroad and automobile bridges that crossed the mighty Rhine River. Hitting these bridges would constitute a significant disruption of the German war transportation network, which brought munitions and materiel to the front-line troops. One of these bridges was only a few blocks away from our home.

Fourth, when Allied bombers attempted to strike a target deeper inside Germany, it was not unusual that the bombers could not reach their initial target because of heavy fighter or flak defenses. At other times, the bombers could not drop their loads on the intended objective because they could not identify the target under heavy cloud cover. In those cases, the planes would return back to their home bases — but they had a problem: they could not land again with their heavy bomb loads and had to drop the bombs before landing. Obviously, the pilots did not want to drop their bombs over Holland, Belgium or France and so they dropped their remaining loads over Germany. Frequently, that meant that Cologne was the last target of opportunity.

And finally, many Allied bombers were simply lost over Germany or had trouble navigating after being hit by German fighter planes or defensive flak fire. As the planes struggled home in a westerly direction, they would eventually encounter the silver ribbon of the Rhine River, which roughly paralleled the western border of Germany. The aircrews knew that it was time to drop their bombs. They could easily spot Cologne and its large cathedral right next to the river and it was a tempting target to drop any remaining bombs there. After that, the planes simply followed the Rhine River in a northwesterly direction to return home to their bases in England. But each one of these overflights by bombers triggered an air raid alarm and maybe a few poorly placed bombs as well.

Over 1,100 air raid alarms spread over roughly four years amounted to about 280 alarms per year that would send the population into the cellars. That meant that on three out of every four days throughout the war there were alarms that sent us below ground. We were true *Kellerkinder* — children of the cellars.

Evacuated to Bad Gottleuba

One of our favorite wartime hiding places was Bad Gottleuba, a community of some 2,500 inhabitants and located only two miles away from the Czech border. Actually, it was the village to which my mother and I were formally evacuated by the German government after the 1,000-bomber raid on Cologne of May 1942. During our stays in Bad Gottleuba, we lived with Frau Erna Pacholzack in her house at Bad Strasse 12-A.

Bad Gottleuba is named after a small river that carries the same name and is situated in the foothills of the Erzgebirge, the Ore Mountains, which form the border of Germany with what is now the Czech Republic. We thought that no bombers were likely to reach us there. Also, there were few military targets in the area. Bad Gottleuba was located only 30 kilometers or 20 miles east of Dresden, which was to become the target of a devastating air raid very late in the war. But for a long time it was as far away as possible from any military actions. During the war, life was reasonably good for mothers and their little children in Bad Gottleuba. I even got to attend Kindergarten together with about a dozen little girls.

We stayed with Frau Pacholzack, whose husband was also off to the war. She owned a small, steeply gabled house on a narrow pathway away from the main street. The house was surrounded by a small garden with fruit trees and she raised vegetables, salads and carrots for all to eat.

Up the steep pathway, along the Bad Strasse, was the *Kurhaus*. Its white glass edifice looked gigantic to me. We would go up the pathway to the Kurhaus to drink the mineral water that gave the village its prefix "Bad." That prefix signifies that the local spring

Kindergarten in Bad Gottleuba. I am second from the right in the picture.

water is a good remedy for all kinds of diseases as well as for taking medicinal baths that are supposed to have magical healing qualities.

Gratitude After the War

One may wonder why I can still remembers the exact name and the rather convoluted address of Frau Erna Pacholzack, Bad Strasse 12-A in Bad Gottleuba bei Pirna über Dresden, a place where I lived as a small child. There is a good reason for that. After the war, my grateful grandmother and my aunts packed every couple of weeks a small parcel with essential foods and mailed it to Frau Pacholzack.

Living conditions were not good in the Soviet occupied Eastern Zone of Germany, which later became the German Democratic Republic. The Russians had conquered this part of Germany at the end of the war. And conquer, they did. Virtually all of the young girls and women were raped multiple times by the Russian soldiers. This part of Germany became the Socialist paradise of the *Arbeiter und Bauern Staat*, the self-styled paradise of workers and farmers. The country's Socialist lifestyle left most of the population impoverished long after Western Germany was back on its feet again.

To help out, my grandmother and my aunts Mia and Li regularly packed small packages with a pound of flour, small bags of coffee and sugar and some powdered milk. They would add a few buttons, needles and thread or other useful supplies. Then it was my job to wrap it all up and write Frau Pacholzack's name and address on the package and take it to the post office. That's why I will never forget her name and address — having penned it at least several hundred times in the post-war period.

This mission of gratitude went on for several decades after the war — because Frau Pacholzack had helped our family when we were in need during the war. The amazing thing was that my grandmother and aunts never actually stayed with her and, as far as I know, never even met her. But this strange woman had been kind to my mother and me in our times of need — and perhaps even helped us to stay alive. And so my grandmother and my aunts showed their gratefulness to Frau Pacholzack when she needed a helping hand years later.

Going Back to Bad Gottleuba

Over half a century later, after the Berlin Wall had fallen, my wife Emily and I drove back to Bad Gottleuba. It was still a sleepy little town with a single restaurant at its town square. A smallish monument in front of the restaurant honored the town residents who had died in the First World War — but there was nothing to remind the people of World War II. The glorious Soviet Union had "liberated" the little town and anybody who had defended its inhabitants against the Russians certainly was a traitor in the eyes of the Communists and not worth mentioning.

I easily found the small pathway leading from the main road down to our former house at Bad Strasse 12-A. I had walked this path numerous times together with my mother when I was four years old and still remembered it after many decades. We rang the doorbell, but no one was home. An elderly woman carrying her groceries approached and I asked her about Frau Pacholzack, our former landlady. Yes, she remembered her, but Frau Pacholzack had passed away many years ago. Her son had become a hairdresser and had moved to the big city of Dresden. That was the end of the story.

The once magnificent looking, glassed-in Kurhaus still stands at the appropriately named *Bad Strasse* or Bath Street. But the Kurhaus looked to me now much smaller. It was also somewhat dilapidated and in great need of repair. No one will come here for medical treatment or to "take the baths" when one can go to truly elegant spas like Baden-Baden or Bad Neuenahr in the West. It made me sad. I had taken a trip into the past. Time had stood still in *Bad Gottleuba* for well over half a century!

Looking back at the war period half a century later, it is utterly amazing to me that my mother and I moved around so much in Germany with Allied planes overhead almost every single day. Trains and railroad tracks were particularly important targets for the bombers as they tried to disrupt the German supply lines and troop movements. To be travelling under these circumstances with a small child in tow was a pretty dangerous endeavor

SAGE ADVICE
When Someone is After You — Keep Moving!

3 **My Dad During the War**

My dad was drafted into the German army at the end of August 1939, just a few days before the German invasion of Poland and he served in the army until he was taken prisoner in 1945.

He had spent several years in the 1930s in Ireland and as a result his English was excellent. Due to that talent, he became a *"Sonderführer Z,"* or "Specialist Leader Z," which made him a

lieutenant in the officer corps. Typically, he was attached to army command units so that he could translate enemy documents for the generals.

My dad was a translator during the entire war: clipping news articles and translating captured documents for the Army command.

Soon after the German invasion of the Netherlands, he was stationed with the occupation troops there and he snapped pictures of the ruins of Rotterdam. Apparently, he himself had a pretty good life in Holland as he stayed in a very nice villa on a canal in Dordrecht and was then quartered at the *Royal Hotel* in Den Bosch. As part of the translator corps, he was able to spend his days off in comfortable mansions, rubbing shoulders with the German generals and other high staff officers.

In June, France surrendered and my dad was posted in Paris. There, he had time to visit all the typical tourist attractions, like the Eiffel Tower, Notre Dame, the Louvre and Versailles.

He sent a postcard to my mother from Versailles sounding more like a tourist than a soldier on duty:

"While passing through I send you cordial greetings. I am doing very well and I get to see many interesting sites. One does not really feel the war here and life takes its customary course. With many kisses and greetings to all! Your Heinz."

My dad's unit in front of the Eiffel Tower. He is the third person from the right in the second row.

The German army parades down the Rue du Rivoli — but there is virtually nobody watching!

He also snapped a picture of a German army unit led by a full drum band marching down the Rue de Rivoli in Paris. But there were only three Frenchmen watching the parade. Or maybe they were just waiting to cross the street? Not surprisingly, the French were in no mood to watch the German troops parade through Paris!

In September 1941, my mother traveled to Munich to meet my dad, who was being reassigned to General Rommel's army in Africa. On his way to Africa, my dad stopped over in Rome, where again he had time to visit all the tourist sights: the Coliseum, Saint Peter's basilica in the Vatican and many of the ancient Roman monuments. Then he flew in a seaplane to Sicily and eventually landed in Tunisia to join the German troops fighting there with General Rommel against the British army in the desert.

From Tripoli in Tunisia, he moved with the German army to Benghazi and Tobruk, where he personally met with General Rommel and snapped a picture of the famous Desert Fox. Because was a translator, my dad also got to interrogate British POWs who looked pretty forlorn as they sat lonely in the desert sand.

My dad posing proudly in his Africa Corps uniform.

The famous "Desert Fox," General Rommel in a trench in Africa. Rommel is second from the left.

It is astonishing to me that my dad, who served in Holland, France, Africa, Greece and Italy, was able to come home as often as he did. In the early years of the war, while he was stationed in Holland and in France, he was able to come home on leave from the Army every two or three months. For a fighting army to devote that much effort to keeping the troops happy by sending them home was truly phenomenal.

Later on, when he was in Libya and Tunisia as part of General Rommel's staff, his home leaves were fewer and far in-between. Nevertheless, he managed to fly home from Africa about twice a year.

During the final phase of the war, my dad was stationed in Italy. History buffs will remember that the monumental Battle of Monte Cassino lasted from the middle of January until the middle of May 1944. During that time, my dad was posted about 60 miles north of Monte Cassino. His position was a bit east of Rome in the Italian mountains near Massa d'Albe. He wrote regularly to my mother and to me, while we were evacuated in Bad Gottleuba in eastern Germany to escape the heavy bombings in Cologne. Here are some excerpts from these letters:

On May 9, 1944, while the Battle of Monte Cassino raged near him, he worried about what was happening at home. He wrote:

"I would love to come home on vacation, but under the circumstances that is unfortunately not possible. I will have to be patient for a long time."

"The attacks on Cologne are still persisting. Today's report says that there was a terror attack on Berlin and that bombs were dropped on Cologne. Also during the night many bombs dropped on Cologne and Düsseldorf. They have to suffer a lot there and I am happy to know that you are not there. I wonder whether we will ever see our property again."

On May 17, 1944 the German General Kesselring ordered the surrender of Monte Cassino. The German troops were now in full retreat. My dad was nearby and wrote on the following day:

"Dear Frauchen," (literally translated, this means 'Little Wife', but it is also generally used as an endearing term)

"In the next days I will probably have to move again. You will have learned though the Armed Forces Report what is going on down here.

Rumor has it that this is the beginning of an offensive or an invasion on all fronts that will be conducted with the utmost force. We hope that we will be able to repel these attacks and that we will achieve the desired victory, which will secure our future and freedom."

"Perhaps it will be impossible to write to you regularly in the near future. But that is no reason for concern. Once we have overcome everything and the offensive has been beaten off, I will again be able to think about home leave. I don't have to tell you, my dear, how much I am looking forward to that. I am not able to truly express my feelings."

"This is a wonderful time in Italy. I have already told you about the delightful interplay of colors when the morning or evening sun shines over the valley. It feels like a wonderful and peaceful time. Many birds start to sing their songs early in the morning and in the evening, the nightingale sings us to sleep...."

A few days later, on May 21, 1944, the German army was in hasty retreat after having lost the Battle of Monte Cassino. But for a staff officer, like my dad, this did not necessarily mean hardship:

"At the present time, I am living like a Lord. I have a large single room with all comforts, which also serves as my work place. Even in the good old days in France, things were not that feudal. But this joy will not last long! That's a soldier's life! Today I am staying in a wonderful villa and tomorrow perhaps in an old shed or under open skies. But that is not all bad. To the contrary, it keeps you moving and elastic and teaches you to act. I will be able to tell you many stories when we are together again. This day will come!"

A few days later, the Americans were advancing rapidly and the situation for the German army was getting worse. On May 25, 1944 my dad wrote to my mother:

"My dear Pinnela!" (*A pet name my father had for my mother*)

"For several days I could not write to you. I cannot tell you what is happening here now. Every few days we have to move. Since May 12 already four times, without counting the small local moves within the same house. That creates always lots of work with packing and unpacking. At night we usually work here until 4 o'clock. For many weeks I have not had a single lunch break. The accommodations are sometimes luxurious

The destroyed village of Massa d'Albe on the foothills of Monte Velino on May 12, 1944.

and pompous and then again extremely primitive and provisional. For 4 days I had a wonderful room in the house of an industrial tycoon. Now I have a simple chamber on a farm. But we will probably stay only for a few days. But the work continues and I have to say that especially in my field of responsibility, the enemy situation, there is a lot of work to be done as I always have to report and brief on the latest developments in the camp of the enemy. Every day I have to work though a pile of 8 to 12 centimeters of mail. But enough said, after all, it is war and I am happy that my work really contributes to the battle."

"Let us hope that the heavy battle that our soldiers are fighting against an overwhelming enemy will turn out in our favor. It is a very uneven battle."

"And now many dear greetings to all at home. To you and Heinerle I want to give the most beautiful and the highest that I can offer to you. In addition, many, many kisses and God's blessings."

"Your Heinzelman" (A diminutive of his name Heinz, but also meaning a little dwarf with magical powers in German)

A few days later, the Germans were retreating further and the situation was deteriorating. He wrote on May 30, 1944:

"My dear little wife!"

"Two days ago we landed at a new place. We are working in tents without tables and chairs. Everything is only improvised. We live and sleep in straw huts that have been used until now as stables. We had to clean out the animal dung ourselves. It is a great contrast to the palace that we had until now. In spite of that, I am feeling well... I took time to climb for half an hour into a cherry tree and ate as many of the wonderful cherries as I could fit into my stomach. They tasted wonderful. Yesterday evening, the major and I took off together and sat in a cherry tree. He is a wonderful guy and we get along very well."

The following letter was written on June 1, 1944:

"My dear Gitschele!" (Still another nickname)

"Now I am finally able to write to you and to thank you for your dear letters.... In a few days, we will probably have to move again. You also have the intent to travel to Cologne for your dad's birthday. I hope that the trip will go well and that you all will be safe from the planes in Cologne. According to the army reports, there are heavy attacks every day. Therefore, I would not stay there very long. It would be nice if you could live with the Giershausens'. I consider a single house in the forest much safer. And you would not have to fear the bombers at night. During the daytime it is possible that a dive-bomber might try to shoot on the house, but such events happen usually in the main traffic centers during the daytime. Here, too, a lot is happening in that regard, as you can probably imagine. There is heavy fighting at the front.... At present, I am eating a big bowl of cherries... Many kisses and hugs to both of you from
  Your Daddy"

That was the last letter he wrote to my mother and me. The German army was in full withdrawal now and my dad moved with his army unit further north towards Florence and Ferrara. There, the Americans took him prisoner in June of 1944 and he remained a POW until December 1945, half a year after the end of the war.

The War at the Front and at Home

When my dad returned from the war, he often remarked that life in Cologne had been much worse than at the front. At the fighting front, the very first groups of soldiers generally took the brunt of the battle, but those further back often led a fairly quiet and uneventful life. As my dad was attached as a translator to the German army command, he was always well behind the front lines. As he himself writes, he was generally quartered in nice villas — until the very last days of the war. He also had plenty to eat and the most work he had to do was to translate a few inches of paper every day. I do not think that he ever fired a shot.

In contrast, and as is apparent in his letters, the war years were pretty scary and intimidating on the home front. Living in the big cities of Germany during the war meant having to be prepared to run into the cellars at any moment of the day or night. Doing that with little children in tow made it even more nerve wrecking and exhausting. Once a bombing attack started, it was like a lottery for life or death whether the bombs would hit your house or that of a neighbor. I often wonder how the women survived and stayed sane.

Life in the rural areas was a lot easier as there were few military targets in the small villages. Small towns like Königswinter, Rottach at the Tegernsee in Bavaria and Bad Gottleuba near Dresden were not subject to bombing attacks until the very end of the war. Life there was pretty peaceful. Consequently, my mother kept running away from the bombs in Cologne and crisscrossed the country west to east and north to south. She kept constantly on the move, but also returned back to her home in Cologne, where her parents lived. In a way, the German women led a life like small and vulnerable creatures, trying to find a safe hiding place when the enemy appeared overhead.

SAGE ADVICE
War is Hell on the Homefront Too!
— *Country Singer T.G. Sheppard*

4 Hiding in the Cave

From Dresden to the Dragon's Rock

It was late 1944 and the Russian army was getting ever closer to Bad Gottleuba. My mother decided that it was safer to return to the West — in spite of the bombers and the Western Allies starting to invade Germany. Given a choice between being overrun by the Americans or the Russians, she opted for the Americans.

Clearly, being in the East no longer provided a secure shelter from the bombs either, as the devastating air attack on Dresden was soon to show. Dresden is a mere 20 kilometers from Bad Gottleuba and it soon became the target of one of the most devastating single attacks ever unleashed upon a city. While Cologne suffered through hundreds of bombings, Dresden was wiped out in a single day.

So, my mother and I boarded a train and we moved westward. As Cologne was virtually uninhabitable, we went to Königswinter, a small idyllic town about 50 kilometers or 30 miles south of Cologne.

Königswinter is located at the edge of the Siebengebirge, literally the Seven Mountain Range, on the eastern shore of the Rhine River. The Drachenfels is the most prominent of these seven mountains and its medieval castle ruin towers over the Rhine valley. Drachenfels, or Dragon's Rock, is the name of the steep mountain jutting up from the river as well as the castle ruin that crowns the mountain and can be seen from miles away. According to the ancient Legend of the Nibelungen, this was the place where Siegfried slayed the fearsome seven-headed dragon inhabiting a cave on the mountain. What young child would not want to live there?

Life on the Drachenfels

We moved into the *Gasthaus Giershausen am Hirschberg*, the "Guesthouse Giershausen on Stag Mountain," owned by friends of ours. Mr. Giershausen worked as a *Wegemeister* or "Path-Master" for the *Verschönerungs Verein Siebengebirge*, a not-for-profit association devoted to the beautification and maintenance of the nature park. He helped to maintain the numerous benches marked with the association's logo VVS, as well as the many footpaths throughout the scenic mountain region.

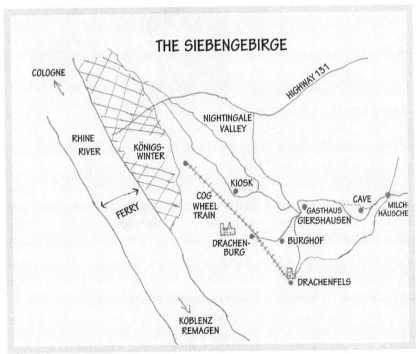

Map by John Swain

The Giershausens' were longtime friends of my grandparents and they lived with their 17-year-old daughter Margaret, as well as their faithful maid Maritz, in the inn. To the delight of us children, there was also Struppi, a very friendly orange and white dog who was always ready to play.

My mother and I play with Struppi, the Giershausen's friendly dog

The sizeable stone building not only contained a restaurant, but also about half a dozen guest rooms that were rented out to vacationers in more peaceful times. Now they became the home for our family. There were rooms for my grandparents, Opa Toni and Oma Lisa, my single aunt Tante Li, Tante Mia and her three-year-old son Toni, as well as for my mother and myself. Yes, it's important to have good friends when times get tough!

Life was pretty good on the Drachenfels. We had a little garden with fruit trees and vegetables and a few chickens ran around that produced eggs for all of us. Nobody told the children what the little rabbits in the wire cage were for, but we were happy to play with them and fed them an occasional carrot. On holidays, the family often enjoyed a stew with some meat in it. The next day, one less rabbit would be hopping around in the cage.

And then there were the donkeys, which could be rented for a ride up the Drachenfels Mountain along a small and winding path. Children could have fun in spite of the war!

My grandfather Toni Hermann celebrates his 60th birthday at the Gasthaus Giershausen on the Drachenfels. From left to right: Tante Mia, Grandpa Toni Hermann holding Toni Hau, Grandma Lisa Hermann holding me, Aunt Li and my mother Karin. The picture was taken at the same spot where Toni encountered the first black American soldier over a year later.

My mother, Margaret Giershausen and me on a donkey ride on the Drachenfels.

The nearest building, the *Schloss Drachenburg*, was about a kilometer away. The Drachenburg looked like a fancy castle — almost like a Disneyland creation. A private entrepreneur had built the castle in the late nineteenth century, when Germany underwent a historical revival period. During the war, the Hitler Youth had commandeered the castle. It served as a home for a few hundred teenage Hitler Youth boys who marched around the countryside with flags flying and drums playing. They were the big kids and they did not have much to do with us preschoolers. They had more important things to do.

Today, the carefully restored Schloss Drachenburg is a favorite location for fancy destination weddings in a romantic setting.

Also nearby was the *Burghof*, an ancillary building to the castle, that housed the horses and cows supporting the Hitler Youth troops and also served as a home for the work crews of the castle.

Not much further away was the *Nibelungenhalle*, which was a small tourist attraction. The exhibits recounted the saga of the Nibelungen in a series of gigantic murals and also housed a replica of Siegfried's slaying the infamous dragon. For us kids, the battle scenes were a frightful and scary sight, but the Hitler Youth troops went there for history lessons and inspiration.

Chased by a Fighter Plane

Life on the Drachenfels was mostly peaceful in spite of the fact that the western front was coming closer every day in late 1944. But there were exceptions. My mother and her sister Mia, along with her little three-year-old son Toni and I walked down to the small town of Königswinter about once a week. There, we traded our government-issued ration coupons to obtain the essentials of life — some milk, butter, flour and other food items that were allotted to us. The walk took about one hour and we descended from the Drachenfels on a long and exposed pathway down to the sleepy town located on the Rhine River.

On one of these trips to the town below, a few Allied fighter planes came cruising along through the Rhine Valley. They were about at eyelevel with us on the hillside. Soon, they spotted the four of us. We were near the *Büdchen*, a small kiosk about half way down the mountain. Before the war, its owner sold drinks and snacks to tourists climbing the Drachenfels. When we saw the approaching planes, we ran to the other side of the small wooden structure to hide. But the pilots had already spotted us and started to circle, chasing us around the Büdchen. As the planes orbited around us, we raced around the tiny wooden structure, trying to evade the fighter planes. Eventually, they gave up without firing a shot and we were able to proceed. Of course, they could have wiped us out instantly if they had wished to. Perhaps they just wanted to take a closer look at us or to scare us a bit.

After that scare, we took an alternative route to town. It lead through the *Nachtigallental*, the Nightingale Valley, and gave us plenty of air cover as the road snaked down to the river trough a deep ravine covered by a canopy of tall trees. No more airplanes could see and chase us.

Watching the V-1 Take Off

Eventually, a small troop of German soldiers moved in with us at the Gasthaus am Hirschberg. They had lots of electronic gear and they strung colored telephone wires all over the area. About the same time, mysterious rocket planes started to appear over the hillside to the east. The rocket planes would first streak steeply towards the sky and then leveled out. With a fiery trail blazing behind the projectile, the rocket planes flew across the Rhine and towards the west. We heard that they were new miracle weapons, Hitler's *Wunderwaffe*, that would assure that Germany would win the war.

These were the famous pilot-less V-1 rocket propelled planes, similar to modern drones, that were being launched from mobile launchers behind the Siebengebirge Mountains towards Allied targets further west. The adults talked a lot about the rockets and speculated that maybe the soldiers stationed in our house were part of the tracking crews directing the flight of the rockets. Of course,

I have no idea whether that was true or not. I never even found out whether the V-1's could actually be controlled from such primitive ground stations. But the soldiers in our house certainly had lots of electronic communication gear and plenty of wires. However, the presence of the soldiers in our house also might have made us a more important target — if the Allies were to find out what was going on in our house.

Heinrich is Born as the War Reaches Us

My younger cousin Heinrich Hau was born on Christmas Eve 1944 in Königswinter, just as the Battle of the Bulge was raging 100 miles to the west. This was the largest and most bloody battle that the United States fought in the entire war and it affected us in Königswinter as well. Bombs were falling all around while my aunt Mia gave birth to the new baby. The doctors asked her to hold her own intravenous device while she and her newborn baby were evacuated into the cellar of the hospital.

Pretty soon, in early March 1945, the Allies appeared on the other side of the Rhine River and we became the target of intense direct artillery fire in our mountain home. Clearly, the Americans were getting ready to cross the Rhine and wanted to "soften up" the Germans on the eastern side of the river.

To everybody's surprise, on March 7, 1945 the American troops captured the undamaged railroad bridge at Remagen, which was only seven miles up-river from us. This was the famous first crossing of the Rhine by Allied forces, which was chronicled in the movie the *Bridge at Remagen*. Clearly, the Allies were advancing and our situation was getting more dangerous by the day.

Many of the locals anticipated heavy fighting and bombing, as the German army would undoubtedly offer the strongest possible resistance to the invading Allies. As the Allied air raids increased, the small town of Königswinter was bombed several times. There was also ever increasing artillery shelling from both sides: the Americans tried to destroy the German defenses and the Germans fired at the Americans to hold up their advance. Life on the Drachenfels was getting very dangerous.

Hiding From the Americans in the Cave

My mother decided that it would be safer for us to hide in an old cave in the nearby woods. The cave was about a mile into the forest and to us it looked like an old natural lime stone cave. Aunt Mia, who had just given birth to my cousin Heinrich and also had three-year old Toni to take care of, decided not to move into the cave. Instead they stayed together with my grandparents at the Gasthaus am Hirschberg. Her doctors told her that she should not move into the cave with the newborn baby. Apparently, the physicians believed that if the baby would constantly live in a dark cave, he would not learn to see and might be blind for the rest of his life. Old wives' tale or not, aunt Mia, her son Toni and little Heinrich never moved into the cave but stayed in the Gasthaus Hirschberg.

This area used to be inhabited by the Neanderthal Men, ancient cave dwellers that lived in this area half a million years ago. The first Neanderthal bones were discovered nearby at the Neander Creek, which flows some 50 miles north of Königswinter into the Rhine River. Hence, the name Neanderthal Man. Allegedly, the Neanderthalers inhabited caves just like the one in our neighborhood. Who knows — maybe we just moved into an old ancestral home?

I often joked that just like the Neanderthal men, I have flat feet, broad hips, bushy eyebrows and a large head. Maybe they really were my ancestors? Many decades later my daughter, who by then was a professor of medicine at Stanford University, gave me a DNA kit to test my hypothesis. I was proud to find out that I was indeed 1.9 percent Neanderthal. Q.E.D.

Eventually, I did find out that the caves were actually underground limestone quarries carved out in the late nineteenth century. Hence, no Neanderthaler ever lived in our cave because the cave was of much more recent origin. Instead, we were the first Neanderthal descendants to live in the cave!

The limestone mined in the cave was prized for its ability to absorb heat and then to dissipate it again very slowly. Because of that desirable quality, the stones were used to build the so-called *Königswinterer Ofen* that used to be very popular. A small mountain ridge near our house consists of pure limestone and is actually called the Ofenkauler Berg because there are so many limestone caves and quarries in the hillside. There must be about 20 or 30 remaining limestone caves in the area. They are all closed up right now, except for small window slits that allow bats to fly in and out. The bats seem to love these caves and today, these caves contain one of the largest bat populations in Germany.

Our cave was called *Kossmann's Kaule*, after the former owner of the limestone mine who created the cavern. One can find the cave by walking about 150 yards west on the Drachenfelsstrasse from the *Milchhäuschen*, which is a popular tourist destination restaurant in the Siebengebirge National Park. At the spot in the forest where the road makes a slight rightward bend, the cave is located about fifty feet down the mountainside.

Over half a century later, I am standing in front of the entrance to "our" cave on the slope of the Drachenfels.

The cave itself was about the size of a large suburban home and some 40 or 50 people took refuge in it in early 1945. Many people moved rudimentary furniture into the cave and there were numerous cots to sleep on. I remember that I had a regular children's bed with big fluffy pillows covered with red and white checkered linens situated in a cozy corner to the left of the entrance. What child would not want to live in a real cave?

At first, my Mom and I just spent only the nights in the cave. During the day we continued to live with the rest of the family in the Gasthaus am Hirschberg. On one of our daily walks from our house to the cave, my mom was a bit tired and wanted to rest. We stopped in a small clearing not far away from the edge of the forest where the cave was located. I was impatient and wanted to reach the safety of the cave quickly. I urged her: "Come on, let's go to the cave!" Eventually, she relented and we continued on the narrow path towards the forest. We had barely walked 200 feet when an artillery shell hit at the very same spot where we had been standing only moments before. A crater maybe 12 feet across was now visible at that location. Undoubtedly, the shell would have wiped both of us out if we had not started to walk away just in time. Some lucky star must have been watching over us!

I remember life in the cave as being very pleasant. I had my red and white checkered bedding and we lived in a cozy corner. Of course, we had no water and all supplies had to be carried into the cave from far away. Also, there were no toilet facilities and one had to go outside and hide behind a tree to go potty. That was easy for a 5 year old, but maybe somewhat embarrassing for a grandmother.

Liberated by the Americans

A few days after the Americans crossed over the Bridge at Remagen, we heard army tanks and trucks rumbling along on top of the cave. We had been in the cave every night for two to three weeks. When we dared to come outside, we saw a long line of American army tanks and trucks snaking along on the road right above the cave. Because it was early March, the trees had no leaves and we could

Inside a neighboring cave. This picture was taken by U.S. soldiers as they occupied the area.

Source: U.S. Army; U.S. National Archives; Reprinted in: Vor sechzig Jahren: Kriegsende im Siebengebirge, Siebengebirgsmuseum der Stadt Königswinter, Rheinlandia Verlag, 2005

see the American soldiers and trucks move towards our home at the Gasthaus Hirschberg.

As we walked home on the path below the street, we noticed that American infantry soldiers were dug in along the forest line. From there they had a good view not only of the highway where their trucks were now rumbling along, but also of the wide-open fields to the east. Any German counterattack would come from that direction. Pretty clever!

As we got back to our home, we were surprised to see that the heavy felt curtains that used to cover our doors and windows during the winter were gone. The soldiers had "liberated" them to line their foxholes along the edge of the forest. Who could blame the soldiers for wanting a bit of comfort in their wet and damp foxholes on a rainy night in March?

Another surprise was that all our precious jars of canned fruit had been opened, but not eaten. The Giershausen family had quite a few pear, apple and cherry trees on their property. It was their custom to preserve the harvested fruits in glass jars that were then boiled and sealed with rubber gaskets. When the soldiers arrived, they must have been hungry and they opened up the jars looking for some fresh fruit to eat. But they did not find the contents to their liking, as we did not have any sugar to sweeten the fruits before preserving them. Instead, all the fruits tasted sour. It was good enough for hungry Germans, but not to the liking of the much better fed American soldiers. The soldiers opened up all the jars in their hunt for some sweet fruits, but there weren't any. Over the next few days, we had to eat the entire fruit supply that had been opened, so that it would not go to waste — when it could have lasted us for many more months.

Mommy, is he out of Chocolate?

The Americans moved into the Gasthaus and we had to leave our rooms. My cousin Toni and I now slept on pillows on the kitchen floor. We would often hide in little cubbyholes under the large wooden counters where the food used to be prepared. In the morning, when we woke up, we would see American army boots standing right in front of our faces. It was quite scary and we kept our mouths shut in our hideaway.

One cute episode took place right after the Americans moved into our place. My cousin Toni was just a little over three years old at that time and none of us kids had ever tasted real chocolate. During the war, chocolate was a rarity and whatever chocolate was available was strictly reserved for soldier's rations. That did not stop our parents from telling us that chocolate was dark and tasted delicious. They also had told us that when the war was over and the Americans came, we would all get to taste real dark chocolate.

Well, the Americans were here now. In our backyard they posted a huge black sentry. I had never in my life seen a black person and I was totally impressed. I still remember his imposing tall figure in full military garb and the several ammunition belts slung around his shoulders. He also carried what looked like an automatic rifle or a submachine gun.

My three-year old cousin Toni was not very much intimidated. Remembering what our parents had told us about chocolate and the Americans, he trotted out the back door, did a few circles around the heavily armed black guard and yelled: "Mommy, Mommy, is he out of chocolate? Can I eat him?"

It is probably fortunate that the black soldier did not understand any German. Tante Mia quickly scooped up her little boy and brought him back to safety inside the house.

The U.S. soldiers were pretty friendly towards us kids. As they rumbled by in what seem to be endless columns of trucks, we would run outside, wave at them and yell: "Bye-Bye!" Maybe it was not the friendliest of greetings, but it was the only English we knew. The soldiers waved back and threw us small packets of chewing gum and an occasional wax-covered K-Ration box, which we would promptly deliver to our parents. We devoured the K-Rations with gusto, and then carefully scraped off the wax that sealed the cardboard boxes. Then we turned the wax into candles that allowed us to see at night. Every scrap was valuable in those days!

The Rest of the Family Arrives

A few months later, my uncle Aedi's new wife, Tante Emma, and her parents Oma Pur and Opa Pur, arrived along with her new baby, little Toni Hermann. Toni — yes, it is a popular name in our family — had been born only a few months earlier in Olmütz, which is now the town of Olomouc in the Czech Republic. Little Toni Hermann was swaddled tightly in several blankets, rendering him essentially unable to move. Not a bad tactic to immobilize a little baby when you were on the run from the Russians.

The Pur family had been overrun by the advancing Russian troops but managed to escape to the West. Oma Pur, as we called her by what was really her last name, told many frightful stories of atrocities committed by the Russian troops against the local population. While I was only five years old at that time, I remember

Grandma Pur telling that some of the Russians cut off the breasts of the women after they had raped them. Even for me as a five year old, that was a horror story that I will never forget. Onkel Aedi, his wife Emma and her parents found a temporary home in the nearby Burghof, which had been vacated by the Hitler Youth troops that seemed to have disappeared from the face of the earth.

Sliding Down the Drachenfels

The stories told by the refugees from the East stood in stark contrast to the generally friendly experiences we had with the American troops in our house. We got our daily chewing gum presents and an occasional candy bar from "our" troops. The only things the Americans took away from us were watches and cameras — valuable items small enough to carry with them. Otherwise, life for us kids was pretty normal. We helped with picking the vegetables in our little garden, played with Struppi the dog, went for walks and played with soccer balls that we stole from the Drachenburg after the Hitler Youth troops were gone. Our parents also "liberated" whole sets of dinner plates with red double rings around the rim. A large German eagle with a swastika was engraved on the backside of all these plates, which served as our regular dinnerware for many years to come. We just hoped that none of our guests would ever turn over the plates and see the swastikas. Everybody took what he or she needed when there was nothing available for purchase!

All the children also engaged in a secret, but fun activity. We never told our parents about it, as we were sure that they would not have approved. A small cog railroad or *Zahnradbahn* ascends the Drachenfels. In better days, tourists took this little train up the mountain so that they did not have to actually hike up "the most climbed mountain in the world." The train's passenger cars were pushed uphill by a steam-powered locomotive that huffed and puffed as it belched black smoke as it ascended the steep mountain slope. Occasionally, the locomotive would emit a loud toot to warn pedestrians of its presence. To help the engine climb the steep mountain slope, there was a cogwheel underneath the locomotive. In turn, the cogwheel fitted into a special center track consisting of two narrow rails with cross bars in-between the two rails.

The cogwheel train did not operate in the months right after the end of the war. So we took pieces of slate found in abundance on the mountain, placed them on the central cogwheel track and slid down the track at breakneck speed. One day, a locomotive that was probably on a test run came up the mountain from the valley, while we were sliding down the mountain at top speed. Somehow or other, we managed to get off the track before we collided with the engine. We escaped into the woods and away from what would certainly have been a severe spanking by the train crew. That's how we had fun in those days. Nowadays, the little cogwheel train still hauls its passengers up the mountain, but a modern electric locomotive has replaced the smoke-belching steam engine.

Unexpected Benefits from the War

The war was over and times were tough. Food was scarce. But there were two unexpected life-long benefits for me: I do not smoke and I do not drink coffee.

During the war, most Germans were unable to smoke tobacco or drink coffee. The reason was simple enough: Germany was essentially cut off from the tobacco and coffee growing regions of the world. The United States, Brazil and Turkey are the major tobacco-exporting countries of the world, while Latin America, Indonesia and Sub-Saharan Africa are the world's key coffee producers. Germany did not control any of these territories during the war. Consequently, Germans who prized their coffee and loved their cigarettes were deprived of these luxuries during the war. What little tobacco and coffee was available was reserved for soldiers in the German army. No young person was ever offered a cup of coffee or allowed to smoke a cigarette.

This situation did not change after the war, when people were hungry and coffee and tobacco were still not widely available. So, enterprising companies started to brew *Ersatz-Kaffee*, a coffee substitute that went by the unlikely name of *Mucke-Fuck*. Nowadays, it is still sold in some German supermarkets in white bags with blue dots on it. While Mucke-Fuck tastes like burned wheat, I actually do like the brew. Various grains are roasted to produce the coffee substitute, but it does not contain any caffeine. In any case, in occupied post-war Germany, real coffee was a most prized luxury for the ladies, some of who literally paid for it with their bodies. The hard earned coffee was never wasted on small children.

The same was true for tobacco. During the war, what little tobacco from Italy or Romania found its way into Germany was a prized possession for the men who craved it badly. Children who tried to sneak a cigarette would do so at their own peril. Instead, we dried strawberry leaves and stuffed them into little white clay pipes. Then we smoked the stuff. I remember doing that right after the end of the war. Every time, I got terribly sick and threw up. I learned my lesson: don't smoke funny stuff in pipes!

As a result of these early experiences, I am neither a smoker nor a coffee drinker. Yes, war and deprivation can have some unexpected life-long health benefits!

SAGE ADVICE:
Very Quickly, Your Enemy Can Become Your Friend

5 Post-War Turmoil and Heartbreak

T he war ended in May 1945 and it was time to return to Cologne.
The city was totally bombed out, but it was time to make a new
beginning and to return home.

Returning to Cologne Without Lice

I still own the official authorization issued by the Military
Government of Germany entitled: "MILITARREGIERUNG —
BEFREIUNG." The English translation is printed right
underneath it: "MILITARY GOVERNMENT —
EXEMPTION." But in German, the word "*Befreiung*" has two very
different meanings. It can mean "Exemption," just like the English
translation stated, or it can mean "Liberation." Most Germans
thought of the word in that second sense, as we had just been
liberated. The war was over and we were free to go home.

The Passport Number 018219 allowed my mother, aunt Li
and me to return to Rodenkirchen, a suburb of Cologne. It was
issued on June 4, 1945, just one month after the end of the war.
The permit specifically notes that we are exempted from the curfew
and the travel restrictions imposed at that time on all Germans.
It orders us "*To report to local Burgomeister on arrival. No travel on
roads other than MER. Person have been examined and dusted. going
home.*" [Spelling like in the original.] That last phrase certified that
all three of us had been "dusted" or deloused with DDT. It was a

MILITARY GOVERNMENT
OF GERMANY

MILITÄRREGIERUNG - BEFREIUNG
MILITARY GOVERNMENT
EXEMPTION

№018219

Datum der Ausstellung / Date Issued: 4/6/45
Wird unwirksam am / Expires on: 10/6/45

Name / Name: Heller Karoline + 2 pers.

Anschrift / Address:
Wohnort / Town: Rodenkirchen

Ausweiskarte Klasse / Identity Card Type: Registr. Nr. No.

Unterschrift des Inhabers / Signature of Holder: R. Heller.

ANWEISUNGEN: Diese Befreiung ist im Namen der Militärregierung ausgestellt worden. Sie ist nicht übertragbar, darf nicht abgeändert oder vernichtet werden und ist nur gültig in Verbindung mit der Ausweiskarte des Inhabers. Der Verlust dieser Karte muss der Polizei gemeldet werden. Gefundene oder unwirksam gewordene Karten müssen an die ausstellende Behörde zurückgegeben werden.

INSTRUCTIONS: This exemption is issued by Military Government. It is not transferable, must not be altered or destroyed, and is only valid when used in conjunction with the holder's identity card. The loss of this card must be reported to the police. If found, or on expiration of validity, this card must be returned to the issuing authority.

The military travel permit issued to my mother, my aunt and me. It allowed us to return to Cologne

GRÜNDE, EINZELHEITEN UND AMTLICHE UNTERSCHRIFT: Die umstehend benannte Person ist, wie unten angegeben, von Beschränkungen betreffend: AUSGANG—REISE—VERBOTENE GEGENSTÄNDE—SPERRBEZIRK befreit. (Nichtzutreffendes ist durchzustreichen).

REASONS, SPECIFICATIONS AND ENDORSEMENTS: The person named on the reverse hereof is granted exemption, only as specified below, from restrictions respecting: CURFEW — TRAVEL — PROHIBITED ARTICLES — PROHIBITED AREA (delete where applicable).

EINZELHEITEN DER BEFREIUNG
PARTICULARS OF EXEMPTION:

To report to local Burgomaster on arrival. Travel on roads

GRÜNDE:
REASONS:

Person have been examined and dusted.

going home.

Ausstellende Behörde: / Issuing Organisation: G. Hermann

Name (Druckschrift) / Name (printed):
Rang / Rank:

Unterschrift / Signature: Paul J. Jenkins
Stammnr. / Serial No:

procedure that every German who wanted to travel had to undergo so that the prevailing lice infestations would not spread.

Somehow, we made our way back to Cologne.

As our house on the Chlodwigplatz was badly damaged, we could not move in there until at least a few provisional repairs had been made. And so my mother and I rented two rooms with a toilet in the back of a building at Alteburgerstrasse 37, about three blocks away from our damaged home. The rental contract also allowed us the shared use of a small kitchen. This building had survived the war largely undamaged, as it was located in the suburbs just outside the medieval city walls. The bombers had considered that area a less desirable target, as the streets were wider and the roofs were not constructed out of highly flammable wooden beams. My grandparents and Tante Li found a similar flat right across the street from us at Alteburgerstrasse 34.

Every German was required to help with the cleaning-up efforts in the bombed cities. There was much rubble to be cleared from the streets in order to make them passable again. Along with all other capably bodied men and women, my mother was drafted for that task.

Along with all other Germans, my mother (at the right) helps to clear the rubble from the streets in Cologne

Dad Returns Home

We moved into the temporary quarters in the summer of 1945 after returning from our inn at the Drachenfels in Königswinter. My dad was still in a prisoner-of-war camp somewhere in Italy. But as Christmas time approached, I had an unusual surprise coming. In Germany, St. Nicklaus is a special holiday where St. Nick gives presents to good children. In any case, in early December St. Nick suddenly appeared. But instead of a bishop's tall miter hat, the strange man had a coffee pot warmer on his head. It was actually my dad, who had just returned from the POW camp and wanted to surprise me as Santa Claus. Understandably, the strange man did not have too many presents for me and apparently, I was not all that pleased to have Dad back.

My dad quickly got a job with the British Military Government that ruled Cologne and the surrounding area. That was proof that he had not been a real Nazi or a member of the Nazi party, as all Germans had to go through an elaborate *"Denazification"* process to weed out the true believers and to punish them. He must have passed the screening easily as the military government hired him immediately. He worked for the British officers in charge of the rebuilding on the destroyed bridges over the Rhine. In that job, he again was able to put his good English skills to work, just as he had done for the German army beforehand.

Punished by Saint Nick

For me as a kid, my dad's employment had certain privileges associated with it. For instance, a year later, I was invited to the official Christmas party given by the British military government for the children of all employees. I remember entering the reception hall, with the real Saint Nick sitting there on his throne in a fancy robe and with two books on his lap: there was the Golden Book in which all the good deeds of us children were recorded. In addition, there was the Black Book, in which all our bad deeds were listed. Unfortunately, my name was found in the Black Book because on a few occasions I had not been very polite to my own grandfather, Opa Toni. To my great embarrassment, Saint Nick read my misdeeds aloud to the entire assembled audience.

This also aroused the ire of Santa's helper, *Knecht Ruprecht*, who was lurking next to Saint Nick in a scary, totally black outfit. For added impact on the little children, his face and his hands were blackened as well. He looked fearsome! Knecht Ruprecht carried a big broom to punish the children that had been bad. He immediately leaped forward to castigate me for my misdeeds. Fortunately, he was attached to Saint Nick's chair with a long rattling iron chain that produced frightening sounds as he leaped forward towards me to mete out his punishment. It was a scary situation for a little kid. Instead of candy, I got a few lumps of coal as a present. But the scene certainly made a big impression on me that lasted for a lifetime. I resolved to be a good kid from then on. Like all the other kids, I must have received a Christmas present as well, but the only thing I can remember are the black Knecht Ruprecht and the lumps of coal.

Playtime in the Ruins and Almost Losing My Hand

Times were tough. Often there was not enough food to eat and there were no coals to fuel the ovens to keep us warm. So, some of the older teenagers and young adults in our neighborhood would go to the train tracks about one mile from our house and place bricks on the tracks. The bricks would cause the trains to derail or at least come to a stop. Then the juveniles would jump on the trains and throw the coal or food to their compatriots below. Like little Robin Hoods, the small bandits would give the ill-gotten treasures to their families or sell the stolen goods on the black market.

People did that to keep alive and the Cologne Cardinal Josef Frings essentially gave his blessings to this kind of pilfering. He announced in a sermon that it was not a sin to steal food or coal for personal use, if needed to survive. Consequently, stealing necessary food and fuel became known in Cologne as *"Fringsen"* and it was considered acceptable, as long as one could get away with it.

Having watched the big kids derail the trains, I wanted to try my hand at it as well. In the street in front of our house there were small train tracks — maybe three feet wide. On these tracks, a small steam train ran with little lorries that were formerly used in underground mines. The lorries carried the rubble from the urban area to the empty fields surrounding the city. There, the rubble was piled up in a gigantic rubble mountain or *Trümmerberg*.

I was just six years old and wanted to be like the big boys. So I placed a small brick on one of the tracks where the little train ran and tried to derail it. But I did not pull my hand back fast enough and one of the lorries ran over my hand. It immediately resulted in a large hematoma on the back of my left hand. The hematoma was a blood-filled swelling, maybe an inch high. Just at that moment, my granddad came back from work at his bar at the Chlodwigplatz. I can still visualize him as he hurried towards me in his white coat that he used to wear when he worked behind the bar. He carried the cash box with that morning's receipts under his arm. When he saw what had happened to me, he grabbed me and took me to the nearby hospital. Fortunately, nothing was broken and my hand was still attached. I had been lucky indeed that an empty lorry was leading the train and not the locomotive, which would have undoubtedly severed my left hand. My future life would have been very different as a disabled person without a hand. I had been very lucky indeed!

Playtime was certainly more adventuresome than anything experienced nowadays by most kids and much more dangerous as well. Our regular playground was the rubble field left by the bombs across the street from our own badly damaged house. Our house at the Chlodwigplatz was located right on the border of the old medieval city, and the Allies had concentrated their bombing on the densely populated area within the city walls. Thus, the houses across the street from us had all been leveled, and the kids used the ruins as their favorite playground.

We would pile up the bricks that littered the neighborhood and build little houses to play hide and seek. Naturally, they would collapse every now and then on top of us, but no major damage was done. We would also try to pry loose old pipes and sell them to the local scrap dealer. Copper pipes were particularly prized and valuable. More dangerous were the unexploded bombs, munitions and hand grenades that could be found in the ruins as well. Kids more adventuresome than I would build little fires and toss the munitions and grenades into the flames — and thus we created our own exciting fireworks! I still find it miraculous that none of my friends were harmed in a major way. Kids will adapt to anything!

I was so thin in those days that my family nicknamed me Gandhi — after the famous Indian leader who was as skinny as a rail. In my case, it was because we did not have enough to eat. To help garner food for the family, my mother would travel to the farms in the nearby Eifel Mountains to go *hamstern*. Hamsters, of course, are the little mammals that scurry about to find their food and bring it back to hide it in their burrows. My mother would do the same. She would travel by train to the rural farms and carry some precious items, like a few silver spoons or a small liquor bottle from our store. Then, she would trade them for food and bring the precious nourishment back to our family in Cologne. That was called hamstern.

Typhoid Fever Strikes

One day in late August 1946, my mother became very sick. I remember that she was moved from our apartment on the Alteburgerstrasse 37 to my grandparents' place across the street, so that they could take better care of her. Apparently, she had some kind of fever. I remember seeing her lying in my grandparents' bed, barely able to move. Everybody was concerned.

A few days later, she was transferred to the hospital. But it was not our little local hospital, the *Klösterchen*, which was only four or five blocks away and where I had been born. Instead it was the *Saint Elizabeth Hospital* in Hohenlind, which was quite far away from our home. I remember my dad and me visiting her in a special isolation ward at the hospital because by now she had been diagnosed with typhoid fever.

Typhoid fever was not an unusual sickness in those days. Because many of the water pipes and sewage canals had been damaged, waterborne infectious diseases were rampant in Germany. My Aunt Li also developed typhoid fever, as did several people in the neighborhood.

A day or two later, when we wanted to visit her again, we were not allowed to enter her room. We had to wait outside the hospital ward for quite a while. When my father and I were finally permitted to enter the restricted area, we were still not allowed to enter her room itself. She was quarantined in an isolation room and only the nuns working at the St. Elizabeth hospital were granted access.

The door to her room had a small window, made out of thick glass with small metal wires embedded in it. It was a strong, unbreakable safety glass that separated her from us. My dad lifted me up, so that I could see her resting in her bed. She gave me a tired wave. That was the last time I saw her. She died a day later on September 9, 1946. I was six years old.

It all went pretty fast. There were no hugs and no kisses. Just that one last glance and wave through the small safety window in the door of her hospital room. That was it.

My mother, who had carefully protected me throughout the war — at first from the bombers and then from the advancing troops — was gone after only a few days of sickness.

The funeral at the family grave on the *Melaten Friedhof* was very large and attended by all our family friends. As the funeral procession snaked its way from the small funeral chapel to the gravesite, we passed a huge statute of the *Sensemann*, the Grim Reaper, which depicts a skeleton carrying a large sickle over his shoulder. It was an impressive and memorable sight for a six-year-old boy on the way back from burying his mother.

My mom was interred in the same family grave where her own grandparents were buried as well. But she was the first of her generation to pass away. Several decades later, her parents as well as her two sisters joined her in the same tomb.

I remember standing at the open grave while the priest

My mother's grave in the family tomb covered with wreaths.

conducted the ceremony. It had been a rainy day and so we stood on a couple of long wooden planks, while hundreds of mourners carrying flowers and wreaths filed by. Eventually, a small mountain of wreaths covered the grave. It was time to go home.

From that day on, I lived with my dad in the small flat at Alteburgerstrasse 37, but I would take all my meals after school with my grandparents — at first in their flat across the street and later on at the rebuilt family home at the Chlodwigplatz.

I have often wondered what my life would have been like if my mother had stayed alive. Would it have been very different? I will never know. Actually, I had a pretty normal childhood. This was largely due to my grandmother and my aunts Mia and Li, who raised me and treated me like their own.

SAGE ADVICE:
Always Rely Upon Yourself and Acquire Emotional Toughness

6   Grade School German Style

At Easter 1946, I enrolled in first grade at a *Volksschule* or a "People's School." Most of these schools were named after their location, and ours was located next to the train tracks. Accordingly, my grade school was the *Volksschule Zugweg* or the "Train Track People's School." Nobody would have called the name of the school motivating or aspirational!

So, there I was in my schoolhouse next to the trains that rattled by all day long and carried coal to a gigantic, smoke-belching power plant right across the street from our school. It was not a very picturesque neighborhood.

A Motley Crew in First Grade

The war had ended just about a year ago, and our first grade class consisted of a motley crew of about 40 boys. Those were the days when boys and girls were strictly segregated and I can understand why. Because of the war, many children had never been in school. Others had recently fled from the distant parts of East Germany, which was now occupied by the Russians or had become part of Poland.

In my first grade class we had not only six-year olds, like me, but also older kids — up to ten years in age — that were just starting

My first day at school. I am carrying the traditional Wundertüte, full of sweets, to make the first day of school more palatable. Note the piles of rubble in the background.

school. Some of these kids were orphans who had survived on their own in the turmoil accompanying the end of the war. They were tough kids who had learned to take care of themselves. A few of them belonged to the train-jumper gangs that would derail the freight trains that lumbered along behind the school. They would then throw the freight, especially food and precious coal, to their waiting compatriots below who would sell the good on the black market. They were tough boys not to be messed with.

One day, four bullies attacked me during a break in the schoolyard. They held me down and took off my shoes and socks. Then they ran away with their loot. When I told my dad about it, he wanted to know whether I had defended myself vigorously against the attack. I told him that the bullies had been much bigger than me and that there had been four of them. I did not consider four against one a fair fight and said that I had had no chance. To my surprise, my dad did not offer any comforting words, but instead got pretty angry with me. He said that if I did not defend myself the next time something like this happened to me, he would "finish the job" by giving me a good spanking that I would remember for a long time. After that stern lecture and threat, I was not sure whether my dad was really on my side.

From that time on, I stayed away from the bullies and made a few good friends so that there would be safety in numbers. There were two nice boys, Friedel Weber and Willi Willpütz. Friedel had a backpack with a picture of an elephant stitched onto it. I guess that was what first attracted my attention to him. The Weber family owned several ships that plied the Rhine River and was considered very wealthy according to the standards of the time. Nowadays, the ships owned by the Weber family still sail on the Rhine under the name *Colonia Schiffahrt* and offer sightseeing tours on the river to visiting tourists. Willi Willpütz's dad was a gym teacher and made his living by offering gym lessons in the basement of his house. The three of us would often walk to the nearby *Römer Park* and play hide-and-seek among the old Roman tombs preserved in this little green oasis that was surrounded by ruins.

Our first grade teacher was Fräulein Quodbach. She was probably about 50 years old and walked with a cane, which she could wield with great effect to restore order. If we spoke when we were not supposed to speak, she would march up to us and order us to make a *Knuetzje*. There is no word for it in the English language, but we had to hold our five fingers together in an upward direction, and then she would smack us with a sturdy ebony ruler on our fingertips. That would hurt a lot and by doing that, quiet was restored.

Another form of punishment in the classroom was that we had to stand quietly in the corner, face against the wall. I remember one time when I was relegated to standing there, but had to go to the bathroom quite urgently. I kept raising my hand to ask for permission to do so, but Miss Quodbach just told me to be quiet. Eventually, nature took its course, and I peed into my pants. As some of the other kids standing against the wall were eventually allowed to move back to their seats, we all had to move one spot over. And each time that I moved, I left a small puddle of pee on the floor. Finally, it was my turn to sit down again and Miss Quodbach spotted the small puddles that I had left as my trail. She got quite angry and yelled that I should have gone to the bathroom. In a meek voice, I told her that I had tried to raise my hand and ask for permission, but that she had ignored me. I guess she realized that she herself was the cause of my predicament and I was not punished any further.

Discipline in Grade School

When I got home from school, my grandmother Oma was in charge. Because no one had enough money for paper, we would write our homework on slates with a *Griffel* or a metal stylus. The slates were made out of a black stony substance that was about seven by ten inches large and set in a wooden frame. With the help of the *Griffel* or stylus, we would etch white letters into the slate. It was a bit like Moses etching the Ten Commandments into his tablets.

I would have to write one whole slate of "a's," then a slate of "e's" and so on. If I did not have the right slant for the cursive letters, or the a's looked a bit like e's or o's, Oma was right there with a sponge, wiped out the entire slate, and I would have to start all over again.

Herr Daners was our teacher in second grade. He had a somewhat different method to maintain order: a simple caning of the offending child would do the trick. He would lift the hapless student off his feet and a few whacks with the cane on the behind of his unlucky victim would generally be sufficient to restore order. There was one little redheaded classmate by the name of Willi Katernberg, who would frequently get into trouble. Translated literally into English, his name meant "Willi Tom-Cat-Mountain." When Willi had done something wrong or had misbehaved, Herr Daners would simply lift him up by the shoulder straps of his Lederhosen. Then, Willi's little legs would start spinning in mid-air like those of Donald Duck in the Walt Disney cartoons in a vain attempt to escape the firm grip of Herr Daners. Without mercy, the stick of Herr Daners would swing at Willi's Lederhosen, which probably protected him from the worst of the beating. As Willi's his little legs would spin futilely in mid-air, his face turned bright red to match the color of his hair. We all witnessed what would happen to us if we did not behave and learned that lesson well. Thus was life.

Willi Kalscheuren was another classmate. He was a bit crazy. During intermissions you could see him racing across the schoolyard. After he had reached top speed, he would crash himself head first into a metal trashcan or into the brick walls ringing our exercise yard. When we would see him starting on one of his sprints, everyone would yell "*Kalscheuren ist los*" and the student closest to him would try to stop him — usually without avail. Even if we stopped him he, he would try again a few minutes later. Things probably did not end well for Willi.

Not that our teachers were immune from violence against them. One day, the dad of one of the kids who had been manhandled by the teacher walked into the classroom. The burly parent strode up to the teacher and essentially lifted him up by his lapels and threatened: "If you ever touch my son again, I'll come to your house and rearrange your furniture!" Rearranging someone else's furniture was about the most severe threat that adults could express towards each other in Germany — short of engaging in an actual scuffle.

Teacher's Pet

By the time that I was in third and fourth grade, I had become somewhat of a teacher's pet. Not only was I one of the smarter kids in the class, but also I was usually fairly well behaved. I remembered the lessons learned from the caning of little Willi Katernberg! So, when our teacher had to leave the classroom to see the principal or attend to some other business, he would often ask me to sit at the teacher's desk on the podium upfront. I had to write the names of all the kids that misbehaved on the blackboard so that he could punish them when he returned. That was actually not a very smart procedure, as the offending kids could see their own names go up on the blackboard and obviously they did not like the prospect of being punished. So, the biggest and strongest of them would simply get up, march to the blackboard and erase their own name from the list of offenders. What could I to do to stop them when they were much bigger and stronger than me? The smaller and meeker kids sat there to await their punishment from the returning teacher and the strong bullies got off free — and I was the implicit accomplice in that unjust system. It was not much fun, but there was not much that I could do about it.

Fed by the Quakers

When I was in first grade, there was little food available at home. As a result, we were all fed at school. The menu every day was the same: someone would haul in a large metal vat of hot *Quakerspeise*, or oatmeal, which had been donated by the American Quakers. We all lined up. Most kids carried an old military canteen that was no longer used by a German soldier. And then each one of us got one big helping of hot oatmeal. The same diet was served on Monday, Tuesday, Wednesday, Thursday and Friday. At the end of first grade, I had eaten enough oatmeal to last me a lifetime.

For the adults, life was harsh as well. The prices of all commodities were rigidly controlled, but money was plentiful. The problem was that you could not buy anything with the worthless money. Instead, people had to have ration coupons to buy a loaf of bread or a pair of sox — if those items were available at all. The economy was essentially at a standstill and people resorted to barter or hamstering by trading their own precious belongings for other essential items. A piece of silverware might be bartered for two loaves of bread or a small rug for a leg of ham.

On my way to school with an old German army canteen. I am ready for my Quaker Oat meal.

Currency Reform

As the economy was at a virtual standstill, the new German Minister of Economics, Ludwig Erhard, instituted a currency reform in 1948. The old Reichsmark became worthless and every German was allotted 60 Deutsche Mark, as the new currency was called. Instantly, the situation was reversed: money was suddenly scarce and farmers and shopkeepers eagerly offered up their wares to earn the new, valuable money. Goods started to appear again on the shelves and people were eager to work even for meager wages.

While Germany was not flourishing by any means, the country's economy was again growing and on it's long road back to prosperity. But rebuilding all the ruined buildings and achieving a comfortable living standard would take several decades.

The Wrong Motto

About that time, my dad gave me a small pocket calendar for the coming year as a present. On the first page, there was a special spot inscribed: "My Motto" and it invited you to write in an inspirational message for the coming year. I wrote:

"Wer Arbeit kennt und sich nicht drückt — der ist verrückt!"

The slogan rhymes very nicely in German and translates into: "He who knows work and does not avoid it — is crazy!"

Eventually, my dad discovered my inscription and flew into an enormous rage because I had selected this indolent slogan as my motto for the next year. Probably as a result of his extraordinary indignation, I never forgot my little slogan for the rest of my life.

SAGE ADVICE:
You Can Learn Something Even Under Trying Conditions;
Dear Money is Good for the Economy;
And, of Course: Avoid Any Unnecessary Work!

7   Almost Failing High School

The late 1940s were a tumultuous time in world history. While hostilities in Germany had ended in May 1945 and Japan capitulated a few months later, peace and tranquility was not restored. There were still massive movements of refugees and displaced people under way all over Europe. All German territory east of the rivers Oder and Neisse became part of Poland. A chunk of what used to be Eastern Prussia was incorporated directly into Russia. All Germans living in these territories were forced to move out. About 10 million refugees from these former German territories moved westward in one of the largest mass migrations in world history.

As Stalin solidified his grip on Eastern Europe, there were further mass movements of people. About one-third of the eastern part of Poland became part of the Ukraine. The displaced Poles had to leave their homes and Ukrainians moved into what had been eastern Poland. In turn, the Poles were moved westwards and resettled in the former German territory next to the rivers Oder and Neisse. It was highly confusing to all and the people who were forced to move out of their old homes and resettle somewhere else endured much hardship.

In 1948, the Soviet occupation forces of East Germany blockaded surface access to the encircled city of Berlin. The famous

Berlin airlift was started by the Western Allies to supply the city with necessary food and fuel for almost a year. Tensions in Germany were at the boiling point and many people thought that World War III was about to start.

At the same time, the Chinese Communists under Mao waged their successful campaign against the Nationalist regime in China, ending with Communist control over that gigantic country in 1949. Just a few months later, the Korean War broke out with North Korea invading the South and almost winning the battle. Communism was on the march all over the world!

Making Plans to Avoid the Third World War

My dad, who had returned from World War II just a few years earlier was convinced that Stalin would seize the opportunity and soon invade Western Europe to consolidate his grip on the entire Continent. He was in no mood to go to war again and he started to make plans to escape from the Russian onslaught that he expected.

But what could he do to escape from what looked like the coming World War III? We did not own a car with which we could have escaped westward towards France or Belgium. But trying to escape by car would probably have been an unsuccessful endeavor anyhow. The roads would be clogged and gasoline would not be available. And in any case, the Russian tanks would probably advance with such high speed that most of Germany would be overrun within a few days.

So he decided to purchase an ocean-going sailboat that the two of us would use to sail from our home in Cologne down the Rhine River and across the North Sea to Ireland. Ireland had remained neutral during World War II, and my dad figured that Ireland would again be neutral during the coming World War III. He had lived in Ireland some 20 years earlier and he had liked the country very much. So he started to make plans to return there if and when hostilities broke out in Europe.

Consequently, the two of us traveled to the island of Langeoog on the Frisian Coast and bought a 35-foot sailboat. The boat's name was *Knurrhahn*, which translates into the *Sea Robin* in English. My dad even bought a somewhat faded flag of North Rhine Westphalia, the state where Cologne was located. The flag was striped Green-White-Red and with its washed-out colors it looked a lot like the Green-White-Orange flag of the Irish Republic. But there was a small problem: the North Rhine Westphalian stripes were horizontal, while the Irish stripes were vertical. But my dad was not deterred. He cut off a part of the rectangular flag so that it was virtually square in shape and planned to turn it sideways after the Russians invaded.

He calculated that the Russians would stop at the Rhine, we would hoist our fake Irish flag, and then the two of us would sail undisturbed down the Rhine River. He expected that the Russians on the eastern bank of the river and the Americans on the western bank would all observe diligently our presumed Irish neutrality. I was very happy that we never had to put his fanciful thesis about escaping from the coming warfare to the test, but he certainly was a careful planner!

After we took possession of Knurrhahn in Langeoog, my dad and I sailed around the island for a shakedown cruise. Also along was Herr Steffens, who presumably knew a lot about sailing and boats. We rounded the tip of Langeoog and were now on the side facing the open ocean. The wind was blowing hard and the tide was running. Pretty soon, we found ourselves in a rapidly narrowing waterway between a seemingly growing sandbank and the island itself. Eventually, we ran out of room and the Knurrhahn ran aground. I was scared and jumped off the boat and waded ashore in the shallow waters.

My dad and Mr. Steffens stayed on board and waited until a cutter from the *Deutsche Gesellschaft zur Rettung Schiffbrüchiger* arrived. It was a boat owned by the "German Society for the Rescue of Men in Peril at Sea." In spite its long name, the rescuers, equivalent to the American Coast Guard, were very quick to show up. They tried to shoot a towing line across our boat with the help of a hand-held device. But the charge in the launching pistol

The Knurrhahn stranded on the coast of Langeoog. After I jumped off the boat, I am standing at the very right of the picture.

exploded and the seaman's hand was badly burned. Eventually, the rescuers were successful and they towed the boat into open waters — leaving me alone ashore. I walked by myself across the narrow island and reunited with the Knurrhahn and my angry dad in the harbor on the other side of Langeoog.

After that, the three of us sailed through the canals of Holland to the Rhine River. It was a very pleasant trip through the Dutch countryside. When we reached the Rhine, we decided to accept a tow from a large steamship instead of powering against the strong river current for almost 200 miles all the way back to Cologne.

Back in Cologne, my dad discovered to his great dismay that the mast of the sailboat would not fit under the Rhine bridges during times of high water — as was usual during the springtime snowmelt runoffs. So he hoped that the Russians would attack during the summer, when the water level of the Rhine was fairly low. Thank God, the Russians never came and we never had to put the Irish flag routine to the test!

Qualifying for High School

At about the same time, I took one of the most important exams of my entire life: the entrance exam for high school or the *Gymnasium*. These were pretty tough exams in writing and arithmetic that essentially determined a person's entire future and career. If you did very well, you could go to the Gymnasium, the German equivalent of high school that leads eventually to a university education. Only about 15 percent of all kids passed the exam in those days and were allowed to go on to the Gymnasium for the next nine years.

If you earned only a slightly better than average grade, you would enter a six-year *Mittelschule* or Middle School, which prepared you for most of the mid-level professions not requiring a university degree. But if you did below average — and about half the kids fell into this category — you continued in the same Volksschule for another four years. You would most likely become a manual worker: a butcher, a baker or a candlestick maker. "No Child Left Behind" was not the order of the day — instead it was all about "Survival of the Fittest."

Life at the Kreuzgasse Gymnasium

Along with my grade school classmates Friedel Weber and Willi Willpütz, I passed the exams to enter the Gymnasium. The three of us entered the *Gymnasium Kreuzgasse*, which was not far away from our homes. I would ride my bike to the suburb where the school was temporarily located because the old building in the city center had been totally destroyed. Just like the Volksschule Zugweg, the Kreuzgasse was an all-boys school. But because so many schools had been destroyed during the war, we had to share our building with a girl's school, the *Irmgardis Schule*. I spent the next few years attending the Kreuzgasse Gymnasium in the Cologne suburb of Marienburg, an elegant and only slightly destroyed suburb south of the city.

Again I was in a class of 30 or 40 children. But the German high schools were different from the American model in that all the students would stay in the same classroom and the teachers would rotate in and out. While we stayed together and bonded pretty well, the teachers for German, mathematics, biology, physics, chemistry, English, French, Latin and all the other subjects would rotate each hour.

German high schools last for nine years, which added to the four years of grade school, amounts to a total of thirteen years of school. That is one year longer than the customary twelve years in America. But the classes were not numbered first, second, third grade as one might expect. Instead, they were numbered backwards, with the lowest numbers assigned to the most advanced classes. Students would start in sixth grade and then were promoted to fifth grade and so on. To make things even more confusing, all the grades were counted in Latin. Starting at the bottom, the classes were numbered: *Sexta, Quinta, Quarta, Tertia, Sekunda* and *Prima*. But to add to the complexity, and for no particular rational reason at all, the last three grades were split into two years each: *Unter Tertia* and *Ober Tertia*; *Unter Sekunda* and *Ober Sekunda*; as well as *Unter Prima* and *Ober Prima*. Each moniker "Unter" stood for "Lower" and "Ober" for "Upper." Thus, the highest class was the Ober Prima, or the "Upper First Grade." I suppose if you could understand which class you were actually in, you were not only an accomplished mathematician but also a Latin scholar! After finishing the Ober Prima, we would be granted the *Abitur* and receive our *Reifezeugnis* — the official attestation that we were "ripe." And that meant that you were ready to enroll in a university.

Many kids actually left school after six years at the end of the Unter Sekunda. They would leave with the *Einjährigen* — the "One-Year Finish" as it was called for an inexplicable reason as it obviously took ten years to get to this point in one's education. Whoever invented this system of numbering high school classes obviously had a few marbles missing!

While we were learning Latin and studying classical literature, we were still subject to pretty barbaric punishments. There was Budda, our gigantic Catholic religion teacher, who would grab our hands and made us slap our own face with our hands when we had done something wrong or had misbehaved. That was because he — as a man of the cloth — was opposed to punishing us directly. Consequently, we were forced to administer the punishment ourselves. Try it! It probably hurts more than having someone else slap your face.

Dr. Voss was our German and French teacher. Always demanding and very stern, he would stand at the top of the staircase when we returned from intermission and make sure that nobody spoke a word. Order and discipline were paramount as we marched back to our classes.

Herr Heuser was our sports and English teacher. He had spent the end of the war years in an American POW camp in Georgia. There, the Americans taught the German POWs to sing all the old Southern slave songs when the prisoners did their work in the fields. In turn, Herr Heuser taught us the old slave shanties in English class, with him standing in front of the class and intoning: "Carry me back to my old Virginny..." I can still sing some of these shanties, which may be an unusual talent for a German, I presume.

The Latin classes by Herr Venten were pure torture. Every day, we had to recite a new set of Latin vocabulary words and then conjugate or declinate them. We even had to read Caesar's writings in the original Latin text and memorize entire sections by heart. Herr Venten rewarded us by flunking well over half of the students in the class. I usually was among the flunkies and I still do not know how to correctly translate a single sentence into Latin.

There was also a smattering of international students in our high school. One of the most prominent ones was Bijan Esfandijari, the younger brother of Queen Soraya of Iran. The father of Bijan and her Royal Highness was the Iranian Ambassador to Germany. Every day, Bijan was chauffeured in a big black Mercedes 300 limousine to school. It was the same model as the German Chancellor drove. The teachers, who could afford no more than a bicycle, stood there in envy as the *Princeling* was dropped off in front of our school. But Bijan was pretty popular with all of us in school as well as with the girls in town. Rumor had it that the father of one of his many girlfriends booted Bijan out of his house after he surprised him and his daughter in a compromising position in the living room. After he had kicked Bijan out the front door, the dad went into the kitchen at the back of the house, only to find Bijan there as he flirted with the maid.

Escaping From Summer Camp

When I was about 12 years old, my father thought I should spend the summer at a catholic youth camp in southern Germany. The group was pretty much akin to the Boy Scouts and we all wore our Lederhosen for the requisite camping trips. I was sent to summer camp at an old castle in Niederalfingen, a tiny town in the mountains near Stuttgart in southern Germany. We all slept in long rows of bunk beds. I had inherited my dad's old German army sleeping bag, replete with several stitched-up shrapnel holes that had been inflicted upon the bag during the Africa campaign. The stuffing consisted of real goose down, and the prized sleeping bags were issued only to members of the *Afrika-Korps*. While my dad considered the old desert-army sleeping bag a historic collectors item, to me it was a bit embarrassing.

Every day we got to march through the hills near the castle behind a leader carrying a flag. We had to march behind the leader singing inspiring songs as we trooped through the forests. I did not like the regimentation one bit and the food was not very good either. We got as much bread as we could eat. It was covered with lots of margarine and jam. On Mondays, it was strawberry jam; on Tuesdays, plum jam; on Wednesdays, apricot jam...You get the picture!

A friend of mine from back home was also in the camp. His name was Rudolf Reinold, but everybody called him *Qualle*, which meant fat jellyfish in German. After one week, the two of us decided that we had enough of the regimentation and the marching and that we wanted to go home. But how could we accomplish that short of just walking well over 200 miles back to Cologne?

Eventually, we devised a pretty ingenuous plan for two 12-year olds. We walked to the post office in the next village and asked to make a phone call back to the camp. In those days, all long-distance calls went through an operator and we knew that the operator was located in Schwäbisch Gmünd, some 20 miles away. We asked the friendly person in charge of the phone calls at the post office whether he could do us a favor and arrange to have the operator announce the call as coming from Gmünd, and not Schwäbisch Gmünd. Gmünd was an entirely different town almost 200 miles away at the Tegernsee in the foothills of the Alps. Qualle's parents were vacationing there at that time and we had a plan to impersonate his parents. After the operator placed the call, Qualle put a handkerchief over the mouthpiece and in a very low voice asked to speak to our group leader at the camp. We knew that all the leaders were on a special trip and so we were sure that the leader would not be able to come to the phone in person. Instead, we left a message allegedly from Qualle's dad that the two of us had parental permission to come home early. We blew a big sigh of relief and left the post office building feeling very accomplished.

As luck would have it, at that very moment all the camp leaders marched by the post office with their flags flying and bellowing their songs. We were petrified that we had been detected, but they never noticed us.

After we returned on shaky legs to the camp, we were told that our parents had called and we had permission to go home. With that, the camp leader handed each of us a one-way ticket back to Cologne. We thought that our plan might work after all.

The next morning, we walked to the train station and boarded the local train to Stuttgart. There, we cashed in the remaining part of the ticket for a few German Marks and headed towards the Autobahn to hitchhike a ride home. Hitchhiking was universally accepted in those days, and several other people stood at the Autobahn with their thumbs out. Two 12-year olds did not arouse any special attention. Eventually, an empty truck stopped and loaded the dozen hitchhikers onto the truck and we were on our way home with quite a bit of money in our pockets.

I still do not know why we never got into trouble at home

because of our wily escape from the camp. But my home life was fairly chaotic at that time as my mother had passed away years earlier and I shuttled between my dad's apartment and my grandparents' home on a regular basis. And, of course, Qualle's parents were on vacation in Gmünd in the Alps. So we got off scot-free!

Repeating a School Year and Almost Flunking Out

I passed the first three years of the Gymnasium without much of an incident. I had average grades, getting mostly grades of 2 "good" or 3 "satisfactory" according to the German grading scale, where the top grade is a 1 or "very good" and 6 "unsatisfactory" means flunking. According to the rigid rules, you could not have more than two grades in the bottom categories of 5 and 6 if you wanted to be promoted to the next grade. Latin was my least favorite subject and I hated all the memorizing I had to do. Typically, I got a 6 in Latin, thereby flunking the class. So that was one more or less permanent strike against me.

When I reached the Unter Tertia, or ninth grade according to the American scale, I had to take French in addition to Latin. I got a 5 in French and as I was already flunking Latin, I had to repeat the entire Unter Tertia. This penalty was imposed in spite of the fact that my overall grades were the second or third highest in the entire class. We called repeating a class doing an *Ehrenrunde* or an "Honorary Lap."

My friend Willi Willpütz even had to take two honorary laps and to repeat two different classes, but he nevertheless managed to found and build up a successful international enterprise with facilities in Turkey, India and Hong Kong. Our Latin teacher would be astounded — and perhaps a bit envious — about Willi's success. Hopefully, he would be a bit chagrined as well!

When I repeated the class, not much changed. Now I got a 6 in French and a 5 in Latin at midterm time. Another rule said that one could not take the same class three times, but would have to leave the school instead. Consequently, there was a real danger that

I would totally flunk out of school at yearend. That would not have been very desirable. My dad had never finished the Gymnasium himself and instead had started an apprenticeship at the Deutsche Bank. He thought I should do the same. While I was disappointed about him not helping me, I was not very surprised and implemented an alternative strategy.

I went to my aunt Mia and asked her to help me switch schools, which she gladly did. With her help, I left the Kreuzgasse Gymnasium and enrolled at the *Albertus Magnus Gymnasium*. At the new school, I did not have to take both French and Latin, and thereby the key obstacle to my progress was removed. Instead of French and Latin, we had much more mathematics, chemistry, physics and biology — all subjects that I liked much better. The new school was a *Naturwissenschaftliches Gymnasium*, or a natural science high school, instead of a *Klassisches Gymnasium* or a classical high school, like the Kreuzgasse was. In English, the word Kreuzgasse means "Alley of the Cross," and I was very happy not to have to bear that cross any longer. I was very grateful to my aunt Mia as her intervention allowed me to continue my studies.

Thriving at the Albertus Magnus Gymnasium

The switch in schools turned out to be a smart decision and I started to enjoy learning. I liked to study what I was good at and subjects that I excelled in. In contrast, I hated subjects like Latin and French that relied mostly on plain memorization. I learned another valuable lesson: That sometimes good can come out of impending disaster and that taking a detour is not always a bad idea.

The AMG, as the Albertus Magnus Gymnasium was generally called, was a UNESCO Model School. Often, delegations of educators from around the world came and visited our classes. It was fun to have gentlemen in turbans and ladies in elegant African tribal gowns attend our classes, and on these occasions the teachers would be extra nice to us as well.

It was an interesting group of students that made up my class. My closest friend was Manfred Peckmann, who later became an engineer for Daimler Benz. A classmate who became quite famous was Winfried Kill. Winfried was not only a tennis champ, but with 50,000 German marks borrowed from his mother, he bought a defunct business and eventually built it into a multi-industry conglomerate called INDUS. At the peak of his career, Winfried was a German mark billionaire. Rudolf Mies became a respected medical professor at the University of Cologne. Willi Wiesdorf always had the best looking girl friends and I envied Hartmut Garding a bit because in his junior year he was able to go to Michigan as a foreign exchange student. That was something that I wanted to do very much myself as well.

Jürgen von Papen was another classmate. Jürgen's uncle, Franz von Papen, had been the German Chancellor just prior to Adolf Hitler. Jürgen himself was also a consummate politician. The annual elections to be the *Klassensprecher*, the Speaker of the Class, often came down to an election contest between Jürgen and myself. I now loved school and I was thriving!

Altogether, we had lots of fun at the Gymnasium and engaged in many practical jokes as well, such as pretending to commit mass-suicide on the train tracks during a school excursion!

Holding forth at a High School event. From left to right: myself, Jürgen von Papen, Hartmut Garding and Rudolf Mies

On a class excursion, it looks like we were sick and tired of high school. I am the third one from the right.

Publishing the School Paper

The most fun I had at school was when I became the editor of the *Antenne*, our monthly school magazine. I had started by writing articles and selling ads for the paper. Selling ads was a very lucrative endeavor as we were allowed to keep ten percent of the proceeds as an incentive commission. That might represent as much as a hundred German Marks in income a month, and that was a lot of money in postwar Germany. I also wrote many articles and pretty soon my fellow journalists elected me editor.

Antenne means "Antenna" in English, and we tried to be a receiver and disseminator of all kinds of news, not just the news that happened in our school. At the time when I became editor, the German army was reconstituted as a fighting force and all young men could again be drafted. I was not too pleased and wrote an article against the "remilitarization" of Germany. A few days after the article appeared, I was called to the principal's office and given a strict lecture that we at the Antenne should stay out of affairs of state. Dr. Honnefelder, our beloved principal, told me sternly that

I was an embarrassment to the German Chancellor Konrad Adenauer, who had been the mayor of Cologne, our hometown. I learned another lesson: keep your nose out of politics!

Die Antenne — Klaus Wallbrecht, our graphics designer, and I hold the Prime Minister's Prize for the best school newspaper in the state.

A few months later, a jury selected the Antenne as the best school newspaper in our state. The Prime Minister of the State of North Rhine Westphalia gave a small reception and invited our principal as well as our graphic designer Klaus Wallbrecht and me as the chief editor to a ceremony, where he presented us with an impressive plaque. Dr. Honnefelder was as proud as he could be of his youthful and successful protégées. I learned a further lesson: if you do well, all misdeeds are soon forgiven and forgotten!

Coming of Age

One of the more enjoyable activities at the paper was to arrange several annual parties. At first, these dances were held in our school gym. As we were all over sixteen years old, we were also allowed to drink alcohol on those occasions. I remember one Saturday evening dance party held at our school where we had a lot of spiked punch left over. I stored the leftover beverage in the Antenne office until Monday morning. Early on Monday, we had a three-hour-long German essay exam. But before beginning the test, I stopped by the office and, feeling a bit hungry, ate several of the peaches that had been left in the punch bowl since Saturday. Of course, it did not take long until I was quite inebriated from the alcohol that had been soaked up by the peaches. So I just sat there in the exam room without writing much. When the teacher observed me doing nothing, he stopped by my desk and asked: "Heller, why aren't you writing?" I answered: "I am thinking about what I should write!" The teacher smelled the abundant alcohol on my breath and exclaimed: "Heller — You are drunk!" Well, right he was. But because I had not really broken any existing laws, I was allowed to continue writing my essay. I forgot what grade I got in the exam.

The Antenne hired increasingly popular bands and pretty soon the parties grew from a few dozen students to hundreds and even thousands that filled the largest ballrooms of Cologne. Students from all the other Cologne high schools attended our popular Antenne parties.

Of course, I had to learn how to dance and so I attended the *Tanzschule Schulerecki*. Our high school was a boys-only high school, just like most German schools were in those days. It did not take me long to discover that the dancing school was a great place to meet girls, and so I repeated the same dancing classes again and again. Foxtrot, rhumba, tango and waltz — they all brought me in touch with more girls. As far as I was concerned, it was heaven on earth and I found my first girl friends there.

During one of these dancing lessons, I met a cute brunette named Anneli Seul. She went to the *Ursulinenschule*, a Catholic all-girls school run by pious nuns. Soon, Anneli became my steady girl friend. Together with a small group of close friends, we would spend many weekends and vacations together. We all had little scooters with which we would travel on holidays to nearby Holland or even to Switzerland and Spain. In many ways, travel was a lot easier and safer in those days. Crime was very low and we would spend our nights in youth hostels or small hotels.

On vacation in Borkum with Anneli and her friend Bibi.

One glorious summer, I told my dad that I was going to travel with a classmate to Sweden. Instead, we both met secretly with our girl friends Anneli and Bibi on the island of Borkum, a small dune-covered island on the northern German coast. We had a great time swimming in the surf and lazing about in the dunes without our parents knowing what was going on. Later on, Anneli and I would travel together to America.

Learning to Fly Glider Planes

When I was sixteen, I spent an exciting and breathtaking summer vacation on the North See island of Langeoog, the same island where my dad had bought his sailboat a few years earlier. I learned to fly glider planes that were either towed aloft or literally catapulted into the sky with the help of a long rope attached to a powerful winch. By now, my dad was working for the newly formed Lufthansa Airline and he was all excited about me learning how to fly. The name Langeoog means Long Island in the Frisian dialect, which is spoken on the island. Langeoog was just that: 10 miles long and only a few hundred yards wide. Consequently, you flew most of the time over the ocean instead of land.

One of the "older" men taking the glider-training course along with me was Harald Quandt. He and his half-brother Herbert Quandt were sons of a rich German industrialist. After Harald's mother divorced, she married Josef Goebbels, the Nazi Minister of Propaganda, making Harald Quandt the stepson of Goebbels. Harald was a Luftwaffe officer during the war and was captured by the Allies in Africa. At the end of the war, Goebbels and his wife poisoned themselves and their own six young children with cyanide. Harald, imprisoned in an Allied POW camp, was the only survivor of the Goebbels family. When the elder Mr. Quandt died a few years later, Harald and his brother Herbert Quandt became two of the wealthiest men in Germany. They inherited a large part of BMW as well as other industrial companies.

Harald Quandt had flown to the island in his own small propeller-driven aircraft — a true rarity in post-war Germany. He knew how to fly propeller planes, but wanted to learn how to pilot glider planes as well.

One day, Harald Quandt was up in the sky with his glider plane. He had journeyed a bit too far away from the very narrow island of Langeoog and did not have enough altitude to make it back to the airport. So we all watched in amazement as he ditched his glider plane a few hundred yards offshore in the North Sea, calmly climbed out of the cockpit and sat on the floating glider plane to await his rescue. For me, this was a familiar spot: it was just about the same location where my dad had stranded his sailboat only a few years earlier.

Eventually, a boat came out to save him, and he did not even get his feet wet. We all learned the lesson not to stray too far from the island and to carefully watch our descent coefficients, something you did not have to pay as much attention to in a motor plane. Unfortunately, Harald Quandt was killed in an airplane crash in Italy when he was not even 50 years old.

Thinking About a Career

Back at school, the subject matters got tougher and tougher. I had a fairly easy time because there was no more Latin and French, my two most dreaded subjects. But even my favorites, like physics and mathematics, became more and more demanding. I had considered studying physics at the university level, but when we started to use difficult mathematical tools like differential equations in our physics classes, I realized that I had reached my limits. While I could master regular calculus, differential calculus was a bit too much for me. The good news was that these demanding high school classes made me reconsider my decision to study physics at the university level. As I liked my journalistic experience at the school newspaper, I decided to become an economic journalist.

There are many examples of people who had started to study physics but then changed to economics, including the very first economics Nobel Laureate Jan Tinbergen. I have often thought of economics as "physics-light" as it uses many of the same tools as physics, but in not as demanding a way. At least that was true in those days. Nowadays, economists use mathematical tools that are every bit as demanding as those used in physics. Well, I guess I caught the economics wave just in time before it crested!

My First Job

During one of the summer vacations I had a job as a bricklayer's helper at the old *Stollwerck* chocolate factory a few blocks away from our house. The chocolate factory had been almost totally destroyed during the war and it was time to rebuild. The Germans wanted to eat good chocolate again!

The big piles of rubble left after the bombings were full of bricks that were still intact, but they were covered with crumbling old mortar. It was my job to scrape the mortar off the bricks and to arrange the rejuvenated bricks in neat piles on wooden boards. Next, I would carry the bricks up on the scaffolding. The actual bricklayers then covered the restored bricks with fresh layers of mortar and cemented them into place.

That was simple enough. The job paid me 50 Pfennigs an hour — the equivalent of 12 American cents! For a tough eight-hour day of hard work I received exactly one dollar as my daily wage! But I thought I was paid pretty well!

There were side benefits as well. Inside the Stollwerck compound we were allowed to eat as much chocolate as we wanted. I especially loved the light-brown nougat and consumed copious amounts of it.

The regular construction workers were pretty tough characters that played pretty crude jokes on each other. One day, a fellow worker wrapped a big chunk of the prized soft nougat into a newspaper and stashed it into the pocket of his coat, which was hanging on a coat rack in the lunchroom. He was probably saving it as a nice desert to eat after lunch. After he left, another worker went to the bathroom, took a big dump, and wrapped the stinky mess into another piece of newspaper. The perpetrator then exchanged the two bundles as the entire bricklayer crew watched and waited. When the unfortunate victim finally returned and finished his lunch, he pulled the substitute package out of his coat pocket. He was eager to enjoy the nougat for desert — only to stick his hand into the gooey mass left there by his "buddy." I am still surprised that nobody was killed in the ensuing melee, as these were rough and tumble times!

When we left the factory at the end of the day, all workers had to hit a red button as they went through the exit gates. A red or green light would light up in random order. If you had a green light, you could exit; if you had a red light, a guard would search you for contraband chocolate. If the guards found any chocolate on you, you were fired on the spot. That simple device was a pretty effective policing mechanism!

Making Friends for Life

Eventually, at the age of twenty, I finished high school. I was the first person of our family to ever do so. My dad had only made it to the Einjähriges before starting an apprenticeship as a banker with Deutsche Bank. My mother had attended a school specializing in arts and crafts and had hoped to make a career out of designing artistic pottery and metal artifacts. None of my grandparents had made it beyond grade school, which was not unusual for the times that they lived in.

Most of my fellow-students with whom I finished high school by passing the tough final exams or Abitur did very well in life. What is astounding is that almost all of my classmates stayed in or near Cologne for their entire lives and remained close friends. The group gets together every year on the day after Christmas.

Our 50th high school reunion in 2010 brought many of the old friends together. I am in the back row on the left.

Obviously, it is difficult for me to attend these regular Christmas-time reunions as I am living over 5,000 miles away. But I did go back for our fiftieth high school graduation reunion, which we celebrated in a monastery in the Eifel Mountains near Cologne. When I walked into the room, where most of my former classmates were already assembled, I thought that I had entered the wrong venue: who were all those old, grey-haired men? But after half an hour of camaraderie, everything was just like in the good old days in high school. We were friends for life!

SAGE ADVICE:
If You Encounter an Obstacle in Life, Don't Give Up. Instead Take a Detour!
Always Keep Your Friends and Bond With Them For Life!

8 My Cologne Heritage

The Center of My Universe

I was born in Cologne and always considered myself more a citizen of that old and venerable city than as a German. When Jesus Christ was born, Cologne was already a Roman settlement. In the year 50 A.D., the Roman Emperor Claudius bestowed formal city rights upon the garrison that he fortified to defend the northeastern frontier of the Roman Empire against the Germanic hordes roaming on the eastern bank of the Rhine.

In the same year, Claudius got married to Agrippina. Because she had been born in the Roman garrison on the Rhine, the emperor named the new city in her honor *Colonia Claudia Ara Agrippinensis*. This somewhat lengthy city name clearly described his intent: "Colony of Claudius, an Altar to Agrippina." He wanted to both memorialize his deed of having founded the new city and also honor his wife. The rather cumbersome and lengthy name was later shortened to simply Cologne. The Germans shortened the name further to Köln.

Agrippina was a lady who had led a most interesting life even before she married Claudius. She was the great-granddaughter of the Roman Emperor Augustus. At the age of thirteen she was married for the first time and soon produced a son with the name of Nero. After her husband's death, her brother Caligula became Emperor and she was accused of having an incestuous affair with him. To clear the air, he declared her a Vestal Virgin. Thus purified, she married a rich man named Crispus, whom she allegedly poisoned to inherit his estate. Free once more, she married her own uncle, the Emperor Claudius, and he named the new city Colonia Claudia Ara Agrippinensis in her honor.

According to Tacitus, the famed Roman senator and historian, her happiness did not last very long. In the year 59 A.D., Agrippina's own son, who by now had become the infamous Emperor Nero, had his own mother killed. Ever since, Cologne has been a freewheeling and fascinating city, with its residents full of never-ending intrigue and *joie de vivre*.

For the first 400 years of its existence, Cologne was essentially a Roman city, populated by Roman legionnaires that guarded the border of the Roman Empire against the wild and uncivilized Germanic tribes on the other side of the Rhine River. As a matter of fact, the two sons of our Cologne neighbor, Heini and Josef Gens, and three of my cousins, Toni, Elisabeth and Wolfgang Hermann, together discovered the three-story-high tomb of Publicius, a rich Roman legionnaire, in our neighbor's back yard. It is the largest Roman tomb ever unearthed north of the Alps. It can now be viewed in the monumental entrance hall to the *Roman Germanic Museum* right next to the Cologne cathedral.

Throughout much of the Middle Ages, Cologne remained an independent city, ruled frequently by an archbishop and eventually by the citizenry itself. Since 1248, the city's skyline has been dominated by the Cologne Cathedral, which was erected in honor of the Three Wise Men who are buried in the Cologne cathedral. According to the gospel, the Three Magi paid tribute to Jesus shortly after he was born.

After the Emperor Frederick Barbarossa conquered the Italian city of Milan with the help of the army of Reinhold von Dassel, the archbishop of Cologne, he gave him the relics of the Three Wise Men out of gratitude for the archbishop's military help. Reinhold von Dassel brought the important relics back to Cologne and in 1248 the construction of the Cologne Cathedral was begun in honor of the Three Wise Men.

The three crowns of the Wise Men are also depicted in the city's coat of arms, along with eleven black flames that are a memorial to the eleven thousand virgins that were slaughtered together with St. Ursula in Cologne by Attila the Hun. However, there is some dispute whether there were actually 11,000 virgins living in Cologne when Attila pillaged the city. That might have been half of the entire population of Cologne at that time. Rumor has it that never again that many virgins lived in the city!

Cologne and Paris were the two largest cities in Europe during the Middle Ages. At the end of that period, Cologne became a member city of the Hanseatic League, an association of free cities that dominated trade in Northern Europe. In addition to Cologne, the cities belonging to the Hanse included Hamburg, Bremen and Lübeck in Germany as well as Bruges in Belgium, Bergen in Norway, Visby on Gotland and Riga on the eastern shore of the Baltic. Many of these cities still call themselves proudly a *Hansestadt* and even the German airline Lufthansa carries the Hanse appellation in its name.

In contrast to this long and proud history spanning two thousand years, Germany became a country only in 1871, when Bismarck unified the formerly independent German states. For centuries, the Saxons had fought with the Swabians, the Hessians against the Bavarians, the Friesians against the Hanoverians and so on. Some of these wars lasted as long as a hundred years. To me, Germany has always been a mélange of different tribes that were frequently at war with each other, but Cologne was a city that had a long and proud history. Cologne was my home and the center of my universe!

My Mother's Family

My mother, Karoline Hermann, was born into an old Cologne family that had lived in or near the city for several generations. Literally translated, the name Hermann means "Army-Man." It was also the name of the Chief of the Cherusker tribe, Hermann der Cherusker, who had annihilated a Roman army of some 20,000 soldiers in the Battle of the Teutoburg Forest in the year 9 A.D. After that, the Romans decided to confine themselves to the western side of the Rhine River and to leave the eastern bank to the uncivilized Germanic tribes. My granddad liked the war stories about Hermann der Cherusker very much and was proud of his namesake.

Both my grandfather's and my grandmother's families made their living by distilling spirits. They then sold the liquor either in bottles or in their own bars and restaurants to the local population.

My grandfather, Toni Hermann or Opa Toni for short, had founded his own enterprise consisting of a distillery, tavern, restaurant and a liquor store next to the medieval city gate, the *Severinstor*, located at the southern entrance to the old city. Together with his wife Elisabeth, my Oma Lisa, they ran the business. Proud of its location next to the medieval city gate, he called his establishment the *Severinstorburg Brennerei und Weinkellerei A. Hermann*. Being in the hospitality business, they were also a pretty friendly and sociable family.

My mother had three siblings: an older brother named Aegidius or Aedi for short as well as two younger sisters, Elisabeth or Li, and Mia. The four children lived together with their parents in the five-story house above the restaurant and bar.

Neither Opa Toni nor Oma Lisa had more than an eighth grade school education, which was not unusual for that time. But it meant that at the age of fourteen, he had entered the work force. Opa apprenticed as a Master Distiller and that was to be his profession for the rest of his life. With the support of his mother, he set out on his own and bought the five-story house right next to the Severinstor and founded his business enterprise.

His highly successful business model was simple: he bought grains and berries from farmers living in the surrounding area and distilled it into many different flavors of liquor. He produced everything from gin to peppermint schnapps himself and sold it in his bar and liquor store. He must have enjoyed a gross profit margin of 80 to 90 percent, something pretty much unheard of in the modern hospitality business. This allowed him to offer excellent prices to his customers, who remained always loyal to him and his liquid creations.

Opa Toni was also an excellent marketer. On many days, he sold more than 100 bottles of schnapps before breakfast! He did so by standing on the street corner in front of our house and offering small flat flasks filled with gin or vodka to the workmen passing by on their way to the nearby factories. They would slip the small bottles into their pockets and enjoy a swig whenever the workday became too monotonous. The next day, they dropped their empty flasks off again and received a small discount on a new bottle.

Another one of his successful marketing techniques was to come into the bar with an entire tray of small crocks filled to the brim with schnapps. He offered this "Special" for 50 pfennig — until all the crocks on the tray were gone. With the regular price being 75 pfennig, the tray would be empty in a matter of minutes. My aunts, who were serving behind the bar, had a hard time filling all the additional orders for beer by the customers who did not want to drink their potent schnapps without something to swill it down with. My grandfather's clever cross selling produced astounding profits.

Opa Toni had been a proud *Ulan*, an elite cavalry unit during World War I. He and his horse *Mäusschen*, or little mouse, served in Belgium and Russia. I still own a picture of grandpa with his Mäusschen standing in front of a small cottage somewhere in the middle of Russia. After the Battle of Verdun in Belgium, he was quartered with a Belgian family. It speaks well for them that the two enemies became life-long friends who would visit each other for many years after the war to enjoy a meal of Belgian mussels and wash them down with a few beers.

A large picture of Opa Toni, dressed in his full Ulan uniform with a feathered helmet on his head, sitting atop his prancing horse dominated the wall at the end of his tavern. He even named one of his liquors after himself: *Alter Ulan* or "The Old Ulan."

The entire greater Hermann family lived under one roof. I am

My granddad Toni Hermann, the "The Old Ulan," on a family painting that also served as the label of one of his liquor brands

still amazed that Opa Toni's small business enterprise provided so well for the entire clan. But perhaps we thrived because all of the adults worked every day in the business as well. Even us children were put to work at a young age to roll barrels in the cellar, tapping the beer kegs and putting labels on newly filled bottles. I still know how to perform all these tasks.

I guess the lesson to be learned is that you need to have a successful business model — vertical integration — and do most of the work yourself in an enterprise if you want to make it a success. In any case, Opa Toni started and ran a thriving business and I admired him for that.

But when the bombs of World War II leveled the entire distillery and tore a big gash into the side of the main house, Opa lost his spirit. He was not enthused about rebuilding and did not want to re-activate the network of commercial customers for his liquor products, which included many restaurants and bars in Cologne. Instead, he wanted to keep things small and simple. So he produced just enough liquor to sell in his own bar and restaurant. Nevertheless, the family earned a decent living also in the post-war years.

My grandparents Toni and Lisa Hermann
surrounded by the entire family

Oma Lisa was the person who really raised me subsequent to the death of my mother and after I had left my father and moved in with my grandparents at age fifteen. Oma was always full of vigor and spirit. She constantly had a piece of good advice at the ready: "Always be there five minutes before the appointment!" she would admonish me. "Never drink the water — it puts lice into your stomach!" was her constant counsel to me, even as I was only a young teenager. Maybe it showed her bias as the owner of a distillery and a bar, but if my mother had heeded that advice, maybe she would not have contracted typhoid fever and have died at such a young age. I still prefer a goblet of wine to a glass of water!

Long after I had left for America, my cousins rebuilt the badly damaged façade of the main house and erected a ten-unit apartment building where the distillery had once stood. Nowadays, the bar is leased out to a well-known Cologne brewery and carries the iconic name of *Früh em Veedel*. Every knowledgeable resident of Cologne knows this popular watering hole.

My Father's Ancestors

My father, Heinrich Karl Wilhelm Heller, was born in 1907 in the Hessian town of Hanau near Frankfurt. Heller is a fairly common name in southern Germany and Austria. Silver mines were

At the top left: a Medieval Heller coin from the 14th century; Top right: a 10 Heller coin from 1907; At the bottom: a 10 Heller and a 50 Heller note issued by the Treasury of Karnten, the Austrian State of Carinthia in 1920.

generally called a *Hall* and a miner working in these mines was a *Haller* or a *Heller*. The small coins struck from the silver in these mines were also referred to as Heller starting in the 13th century. A Heller was generally worth half a penny. These Heller silver coins used to circulate widely in Germany, Austria and the Czech Republic.

As a youth, my dad went to a *Realschule* that finished at the tenth grade level, when the students were about 16 years old. He then served an apprenticeship as a banker with Deutsche Bank. Soon thereafter, he decided to move to Ireland and tried to make a living by selling Madonnas to the Irish. That enterprise was not too successful and by the mid 1930s he was back in Germany selling paint. Together with some friends, he then started a factory that manufactured tall poles out of pre-stressed concrete that were used as posts for streetlamps and to hold up the overhead wires for electric street cars. During the war, that factory in the suburbs of Cologne was hit by a bomb and was totally destroyed.

While staying in Ireland, my dad learned to speak excellent English and he always loved that country. This linguistic talent would come in very handy during World War II, when he spent the entire war well behind the front lines as a translator. Towards the end of the war, he was taken prisoner in Italy near Monte Casino in Italy. Right after the war, he was released from the POW camp and he was hired as an administrator by the British military government in Cologne to help rebuild the bridges across the Rhine River.

After the bridges were finished, he returned to his initial profession of banking. His first job was with the private banking house of Salomon Oppenheim jr. & Cie., which was owned by a prominent Jewish family that had survived the war unscathed. Eventually, the bank grew into the country's most prominent private bank, before being acquired by Deutsche Bank. When Lufthansa Airlines started up again in Cologne in 1955, he became one of their first employees. At Lufthansa, he worked in the Central Planning and Policy Department of the airline until his retirement.

My dad was the son of a so-called *Zwölfender*. That meant that his father had served in the Prussian military for twelve years. But a Zwölfender is also the German word for an adult buck that sports a full rack of antlers with twelve points. In the view of many Germans, it was quite an appropriate comparison.

After serving for twelve years in the Prussian military, a Zwölfender was automatically eligible to become a schoolteacher! It was an interesting qualification to teach young school children. Grandpa Heller, whose full name was Heinrich Wilhelm Emil Ernst Heller, had been born in Wolgast, a small fishing village on the coast of Mecklenburg on the Baltic Sea. I never met my paternal grandfather who passed away a year before I was born.

His dad, my great-grandfather Friedrich Albert Heinrich Heller was a blacksmith on the "*SS Polaria*." The Polaria was a 300-foot long steamer that also carried two square-rigged masts. The ship sailed under the flag of the Carr Line and was specifically built to carry immigrants from Hamburg to New York. According to contemporaneous sources, life aboard ship was a "living hell" for the Russian and Polish emigrants from the "troubled dominions of the Czar" as well as the German emigrants that were unhappy after the German Empire was formed in 1871. Most of the passengers on the S.S. Polaria were in their twenties or thirties and many were accompanied by small children, with more being born during the passage to New York. It is easy to imagine the terrible conditions on board as there were up to 1,100 passengers on this 300-foot long vessel, each one of which would pay five Pounds for the trip to the New World. My paternal great-grandfather died on August 12, 1883 aboard the Polaria at the age of 34 due to a heatstroke. Undoubtedly, his job as a blacksmith aboard the ship had something to do with it as he probably toiled at an open hearth below deck near the boiler room in the hot summer heat.

My father had a younger brother, Kurt Heller. Kurt went to law school, and my dad had to contribute money to the family to help finance his brother's education. He always seemed to resent that. When their parents died, they left a house to their two sons. My dad thought that he should inherit the entire house because he had helped to put the younger brother Kurt through law school. So, the two brothers had a good argument over the issue and never spoke with each other again for the rest of their entire lives!

I never got along particularly well with my dad either. When I was 15 years old, I moved into my grandparent's house on the Chlodwigplatz and lived there permanently with my deceased mother's family. This was my true family and I was happy at that home above the restaurant and bar owned by my grandparents.

The Name Game

My father's formal name was Heinrich Karl Wilhelm Heller. He shortened that cumbersome name to Heinz. When I was born, my parents named me Heinz as well. That was the beginning of the confusion. To differentiate between the two of us, most people called me by different and ever-changing names, such as Heinerle, Heino, Heiner or simply Hen so as not to confuse me with my own father. During the hunger years right after the war, I was also called Gandhi because I was as skinny as that famous Indian leader. But throughout my childhood, my mother always called me Bubbie, which means "little boy" in German. In virtually every letter that she wrote to my father, I am referred to as Bubbie.

When I came to America, my friends Anglicized the spelling and called me Boobie or Bob for short. I kept that name and when I got my permanent residency papers and later my citizenship documents, I added the more official sounding Robert as my middle name. Not using the Heinz moniker, I became H. Robert Heller.

After the 9-11 terrorist attacks in America, that lengthy and yet abbreviated name was not very helpful to get me through the airport security controls. Every time, the security officers pulled me out of the line of people boarding the plane and took me aside for a special interrogation. "How come the names in your passport and on the ticket are not identical?" they inquired. What was my "real" name, the officers wanted to know. To top it off, my driver's license said H. Robert Heller and my passport Heinz Robert Heller. Was I the same person?

When the local hospital, where I served on the Board of Directors, adopted a new convention designed to preserve the anonymity and confidentiality of patients, things got even more confusing. The hospital decided that only first names should be written on the whiteboard in the nurses' station that showed all the patients admitted to the ward. I would have been listed only by my first name Heinz, but none of my doctors would know me by that name. What would happen if I were unconscious after an operation or an accident? My doctors would not be able to find me readily. I did not like that prospect very much.

Finally, I had enough of all the confusion and went to the courthouse and changed the name to simply Robert Heller. That solved the security problem and now I can board any plane without being challenged and relegated to the end of the line. Problem solved!

SAGE ADVICE:
Always Be Proud of Your Ancestors

PART II
Coming to America

After graduating from high school, I decided to follow my girlfriend to America for a year. As luck — or lack thereof — would have it, I went to one of the worst colleges in America, which became known as Flunk-Out U. Life at Parsons College often bordered on the hilarious, but it allowed me to graduate from college with a bachelor's degree only one year after finishing high school in Germany.

The degree allowed me to attend the University of Minnesota, where my advisor promptly tried to get rid of me. To avoid that fate, I changed majors and decided to become an economist. But Minnesota was too cold for me, and so I transferred to the sunny University of California at Berkeley.

In those days, Berkeley was not only the scene of the Free Speech Movement, but also a hotbed of student activism and labor union activity. Nevertheless, I managed to earn a Ph.D. in economics only five years after graduating from high school. I was off on a fast and promising career.

9 Coming to America

Coming to the Promised Land

In post-war Germany, the United States was the Promised Land. First of all, the Allies had defeated Germany soundly in the war and everybody likes a winner. Even if you have been trounced! Second, Americans had everything that one could imagine and that Germans only dreamt of: big cars, fast airplanes, lots of food, beautiful scenery, Hollywood, and — very important for a young kid — cowboys and Indians. The real ones! Just like many of my compatriots, I always wanted to see and experience all of that.

My First Attempt to Visit the U.S Fails

Already in high school I tried to come for a year to the United States. The American Field Service, an organization that arranged exchange visits for high school students, selected me as one of their candidates for a yearlong visit. But when they found out that my mother had passed away, I was told that I was no longer eligible. They said that they did not want to take me, as an only child, away from my father. While I thought that this was grossly unfair, that was the end of my first dream to visit the land across the Atlantic Ocean.

Following My Girlfriend Across the Ocean

A few years later, when I graduated from high school, my girl friend Anneli Seul was accepted to study at the College of St. Teresa in

Minnesota. A good friend of hers was already studying there and she arranged for Anneli to obtain a work-scholarship at the college. In return for free food, a room in a dormitory and free tuition, Anneli had to work a few hours each week in the German Language Lab, helping American students to learn German. That was an easy way to finance her education and it sounded like great fun to me.

So I decided to try to come to the U.S as well. We both thought that the Mid West was the *real* America. During long debates, we decided that New England was just like Old England, that the people in the South were bigoted, and that the West Coast was full of nutcases. The Mid West was the true America that we wanted to experience!

The two of us drew a circle of about 250 miles around Winona, Minnesota, where the College of St. Teresa was located. Then, I wrote letters to all the colleges within that circle. We had decided that 250 miles was probably the maximum distance that we should be apart if we wanted to be able see each other every now and then during our stay in America.

I must have written to some 80 colleges, big and small, within that 250-mile circle, which covered most of Minnesota, Iowa and Wisconsin. About a dozen institutions sent me further information and after filling out endless forms and applications, I was admitted to six or seven of them. There were some pretty fine colleges in that group, including Carleton College and St. Olaf College, both in Northfield, Minnesota as well as Grinnell College and Cornell College in Iowa. Some of them even offered me some limited financial assistance.

While I was still mulling my choices and tried to find the various places on the map, I received a letter from Parsons College in Fairfield, Iowa, which offered not only free tuition, but also room and board in a residence hall plus a stipend of $50 a month. Fifty dollars was a lot of money in those days. It amounted to 200 German Marks. It looked like a small fortune to me. And so I quickly accepted the generous offer, in spite of the fact that Parsons was the maximum "allowable" 250-mile distance away from

Anneli's College of St. Teresa in Minnesota. In Germany, with its no-speed-limit Autobahn, that would have been only a few hours drive. But in Iowa, with its narrow two-lane highways populated by horse-drawn Amish buggies, it would take almost a whole day to cover that distance.

Crossing the Ocean

My dad, who worked for Lufthansa Airlines at that time, was able to get me a standby plane ticket to New York. Anneli booked a cheap cabin on a freight ship that also took a few passengers across the Atlantic. Together with Anneli's family we drove to Rotterdam to see her off on her trans-Atlantic voyage. I was planning to be in New York to welcome her when her ship arrived there a week later.

Saying good-bye to Anneli as she boards her ship to New York. From the left: Anneli's parents, Mrs. and Mr. Seul, Anneli's best friend Elfi Pallien, Anneli and me.

My flight was not without obstacles. As I arrived at the Frankfurt airport with my standby ticket, the Lufthansa counter staff informed me that my planned flight was fully booked and that I would have to wait for a day. I learned an instant lesson about the perils of flying on a standby ticket. But the Lufthansa staff was also ready to help one of their colleague's children in need, and so a friendly ground hostess suggested that I might want to take a Lufthansa freighter that very same evening. I jumped at the opportunity to get to America as fast as possible, although the freighter was a pretty slow Lockheed Super Constellation, driven by four propeller engines.

On board, there were only three rows of seats for pilots and other Lufthansa staff members "dead-heading" to the United States. I was invited to join them. Food consisted of a few sandwiches and I spent the night watching the flame-spewing aircraft engines powering our freighter across the Atlantic. As a propeller-driven aircraft, we were not able to fly above the clouds, and so we flew through several severe summer storms. The plane bounced around a lot and there was probably as much up-and-down motion as there was forward progress. But eventually we made it to New York.

After we landed on a hot August day at Idlewild Airport (now JFK), the U.S. Agriculture Department inspection service came on board to examine the plane and spray anti-insect disinfectant on the few passengers. But to our horror, they also detected that one of the freight crates aboard the plane had broken open during the bumpy ride. To everybody's dismay, a small herd of white mice had escaped from their cages. The mice were medical mice being shipped to the U.S. and destined to serve as Guinea pigs in medical experiments. The stern governmental inspectors insisted that all the mice had to be caught before we were allowed to disembark from the steaming-hot plane. And so the off-duty pilots and I spent an hour or two chasing the little white critters around the plane and we returned the ones we could find to their cages. Eventually, the inspectors felt pity for us and let us disembark the plane. The heat outside was stultifying: the temperature was in the high 90s and the humidity close to 100. Welcome to summertime in America!

To top everything off, I had a brand-new overcoat for the expected cold Midwestern winters. My stepmother Liesel had bought it for me at the Congress der Moden, the Cologne fashion house where she worked. I still own that coat, having worn it less than half a dozen times in the more half century since I came to America. Anybody interested in an almost-new white-grey peppered overcoat that was just the rage in Germany in the middle of the last century?

Welcome to New York

Together with my two heavy suitcases, I made it to a small modest hotel in Manhattan. It was located in one of the small side streets, away from the elegant Avenues. The hotel was pretty much of a flea-bag and had no elevators or air-conditioning. After I checked in, a huge, black porter helped me with my two weighty bags to the top floor. When we arrived there, I generously tipped him with a quarter. In Germany that was equivalent to almost two marks and certainly enough for a beer or two. My grandmother, who knew all kinds of good rules, always told me that a tip was a *Trinkgeld*, or drinking-money in German, and that I should always tip the equivalent of the price of a glass of beer for good services rendered. Well, the porter did not think that my quarter was enough of a reward for dragging my heavy suitcases up all those stairs and so he intoned: "That's not good enough, BOY!" I understood and pulled a precious dollar bill out of my pocket. He grinned: "That's much better, BOY!" Oh well, I had a lot to learn in my new country.

A few days later, Anneli's ship arrived and together we waited until my sporty Karmann-Ghia was unloaded from the ship. My dad had bought the car for me so that I might sell it at a profit in America. In those days, there was a considerable price difference between cars in Germany and the U.S. and he figured that the profits made might help to subsidize my stay in America.

Anneli and I spent a few fun days in New York, staying at the International House at Columbia University. We did all the touristy things, like visiting the Statue of Liberty and ascending the Empire State Building, which was at that time the tallest building in the world.

Anneli and me in the front seats of my Karmann-Ghia during a test-drive in Germany.

Driving to the Midwest

Then we set out on our drive to Iowa. We went to Philadelphia, which we both found very disappointing with its dilapidated downtown and a Liberty Hall that was not all that grand. Washington D.C. was much more impressive and we visited all the famous monuments and museums. Little did I know that decades later I would have my own office on Constitution Avenue with a head-on view of the Washington monument. But for the time being, we just gawked.

We drove through Shenandoah National Park, where we almost ran over a turtle. When I picked up the little creature, she raised two flaps to completely cover her head and leg openings. I was most impressed, as I had never seen a turtle in Europe that could do that! We had found a Box Turtle and I thought even the animals in America were more advanced than those in Europe.

Next came Kentucky, where Anneli and I had the first huge American hamburgers of our life. Neither one of us could open our mouth wide enough to wrap ourselves around that burger — we were impressed!

St. Louis was our subsequent stop. We spent some time sightseeing and were fascinated to find an almost totally black neighborhood. All the men were in dapper suits and wore white broad-brimmed Panama hats made out of straw. Some even carried little walking sticks that they flicked lazily through the air. It looked like a scene from a movie and we were amazed to experience a totally different world.

Not so memorable was our first experience with root beer. We had driven all day through the cornfields of the Midwest in the hot August heat and had gotten very thirsty. Back at home we both regularly drank beer as refreshment, which was perfectly legal for any German kid above 16 years of age. In the middle of the cornfields, we spotted a refreshment stand that advertised *"Root Beer"* for sale. We stopped, ordered two Root Beers and gulped them down — and instantly spit the brew out again. We had expected a nice cold glass of beer, like we were accustomed to from home. Instead, we got a lukewarm and terribly tasting concoction that I have stayed away from ever since. We wondered: how could Americans drink that kind of awful brew?

Slowly we meandered towards Winona, Minnesota where we were met by Anneli's girl friend Ursula Junk, who had gotten Anneli the job at the College of St. Teresa. Ursula was a pious and demure young lady, but for some reason I nicknamed her *Drachen* or Dragon. Just like Anneli was *Leu*, the Lion. All my girlfriends had animal names!

Later in life, Ursula was to become a radical left-wing activist and knew all the leading revolutionaries of the Sixties, like Rap Brown and his Band of Black Brothers. Rap was the Chairman of the Student Nonviolent Coordinating Committee or SNCC, which was anything but non-violent. Years later, he was convicted for killing a black policeman. His autobiography is entitled *"Die Nigger Die,"* but Ursula always thought that he was just a sweet young fellow. Several decades later, Ursula committed suicide on Adolf Hitler's birthday, which was probably not a coincidence. But in those days in Minnesota, Ursula was just a gentle soul who would stop the car to admire a flower blooming alongside the road.

After dropping off Anneli at her college in Winona, I headed south to Iowa in my little Karmann-Ghia. I drove through the endless cornfields covering the rolling hills of southern Minnesota and Iowa to Parsons College in Fairfield in the southeastern corner of the state.

The next order of business was to sell the Karmann-Ghia and to send my dad his money back. Only then did I find out that little Karman-Ghia sports cars, while presumably the rage in California and Florida, were not at all popular in the Midwest. The Iowa farmers loved their Ford and Chevy pickup trucks — or a Plymouth with big tailfins!

Eventually, I was able to sell the car for just a few hundred dollars more than my dad had paid for it. I sent my dad his money back and with some of the slim profits, I bought a very old Ford Fairlane for one hundred dollars. I was on my own in a big country.

SAGE ADVICE:
Head West Young Man!
        Horace Greeley

10   Welcome to Flunk-Out U

Parsons College and Dr. Bob

The same week that I realized my dream to come to America, *TIME* magazine published an article entitled *"Academically Average"* about Parsons College. A while later, *LIFE* followed suit with an article headlined *"Welcome to Flunk-Out U"* and described the college as a haven for students who could not get into any other college, but whose rich parents wanted them to go just somewhere.

Even today, the Parsons College website describes the spirit of the college proudly:

"What it is above all else is a college for students who can't get into any other — or have been thrown out of another college. In fact, some boys have been thrown out of four or five. Nobody on the campus feels slandered when Parsons is called 'Flunk-Out U.' Nobody resents the description of Parsons as a college for rich dumb kids." (www.parsonscollege.org)

Parsons College was located in Fairfield, Iowa, a typical midwestern town of some 7,000 inhabitants. Prosperous farms, where corn was cultivated and hogs thrived, surrounded the town. Along the highways, one could also find many marijuana plants that were growing wild. Most of them were left over from the hemp fields that used to cover Iowa during World War II to grow hemp for the ropes used by the U.S. Navy. When I got there, quite a few of the students did their best to free the countryside of the unsightly weeds and they inhaled the stuff to bring some excitement to the otherwise sedate Iowa lifestyle...

Fairfield itself was a typical Midwestern town, built around a central square with a bandstand. On Saturdays, local musicians would strike up patriotic tunes along with favorites from the popular musicals. "Oklahoma — where the wind comes whistling down the plain..." and "the corn as high as an elephants eye..." were the local favorites for rather obvious reasons.

Many students drove around in brand new Corvettes and Jaguar convertibles. This was in stark contrast to the Dodge and Ford pickup trucks favored by the farmers and the regular town residents. I did fit right in with my 10-year-old Ford Fairlane that I had purchased after selling the Karmann-Ghia.

Just a short time before my arrival, Parsons was on the verge of going broke. The college catalogue stated that there were 212 students at the college when I applied. But thanks to an energetic new president, Dr. Millard G. Roberts, the college had expanded to over 800 students by the time that I arrived. When I left only a year later, it had 1,600 students. Parsons was not only America's worst college, but also its fastest growing college. Coming to think of it, maybe these two phenomena were closely related to each other.

Dr. Bob, as everybody called the President, had set out on a mission. He wanted to create a new type of college that was open to all students and that offered an excellent education. To that end, he raised the tuition to the same levels as charged by the best Ivy League colleges. At the same time, he increased the salaries of the professors to the level prevailing at these elite universities as well. When I first heard this story, I did not quite believe it. I marched to the usually deserted library of the college and checked the official statistics of the American Association of University Professors. There was the official salary list: Harvard, Yale, Chicago were the top three in the country and next in line was Parsons College. Stanford University followed right after Parsons on the list. Not bad for America's worst college! While in the past Parsons College had had almost no professors with Ph.D.'s, it was now awash with them. The excellent salaries and the free membership in the country club attracted them. The academic processions of the professors during the many college festivities were something to behold: the crimson gowns of Harvard and the deep blue of Yale, along with the fabulous costumes and fur-brimming four-cornered mortar boards and bonnets from Oxford, Cambridge and the Universities of Geneva and Budapest. They all were testimony to the recognition, pomp and circumstance that Dr. Bob paid for so dearly.

One of the many faculty parades entering Barhydt Chapel on the Parsons College Campus

My Professors

Parsons had a rather illustrious and distinguished faculty. There was my history professor Dr. Robert Tree, with a Ph.D. from Northwestern. My sociology professor was Dr. Sedelow from Harvard. Dr. Howard Dorsett, my first economics professor, would frequently climb on a trashcan to make an unforgettable point. I still can see him standing up there, but I forgot what the important lesson was. Ray Greenhalgh taught political science and sports and Dr. Merey-Kadar, with a doctor's degree from the University of Budapest in Hungary, would get mad at anybody who mispronounced his unpronounceable name.

My favorite professor was also my advisor, Dr. Lewis F. Wheelock, who had a degree from the University of Geneva. When I went to him for help in selecting my classes, he intoned: "Young man! You are now in America! And you will study American History, American Government, American Politics, and everything else American." When I meekly inquired whether I could also take some economics courses, he grudgingly let me take the introductory course in the field that I really wanted to study. But in the end, I was very grateful to him — not only for his guidance — but also because he was a true friend to his students. He and his wife often invited us to their home for dinner and many evenings filled with animated discussion about world history and politics. That was truly one of the advantages of attending Parsons College — the faculty cared about the students and was most friendly and approachable.

Testing Out

There was one other action I took when I arrived at Parsons that proved to be of enormous benefit later on. I had gone to a German high school specializing in the natural sciences. Consequently, I had no need to take all these classes over again. Instead, I took advanced placement tests in mathematics, physics, chemistry and biology. To my great delight, Parsons awarded me 30 college credits for all these high school courses.

Furthermore, the Albertus Magnus Gymnasium had given me a total of 13 years of pre-college education, instead of the 12 years typical for American high schools. Generously, Parsons allowed me 30 credits for having finished that additional year of high school, making me a sophomore. Then they gave me another 15 credits for my one summer semester at the University of Cologne. Add the 30 credits for the advanced placement tests in the natural sciences that I took when I arrived, and to my own surprise, I was suddenly a second semester junior as I entered Parsons College in the same year as I had graduated from high school! I somehow suspected that they should not have counted *both* my extra year of high school and the advanced placement tests because I had taken most of these advanced courses during the last year of high school. But I decided not to complain about this unexpected generosity. My rate of progress, before I had taken even a single class, truly astounded me! I was sure that I would love American colleges!

College Roommates

I lived in a dorm, along with two freshmen in the same room. One was Scott Scot, a huge black fellow from the South Side of Chicago. Over Thanksgiving vacation he invited me to his home, which was in the "Projects" on the South Side of Chicago. While the area was right next to the University of Chicago, it was also an almost totally black ghetto. His mother was quite surprised when a white boy showed up with her son to stay at their high-rise tenement. Something like that did not happen often in the early Sixties in the Chicago Projects. Mrs. Scot was a most gracious lady and an excellent cook who admonished her son to be nice to his white European roommate. And he was.

My other roommate was Gene Gerth, a farmer's son from Iowa. Gene played a big tuba in the Parsons College marching band and most students in the dorm considered him something of a dork. As a result, the other kids in the dorm often played pranks on him. One evening, Jimmy Mays, who had grown up in the swamps of Florida, caught a snake and killed it. Those were the days when college kids used to spray the insides of each other's beds with shaving cream as a joke. But instead, Jimmy put the dead snake into Gene's bed. The room filled quickly with many students who wanted to see the surprise in Gene's face when he finally went to bed and discovered the snake. But Gene was not very cooperative. As our room was full of kids, he thought that this was just a wonderful gathering and he refused to go to bed. Instead, he sat on his pillow with his knees pulled up to his chin and enjoyed the company with a big grin on his face. After a long time and way past curfew time, he finally stretched out and put his feet under the sheets. But to everybody's astonishment, Gene just lay there and did not seem to mind the dead snake in his bed. Eventually, he pulled back his blanket — and with one screaming leap jumped all the way across the room and landed on one of the study desks. He was shivering like a leaf. He told us later that when he stretched out in the bed, he felt something cold and slimy between his legs and thought that is was the ubiquitous shaving cream, but not a snake. For many months, he did not forgive us. I am not sure whether he ever found out who really did the dastardly deed.

College Pranks

College pranks were commonplace at Parsons, which was well known for its over-the-top and crazy student shenanigans. It was the homecoming game weekend for Iowa Wesleyan College in the neighboring town of Mount Pleasant. The night before the Wesleyan homecoming game and parade, a couple of Parsons students snuck into Mount Pleasant and burned down all the homecoming parade floats. With outrage and grief, and to shame the perpetrators, the Wesleyan Tigers paraded all the burned-out floats through town. Dr. Bob, our President, was very embarrassed and we were all required to attend a stern lecture at the Parsons field house the following day.

But the ultimate Parsons prankster was an anonymous character who called himself Benny Belch. Almost every week, Benny Belch played some innovative and hilarious pranks on the community. One day, as we all walked to class, we saw a huge white linen flag inscribed with the words "Benny Belch" fly from the campus flagstaff where the American flag usually waved proudly in the breeze. But Benny had cut the ropes used to hoist the flag and thus there was no way to lower the Benny Belch flag. Finally, someone called the Fairfield fire department to come for assistance. They arrived with a huge red fire truck and ladder on campus and cut down the flag accompanied by the boos of the entire student body.

The oldest building on campus was an old red brick building used mainly for faculty offices. On the second floor was a screen door that led to literally nowhere. The door was usually not well secured, and one day there appeared a nice sign on the door that read: "Office — Dr. Benny Belch — Enter Without Knocking." Anybody who would have done so would have fallen through the opening down to the portico below. Oh well.

Benny Belch was omnipresent. A few weeks later, he opened a second office. The inscription: "Office — Dr. Benny Belch" appeared on a trap door located at the very bottom of the campus swimming pool some 10 feet under water. The workmen drained the entire pool to the applause of the students in order to remove the offending sign. Nobody ever figured out how Benny Belch managed to affix the sign to the bottom of the pool in the first place.

Mysteriously, Benny Belch was also enrolled in several classes. When the grades were posted outside the lecture hall, Benny Belch's name would frequently appear on the grade sheets as well. He usually got fairly good grades because someone had taken the exam for him — without the faculty ever noticing. I never found out whether Benny Belch managed to graduate with honors.

Making the Grade

Instead of being the college prankster, I studied hard and got pretty good grades, although it was not always easy. I remember that in my Introduction to Sociology class I got an "F" grade in my first mid-term exam. Questions like: "The Queen of England is comparable to the...... in the U.S. government" always flummoxed me. But in the end, I managed to get a "B" in Sociology. I must have accidentally aced the final after the slow start. Also in Psychology, I managed to get only a "B," but I received an "A" in all of my other courses.

As I approached the end of my second semester, it occurred to me that I might actually graduate if I would attend the summer semester as well. Wow, I thought, getting a bachelor's degree only one year after graduating from high school — that would be great! So I went to see my advisor, Dr. Wheelock, and we tallied up my course credits. To my great surprise he figured out that I could indeed graduate, as long as I majored in political science. That was because at his insistence I had taken so many American government and politics courses. I guess a degree in political science was better than no degree at all, but this choice would later on come to haunt me.

College Life

College life was pretty stimulating, and I participated in several student groups. One was *Clio Clio Clio*, which was run by my history professor, Dr. Robert Tree. It was an intellectual discussion society that focused on history and public affairs to present a counterculture to the fraternities and their pranks. To set us apart from the members of these organizations with their college jackets emblazoned with large Greek letters, we would wear black and white striped ties that would make us look like the geeks that we were.

On another occasion I was asked to participate in the play *"The Diary of Anne Frank."* Greg Wannamaker, a Big Man on Campus and a scion of the department store chain with the same name, was to be the lead actor. His presence alone would assure a sell-out crowd as all the female students rushed to see him perform on stage. I had never been an actor before and I was cast as one of the Dutch relatives of Anne Frank in the play. Afterwards, the reviewer of the *Fairfield Daily Ledger* thought that I had done a great job imitating the Dutch accent of my character. Little did he know that I did not have to try to mimic that accent — it was the way that I talked all the time!

Along the way, I made friends with many kids from rich families. We would drive around in their fancy cars and visit other places nearby. Nicholas Papadakis, another foreign student, was a particularly good friend. Nick hailed from Greece and his dad was a very rich Greek ship owner. Maybe not quite as rich as Onassis, but rich. Nick drove around in a black Mercedes — and there were not many of them in Iowa in those days! He lived in a neat apartment on top of a garage in town. One day, as I visited him there, I noticed the Coat of Arms of the Principality of Monaco hanging at the top of the staircase. Assuming that he had stolen it somewhere as part of the ubiquitous student pranks, I asked him how he got it. He told me that Prince Rainier of Monaco had officially made him a Consul because His Highness, the Prince, and Nick's father were the best of friends. So, Nick actually was the Consul General of Monaco for the State of Iowa! I was most impressed.

On a cold day in December, Nick declared that one of his dad's ships was stuck in Duluth and asked me whether I wanted to accompany him there. I said yes, and the two of us took off that wintery night on a 500-mile non-stop trip. It was close to Christmas, and we drove through many small Wisconsin towns in the pitch-dark night. From total darkness, we would suddenly enter small towns with brightly lit Santa Clauses and nativity scenes alternating with neon signs that flashed: "Eat-Eat-Eat" to lure drivers to always-open hamburger stands. Some impressions never fade away.

While studying took most of my time, I had time for a few dates with the girls attending Parsons as well. But nothing serious ever developed. After all, I still had my girl friend Anneli in Minnesota. But eventually, the two of us drifted apart and she returned to Germany. That did not stop us from staying friends until she passed away many years after returning to Germany.

The Reason for All the Largesse

Every now and then I was invited by a local service club or a church to speak about life in post-war Germany. I eagerly accepted these invitations to the Lions Club, the Rotary, the Presbyterian Church and other organizations, thinking that I was a pretty popular guy. But eventually, I noticed that whenever I went to one of these events, either a young lady by the name of Georgina Laux from Mexico or Joe Slagle from Ghana had been there before me. I started to wonder about these amazing coincidences and finally figured out that all three of us were there for the same reason: the college was trying hard to live down its playboy reputation and had offered scholarships to the three of us to counterbalance that view. Behind the scenes, the college administration suggested to the various service clubs and churches that they might want to invite one of us to hear what we had to say about life in Africa, Mexico or — in my case — Germany. That's why I had received the generous scholarship that paid for my room, board and tuition at one of the highest priced colleges in the country. I learned much later from Milton Friedman that there is no such thing as a free lunch! But I loved the experience nevertheless.

I gained an additional insight by going to Parsons College. Because many of the other students were either not very smart or did not study very much, I was one of the best students in that motley group. I graduated with the third or fourth highest grade point average in my entire class. If, instead, I had gone to an Ivy League college after coming straight from Germany, I probably would have been near the bottom of the class. I might not even have graduated because I would not have gotten all those extra credits required for graduation. I would possibly have gone back to Germany after one year, and my life would have turned out very differently.

SAGE ADVICE:
Sometime It Pays Off Being a Big Fish in a Small Pond

11 The Golden Gophers of Minnesota

When I got close to finishing my degree at Parsons, I began to realize that I would be able to obtain a Master's Degree much faster in the U.S. than it would take me in Germany. I had graduated from my high school in Germany in April of 1960 and received my B.A. from Parsons a year later. If I managed to get an M.A. within a year, I would get that degree only two years after graduating from high school. In contrast, if I returned to Germany, it would take me four or five years to obtain a *Diplom Volkswirt* degree, the equivalent of a Master's in the United States.

I figured that faster was better and so the decision to stay was not difficult to make — especially in view of the fact that due to my own past laziness it had taken me an extra year to finish high school. Now I wanted to catch up on the fast track.

Becoming a Golden Gopher

But there was a problem: because I had taken so many courses in American history and government, I got my degree at Parsons College in political science. I had taken only two introductory courses in economics. With that little preparation, how was I going to get into graduate school in economics? But I still wanted to become an economist!

Clearly, I needed a bridge between political science and economics. After some analysis of the various degree requirements,

I decided that a degree in International Relations would constitute the best compromise.

Consequently, I applied at various graduate schools for admission to their international relations programs. I picked the usual famous suspects: Georgetown University and its School of Foreign Service, the School of Advanced International Studies at Johns Hopkins and the Fletcher School for International Law and Diplomacy at Tufts University. For good measure, I also applied at the University of Chicago and the University of Minnesota. Not a bad bundle. Would my degree from one of America's worst colleges get me in there?

My other problem was how to finance my studies. Therefore, I applied for fellowships and work-study programs as well. With the help of my professors, I even got a tuition scholarship for the prestigious program of the University of Chicago. But I had to eat and live somewhere as well. And that would cost money that I did not have.

So it was indeed fortunate that the University of Minnesota offered to me a Counsellorship in a Residence Hall. The job required me to live in Frontier Hall, a university owned dormitory. My job was to play "housemother" and to supervise some 50 students also residing on the same floor. In return, I would get free room and board in the residence hall and a small stipend. I would also be allowed to pay sharply reduced tuition at the in-state resident rate of only $71 per quarter. Not a bad deal. Soon I was headed to Minneapolis and became a *Golden Gopher*, as the mascot of the university was called.

The Ice Hockey Team Is Out Of Control

When I arrived, the director in charge of all the residence halls asked me whether I would like to supervise a freshmen floor or an upper-classmen floor. Not knowing what I was getting into, I thought that juniors and seniors might be more mature than a bunch of rowdy and raucous freshman, and so I opted for the upper classmen assignment.

Quickly, I realized my profound mistake. I got to supervise the entire ice hockey team of the University of Minnesota on the uppermost or fourth floor of Frontier Hall. If you are not familiar with sports at the University of Minnesota: at that time, the Golden Gophers were regularly one of the best ice hockey teams in the entire nation. And those athletes quickly realized that the skinny foreign kid in the corner room was no match for them.

Certainly, I was not going to stop them from partying at any time of their choosing — be it day or night! One evening, my boss, the director of the residence halls, was patrolling the floor on an unannounced visit. He heard a lot of noise emanating from one room. He knocked on the door and somebody from the inside yelled: "Come in and have a beer!" Needless to say, no alcohol was allowed in the residences and I was the one who was in big trouble for lack of supervision. All too often, I would hear the little clicks of high-heeled shoes leaving the rooms of my boys at 2 o'clock in the mornings — at a time when co-ed dorms existed only in student dreams.

A few years later, when I turned on the television set to watch an ice hockey game at the Winter Olympics, I saw a toothless player being relegated to the penalty box for reckless play. Needless to say, he was one of my former Golden Gophers!

Switching to Economics

Soon it became time for me to enroll at the graduate school of the university and to pick my classes. The advisor assigned to me by the international relations program was Dr. Werner Levy, a professor who also had been born in Germany. Being Jewish, he had to leave Germany several decades earlier when the Nazis came to power. He was obviously very familiar with the German educational system and when he discovered that I had graduated only one year earlier from a German high school, he frowned at me and growled: "Who let you in here???" I showed him the admissions letter signed by the chairman of the department, Professor McLaughlin. He took one skeptical look at the letter and immediately started to dial the chairman's number. Fortunately, the chairman was not in. Professor Levy sternly looked into my eyes and with some irritation in his voice asked me what classes I wanted to take.

Realizing that I was in deep trouble, I answered meekly: "Well, Professor Levy, foremost of all I would like to take your classes in International Relations and also in International Diplomacy!" I was hoping that this might mollify him. But then I added that I also wanted to take a class in International Economics. And in order to do that, I needed to fulfill the required prerequisites for that class. I would have to take one course each in Macroeconomics, Microeconomics and Money and Banking. Immediately, Levy shot back: "If you want to take all those economics classes, why don't you just major in economics?" I replied that I had only taken the principles of economics course as an undergraduate at Parsons. How could I possibly enter the graduate program in economics with that skimpy a background? He was not deterred and said: "Well, you can try, can't you?"

It was totally clear to me that he did not want me there and so I trotted over to the Economics Department with my transcripts in hand. Professor John Buttrick was the director of the graduate program in economics and after taking a look at my transcript he said: "OK, I will let you into the department. If you make it, you make it. If not, that will be your own problem!" In a way, that was typical for the thinking of free market economists and their freedom of choice attitude.

Suddenly, I was an economics graduate student. This was exactly what I wanted to be. The question was whether or not I was prepared enough and if I would survive the rigorous program. It was swim or sink time!

Becoming an Economist

Fortunately, the University of Minnesota was on the quarter system, and so I was able to take most of the prerequisite courses in economic theory in my first quarter. To my own amazement, I did very well.

My favorite professor was Martin Bronfenbrenner, a somewhat idiosyncratic scholar who would sometimes show up in class wearing an apron that read: "Read the Wall Street Journal — It Brings You Business!" At the same time, he taught classes on Marxism and on the Japanese economy. He was truly eclectic in his views, but always rigorous in his analysis. He was also an extremely methodical teacher, who would write all the important points on the blackboard. I loved his well-organized lectures just as much as his sarcasm and humor. Most of the economics that I ever learned, I learned from him.

In later years, I dedicated the Japanese edition of one of my textbooks to Professor Bronfenbrenner. One day, a Japanese student asked me with puzzlement why I had dedicated my book to a hops distiller? The editor back in Japan had translated the German name *Bronfenbrenner* literally into Japanese as a "Distiller of Hops." I guess that got the Japanese wondering.

I studied international economics with Ed Coen and Anne Krueger. Our paths crossed several times in later years, when Anne Krueger rose to become the Chief Economist of the World Bank and the First Deputy Managing Director of the International Monetary Fund. Together, we went on a mission for the World Bank to Korea as advisors to the government. Both of us inspected a Korean shipyard, and I climbed up a steep ladder in front of Anne. My suit pants were not built for that kind of exertions and suddenly the seat of my pants split wide open. Anne started to laugh uproariously at my predicament. I was somewhat chagrined and thought that professors should not be amused when their former students were in a quandary. We all had fun!

There were quite a few eminent economists in the department, among them Leonid Hurwicz, Oswald Brownlee, Francis Boddy and David Henderson. But the most well known of all of them was Walter Heller, who was unfortunately on leave as President Kennedy's Chairman of the Council of Economic Advisors while

I was at Minnesota. But because we shared the same last name, everybody immediately remembered me and called me by name.

Making Lifelong Friends

The students at Minnesota were a friendly group, like Midwesterners are apt to be. One day, I sat next to a pretty girl in class. When I introduced myself, she said: "Oh, I am Sue Rhame and I am your American sister!" I was surprised, as I did not know that I had an "American sister" or any sister at all for that matter. She explained that there was an American brother-sister program for foreign students at the university and that I had been assigned to her. Consequently, she was my "American sister." But the committee responsible for the assignments eventually thought that a fellow from Ethiopia needed her more. So she dropped me without me ever knowing about the adoptive relationship. Nevertheless, we became life-long friends and our paths crossed again and again in California and Washington D.C. Some things are just meant to be.

Assibi Abudu was a foreign student from Ghana and he, too, became a good buddy. In later years, we were both together at UCLA while he earned his Ph.D. in economics. We met again when both of us taught at the University of Hawaii. Eventually, Assibi returned to Africa and worked for the Central Bank of Ghana as well as several international organizations.

Every now and then another foreign student from Ghana, who attended nearby Macalester College, joined us. His name was Kofi Annan and later on, he became Secretary General of the United Nations. When Kofi showed up, someone usually remarked: "Oh, little Kofi wants to join us!" He was a rather quiet and unassuming man in those days and he seldom said a word. He told us that he was named Kofi because he was born on a Friday, and Kofi meant Friday in his native language, just like Assibi's name meant that he was born on a Saturday.

We enjoyed our free time as long as it was not freezing outside. There was Dinky Town, with many ramshackle stores that catered to the students at the university. There was also the Big Ten Tavern, a sing-along bar, where nobody checked ID cards and a blind piano player hammered out Big Ten fight songs all night long. Life was much more civilized and enjoyable than in staid Iowa!

We all regularly went to the football games in nearby Memorial Stadium, where Sandy Stephens had led the Golden Gophers in the previous year to a Big Ten Championship and also to the Rose Bowl. In my year at Minnesota, the Golden Gophers won the title as the best team in the nation and also repeated their win in the Rose Bowl over hapless UCLA.

Needless to say, I also went to many of the ice hockey games to see "my boys" play against the other Big Ten teams. Life was good for a foreign student!

Going For the Master's Degree

As the year progressed, I started to realize that I had made a potentially fatal mistake by taking only four graduate courses during my first quarter at the university. The reason was that in order to graduate with an M.A. in economics, a student needed a total of 45 credit units. Each course was equivalent to three credits, and so I needed a total of 15 courses to amass the 45 credits. What to do? I devised a plan to take 15 units in the second quarter and then 18 units in the last quarter to accumulate the required 45 units. That meant I had to take an unheard of 6 courses for 18 credits in my last term in graduate school, while most students took only half that load.

In order to be granted the master's degree, I had also to fulfill certain distribution requirements. This forced me to take two courses that were actually given at the same time, three days a week. So I went to the courses on alternating days and studied the remaining material from class notes that I borrowed from my classmates. Fortunately, these were the days before computer systems were used to enroll all the students, or the machines would have undoubtedly have caught my double-enrollment during the same time slot.

As we came to the end of my last quarter, there was one additional hurdle to overcome: the final exams for all courses were usually given at the time of the last scheduled class meeting. I started to worry: how was I going to take two exams at the same time? Fortunately, luck was on my side because in one of these two classes we had to write a term paper instead of taking a final exam. Consequently, nobody ever noticed that I was enrolled in two classes at the same time period.

I accumulated my 45 units and graduated without problems with my M.A in Economics in 1962 — two years after my high school graduation.

The graduation ceremony took place in the monumental football stadium of the university. There must have been several thousand students assembled on the stadium turf, with all their proud patents and friends looking on from the regular stadium seats. When O. Meredith Wilson, the President of the University, started his speech, I noticed a small black cloud far on the horizon. As his commencement speech progressed, the cloud was almost overhead and it started to drizzle lightly. President Wilson said: "I am afraid, we will have to speed up the ceremonies somewhat and therefore I would like to ask all the students to come on the stage two at a time to receive their diplomas." He had barely finished his sentence when a typical Midwestern cloudburst drenched the audience. Nonplussed, President Wilson grabbed the microphone and announced: "I herewith confer upon you the degrees that you are entitled to!"

And with these words, all the students in their festive black graduation gowns turned around and ran for the tiny opening in the U-shaped Memorial Stadium where the football players usually entered the arena. Obviously, there was a huge traffic jam and everybody soon was totally drenched. When we finally reached dry territory under the stadium, all the graduates' hair was totally wet and hanging down listlessly. The women's black and wet graduation robes left ugly dark streak marks on their best party dresses that they were wearing underneath. It was a sorry and dispirited crowd to behold. When we emerged out of the stadium only a few minutes later to be greeted by our relatives and friends, the sun was shining again brightly, but it was too late. The most festive day of our young lives had been totally ruined!

Deciding to Move to Warmer Climes

The winter of 1961/62 in Minnesota had been extraordinarily cold and sometimes the thermometer had dropped to minus 20 or even minus 30 degrees. When March rolled around and it was still freezing and snowing outside, I had had enough! I thought that this climate was better suited for polar bears than for humans. Consequently, I decided to move to warmer climes and applied at Berkeley, Stanford, UCLA and USC — any place that was warmer than Minnesota!

> **SAGE ADVICE:**
> If you want to Accomplish Something — Do it Fast!

12 Protests at Berkeley

Crossing the Rockies

In late August 1962, I climbed into my little blue Sprite convertible with its two bug eyes and headed out West. Almost 2,000 miles of highway were in front of me. The rolling hills of the Midwest were followed by the seemingly unending plains of Nebraska and Colorado. I veered a bit south to see Denver and for the first time in my life saw the imposing peaks of the high Rocky Mountains in front of me.

When I ascended the steep grades towards Estes Park and Rocky Mountain National Park, it not only started to snow heavily, but I also blew out one of my tires. This was August and I certainly had not expected a snowstorm. Would I make it across the Continental Divide in my rickety British sports car? I changed the tire in the snowy cold and contemplated the situation. I decided that it was best to be safe and drove back to Denver, where I found another tire that fit my little foreign sports car. Fully equipped and with new confidence, I took another run at the Rockies.

This time, I took Highway 40, which was a bit further south of Rocky Mountain National Park. The route took me past the Dinosaur National Monument and through Starvation State Park to Utah and the Great Salt Lake. I enjoyed seeing the Great Salt Flats, where all kinds of automotive speed driving records had been established. Pretty soon, I was crossing Nevada and its endless desert. I vividly remember one sign in the middle of the desert that proclaimed:

"THIS SPACE RESERVED FOR AMERICA'S POPULATION EXPLOSION!"

Yes, America was a big place! I thought that it would have to be a very big population explosion indeed to fill up all that empty land. Actually, many atomic test explosions had occurred nearby in the desert, which was also used as a nuclear test site. I guess that made the territory uninhabitable for humans — at least for a while.

Speeding though the dilapidated desert towns of Elko, Battle Mountain and Winnemucca, I reached Lake Tahoe, which truly looked like a jewel after all that desert driving. Descending the western slope of the Sierra, I quickly reached the San Francisco Bay area. With gratitude, I saw the highway sign that read: "EXIT — University of California Berkeley." I had reached my dream destination, almost 6,000 miles from home!

Surviving the First Few Days

Berkeley was a peaceful little university town in those days. The tall white spire of the Campanile dominated the scenery. Unlike my experience at the University of Minnesota, enrolling in the graduate economics department was a very welcoming occasion. I had been appointed to a teaching assistantship, and so the members of the orientation committee immediately embraced me and informed me of my duties.

Now that I had a paying job, I decided to live off campus and rented a charming small apartment in an old redwood-shingled house at 2329A Dwight Way. While the rent was only $80 for the month, the landlord also required a month's deposit, and that ate up all my meager cash reserves. I was left virtually penniless for the first four weeks until I would get my first paycheck. I ate dry bread and drank water until the university paid me a princely $215 for the month.

I thought that Berkeley was a fabulous place. I walked to campus along Telegraph Avenue, which was always a lively hangout for all kinds of early hippies. Nice restaurants lined the street and you could buy a fried chicken and spaghetti dinner for $1.75 — so why cook?

Every day, I would walk to campus and returned to my apartment when the sun set in bright orange over the Golden Gate Bridge. It was truly spectacular and I never got tired of watching the scene.

The Cuban Missile Crisis

All the new graduate students had to take several classes together. There were the required economic theory courses as well as courses in statistics and economic history. I remember all too well one economic theory class taught by my advisor, the Hungarian-born Professor Tibor Scitovsky. The class was held in Giannini Hall, which was located on the Western edge of the campus and overlooked the Bay and the Golden Gate Bridge.

One day in late October 1962, the Cuban Missile Crisis came to a head. Instead of going to classes, all the students were listening on their portable radios for the latest news. Would the Russian freighters carrying nuclear long-range missiles from Russia to Cuba turn back in front of the American blockade or would they make a run for it and thereby possibly trigger an instant nuclear missile exchange?

All of us surmised that San Francisco would be a major potential target for the incoming nuclear rockets. Instead of going to class, the entire class gathered at the critical hour outside of Giannini Hall. We all watched the horizon over the Golden Gate for the arrival of the first Russian nuclear missiles that would spell our certain demise. Eventually, the radio announced that the Russian freighters had turned back from Cuba. Satisfied that we were not going to be annihilated by the Russian nukes on that day, we went back into the classroom and Professor Scitovsky got to finish his lecture. Those were exciting days!

The Nobel Faculty

Quite a few of our professors were eventually awarded Nobel Prizes, but the prize itself did not yet exist when I was a graduate student. Dan McFadden, Oliver Williamson and Peter Diamond all taught our economic theory classes when they were freshly minted Assistant Professors at the university. All three of them would go on to win Nobel Prizes in Economics.

One day, we were sitting in one of our discussion sections of the economic theory class when Pete Diamond walked into the windowless interior classroom. We all sat there quietly when he marched in and asked abruptly: "Does anybody have any questions?" Hearing none, he turned on his heels, flipped off the light switch and walked out of the room. Yes, he was probably a lot smarter than any of us, but we thought that leaving us in a pitch-dark classroom was nevertheless a bit arrogant. Half a century later, President Obama nominated him for a seat on the Federal Reserve Board, but the Senate refused to confirm him in spite of his Nobel Prize.

Another future Nobel Prize winner, Amartya Sen, was a congenial visiting professor from India who taught one of my classes. All students liked his friendly and courteous demeanor and appreciated his well-prepared lectures.

Gerard Debreu, a distinguished Frenchman who always seemed to float above the clouds, also won a Nobel Prize for his contributions to economic theory. I did not dare to enroll in any of his high-powered and mathematics-laced classes that where more suited for an advanced mathematics symposium than to illuminate basic economic relationships. I certainly knew my limits.

Professor Andreas Papandreou definitely knew his mathematics. Many graduate students loved his courses in economic theory and linear programming and he was known and appreciated for his systematic and well-organized lectures. He also taught the Principles of Macroeconomics course in which I served as a teaching assistant. Well over 400 students were enrolled in his class, which he taught in the cavernous Wheeler Hall Auditorium.

He would pace back and forth on the stage, droning on with his lectures. The students were often bored. Just after the first midterm, Papandreou noticed that the class size had shrunk precipitously. At the next meeting of the half-dozen teaching assistants, he asked plaintively why the students were dropping his class in droves. "Are my lectures too demanding?" he wanted to know. "Is the textbook too difficult to read? Are the exam questions too challenging?" he questioned. I noticed that all my fellow teaching assistants were looking straight down at the table in front of them to avoid his probing glances. There was an embarrassing silence. Finally, one of the more outspoken teaching assistants piped up: "Professor Papandreou, have you ever considered that you are a boring lecturer?" More embarrassing silence.

Soon thereafter, his father George Papandreou became the Prime Minister of Greece. "Our" Professor Andreas Papandreou returned to Greece, renounced his American citizenship, and became active in left-wing politics. He soon became known as an inspirational and exciting orator who brought the Greek masses to the barricades. His slogan was "Change" and he formed a new radical Socialist party, the *Panhellenic Socialist Movement* or PASOC for short. The Greeks loved him and twice they elected him as their Prime Minister. I figured that there must be some-thing about the Greek language that turned the dull and monotonous professor that I knew into the most exciting Greek orator since Socrates.

My Fellow Teaching Assistants

All the teaching assistants formed a friendly and congenial group. Together, we would all hang out in our large office, the "bull pen," in Wheeler Hall. We also held the office hours for our students in that room. At the beginning of each semester, our favorite activity was to sort the enrollment cards of all the pretty female students taking Principles of Economics into our own discussion sections. Why not?

Among the teaching assistants there were quite a few interesting personalities. One of my best friends was Gunter Wittich, a rather serious character, who also hailed from Germany. Our careers overlapped years later at the International Monetary Fund, where he rose to be Deputy Treasurer.

With my friend Gunter Wittich at the Berkeley Student Union

Ever jovial, Charles Vars hailed from Rhode Island. He later taught at Oregon State University and became the mayor of Corvallis in his spare time. Hamdy Loutfi grew up in Egypt and eventually married fellow-student Martha Fetherolf. Both of them wound up working for various international organizations like UNCTAD and the ILO. Joe Swaffar was a close friend and we roomed together for a while. He later transferred to UCLA and then taught at the University of Hawaii, both of which were also to be future way stations in my own life.

Not finishing the doctoral study program was a problem for quite a few of the graduate students at Berkeley. As far as I could tell, there were two basic reasons for it. First of all, as a public university, Berkeley cast a wide net in its admission procedure. The Economics Department admitted maybe 30 or 40 graduate students every year. But then the economic theory classes were used to "weed out" the students who could not quite make the grade. They were sent on their merry way with a M.A. degree in hand, but were not allowed to continue in the Ph.D. program. A second reason for the high dropout rate was the rather distracting environment in Berkeley. There were the constant student demonstrations and riots, which started soon after my arrival. Many of the students got deeply involved in the demonstrations and that took time and energy away from their studies — and good-bye to the Ph.D. degree it was. Distraction never helps to achieve a tough and demanding goal!

Sid Ingermann was a bit older than the rest of us. Sid was a rather diminutive guy and he was married to an always-smiling and genial black lady who was much larger than he was. Everyone liked this somewhat incongruous, but most pleasant couple. Prior to enrolling at Berkeley, Sid had organized the steelworkers in Buffalo and now he practiced his considerable organizing skills on his clueless fellow teaching assistants. He was one of the most effective organizers on campus. As soon as the student demonstrations broke out, he decided to organize the teaching assistants. After giving a few speeches and convincing his close buddies to join the newly formed TA Union, he posted the signed union cards of those who had joined the cause on the bulletin board. After a few more TA's signed up, Sid changed his organizing tactics. From now on, there were two lists: one of those who had joined the union and a second list of those who had not joined. The tally soon showed that the union members now outnumbered the non-unionized TAs. That clearly increased the pressure on the reluctant minority. Then, the next stage started. Only the names of the ever dwindling group that had not yet joined the union were posted under a big sign that asked the rhetorical question: "Most of your colleagues have joined the union — Why haven't YOU?"

All that was fine with me. They could organize, if they wanted to. But then the exhortations started that we should not buy gasoline from Standard Oil of California and to boycott Bank of America. I thought that had little to do with our working conditions and salaries, which I found to be quite comfortable and generous.

I was a happy student and proud to be a TA and certainly did not feel the need for union representation.

Thus, I slowly turned against the radical tactics used by the organizers. While I was fairly sympathetic towards unions when I arrived on campus, I disliked the aggressive methods used by the organizers and other left-wingers. Furthermore, I thought that Standard Oil produced good gasoline and Bank of America was a fine bank, where I had enjoyed a most pleasant internship during the previous summer. In the end, I believe that I was the only teaching assistant in the Berkeley Economics Department who did not join the union. A smart choice!

Student Protests and Riots

While students were free to express their views and solicit donations for their causes at the entrance to the Berkeley campus on Telegraph Avenue and Bancroft Way, a student was arrested in late 1964 because he violated some of the rules. Immediately, a huge outcry started and several hundred students surrounded the police car in which the hapless young man was confined. In the following days, Mario Savio and several friends of his started the "Free Speech Movement," which featured daily protest marches across campus.

Many of my fellow graduate students were distracted by the endless student demonstrations and the progress towards their doctoral degree slowed down. There were numerous other distractions in Berkeley that were not only fun to watch or to participate in, but that also took a lot of time. Telegraph Avenue was morphing into a hippie hangout and the street teemed with hippie vendors that offered their wares: cheap jewelry, silver rings and bracelets, small pictures and anything else that could be produced at home and sold for a few bucks. The pot peddlers were also out in force and one could get an involuntary high just by walking down Telegraph Avenue and breathing the air.

And then, there were the tree climbers who sat in treetops for weeks at a time in order to save them. In addition, there were the amateur gardeners who took over an empty city lot and wanted to

In late 1964, almost daily protest marches took place on the Berkeley campus as part of the "Free Speech" movement.

grow their vegetables there. Eventually, the whole garden turned into a sacrosanct field of weeds when they lost interest.

On campus, all kinds of groups vied for the attention of the students walking to class. In front of Sather Gate, the main entrance to the campus, you could always find students manning small tables with leaflets and pamphlets. One day, the Young Marxists put up a large poster that announced: "GOD IS DEAD!" Promptly, a Christian group nearby put up their own poster: "MARX IS DEAD!" That settled the score!

Of course, there were the regular demonstrations for free speech, for filthy speech, or any other cause that might strike the fertile brain of a twenty-year old. Many of these protests took place in front of Sproul Hall or Sather Gate. The police would come, but usually not touch the demonstrators. On other occasions, they would grab one or two of the demonstrators and then a crowd would gather around the police car. The police would just sit still, with their prey inside the police car. One time, one of these standoffs in front of Sather Gate went on for well over a week with the hapless arrestee confined to the police car and forced to relieve himself into a Coke bottle. Oh, those were the days!

The university administration treated all the students with kids' gloves and when the students occupied a university building, the administration typically retreated. Chancellor Strong was anything but a strong leader. He was a Professor of Sociology and Philosophy, and it showed. He was a courtly gentleman, who was hopelessly overpowered by the radicals who did not care whether they stopped the learning process or damaged university property. The more the students succeeded with their protests, the more power they accumulated. Any event became a media spectacle — all to the delight of the news reporters who were camped almost permanently on campus with their TV cameras.

All that turmoil, as well as the graduate students organizing their unions to fight against the corporate world, convinced me more and more that these radicals were not a constructive force. But I still loved Berkeley and the fabulous natural environment of the Bay Area surrounding the campus. I liked walking home from the library at sunset time when the sun dropped into the Pacific Ocean behind the Golden Gate Bridge and turned the sky into brilliant shades of red, orange and scarlet. Sitting at that magic time on the terrace of the Student Union was a wonderful and relaxing experience after a hard day of study.

But there were other pleasures as well. The chicken cacciatore at the Café Mediterranean on Telegraph Avenue was delicious and cheap as well. Larry Blake's Rathskeller was a funky watering hole next to campus that had plenty of sawdust on the floor to soak up any spilled beer, and there was always plenty of that! The more hip students retreated for their cappuccino to the Steppenwolf and played chess until late in the night.

But seeing all the riots and turmoil and wasted energy around me, I grew more and more determined not to let that slow me down or to derail my progress toward the doctoral degree that I wanted to obtain so badly. If I could earn it, the degree was going to be my ticket for a professional career. I retreated to the library and resolved to write my dissertation as quickly as possible just to get out of there.

Internship at Bank of America

During one of my summers at Berkeley, I was able to obtain an internship in the Economic Research Department of Bank of America in San Francisco across the Bay. The bank had several fine economists on its staff and I enjoyed the professional atmosphere there. There was Chuck Haywood, who was the Director of the Department, puffing on his ever-present pipe. The Chief Economist for the bank was Howard Craven, who was also a speechmaker par excellence. Kimi Narita was a young Japanese economist who spent her entire career at the bank. Carol Beaver, who eventually became Carol Singer, was a fine analyst and a good colleague. And then there was Sandra Johnstone, a young research assistant whom I started to date a bit later and eventually we got married.

During that first summer at Bank of America, I was asked to undertake a research project on what the government should do about the growing imbalance in the U.S. balance of payments, which had swelled to almost $3 billion dollars. Nowadays, that would be an insignificant rounding error, but it was a topic of great public interest and policy debates at that time. To my great surprise and delight, I was asked to present my findings to the Managing Committee of what was at that time the world's largest bank. If I recall correctly, Bank of America had a balance sheet of some $65 billion at that time. It was small by today's standards, but huge at that time.

As a lowly intern, I felt greatly honored to be asked to present my conclusions to the Managing Committee, which included the bank's President Clark Beise. At that time, the international monetary system was still operating under fixed, but adjustable, exchange rates under the aegis of the International Monetary Fund that had been created at the Bretton Woods Conference in 1944. In my presentation I made a few favorable comments about flexible exchange rates, arguing that increased flexibility of exchange rates might solve the persistent U.S. balance of payments problem and thereby stop the gold outflows from the Treasury that everybody was worried about.

After I had finished the presentation in the bank's ornate boardroom, President Beise and I happened to ride down together in the same elevator. Always dressed to perfection in a dark blue suit, a white starched shirt and a conservative, but elegant tie, President Beise turned to me and said: "Young man! You said a lot in favor of flexible exchange rates. Let me tell you: Never again! Never again!" He got quite agitated and maybe a bit red in his face when he continued: "When I was posted in London in the late 'twenties, they used to get me out of bed in the middle of the night when the Pound was falling against the dollar — never again!" I had learned another argument in favor of fixed exchange rates that I had not thought about before: getting a good night's sleep! I remember the exhortation by the very upset Mr. Beise to this day.

A few years later, the fixed exchange rates of the Bretton Woods System broke apart and the world adopted flexible exchange rates, just like I had recommended. In the following decades, earnings from foreign exchange trading operations became one of the main sources of profit for Bank of America and most large banks around the globe!

Getting My Doctoral Degree in Record Time

After I returned to Berkeley, I finished my "Comprehensive Exams." They were a grueling set of written and oral exams that qualified you to begin writing your Ph.D. dissertation. I had worked as a research assistant for Professor Tibor Scitovsky, a courtly Hungarian émigré, who specialized in international economics and who had written a well-regarded textbook in that field. He was one of the main reasons, besides the climate, why I had decided to come to Berkeley. He asked me what I wanted to write about in my thesis. I told him that I wanted to explore what level of international reserves would be optimal for a country to hold. He was not too thrilled and told me that there were already three other students that had selected very similar topics. I bluntly answered him: "Yes, but I will do it faster than any one of them!" And with that promise, he accepted me as his doctoral student.

All day long, I would do my research in the library and collect relevant data. Then, I would punch up the data on IBM cards and submit the stack of data cards to the IBM 7040 computer that took up the entire basement of the building next door. The gigantic computer lived in a hermetically sealed air-conditioned room and would swallow up my IBM cards. Then, the machine would put its 8 GB of memory to work and produce a stack of printouts that I would collect the next morning. Nowadays, any handheld iPhone has a larger capacity and will produce the same results in a fraction of a second. But in 1965, the IBM 7040 was cutting edge technology.

Some of my fellow students produced dissertations that were hundreds of pages long and took years to write. That was not for me and certainly not compatible with my goal to beat the others working on the same topic. So I developed a very simple, but elegant analysis that compared the cost of holding more international reserves, like gold or foreign exchange, with the benefits of not having to adjust to the imbalance. The topic was similar to the subject matter that I had already addressed in my work at Bank of America. Entitled "Optimal International Reserves," my thesis not only developed a simple theoretical model of a country's reserve level, but also calculated the actual optimal reserve levels that countries should hold. The results made eminent common sense and I presented all my conclusions in some 50 typewritten pages. My dissertation was written in five or six months, a near record time. After the official defense of the thesis in front of a faculty panel, Professor Scitovsky turned to me and commented: "Hmm, your model is so simple and straightforward — there must be something wrong with it!" I was thunderstruck, but got my Ph.D. nevertheless.

Not being timid, I submitted the dissertation in an abbreviated form to the *Economic Journal*, one of the most prestigious economic journals in the world. To my absolute delight it was accepted for publication and published. I was on top of the world!

A Short-Term Marriage

During that last year at Berkeley, Sandra Johnstone and I got married. I had met her during my summer at Bank of America and we loved debating economic issues. We lived in a comfortable apartment near the university on Shattuck Avenue from where I could walk to the campus library to work on my dissertation and she commuted to her job at the bank in San Francisco.

Life was good, and she was ready to start a family and have kids. Not so fast, I thought. I wanted at least some time to enjoy life and have a good time before we would have to care for little screaming children. We both argued until we both thought that it was better to split up again to pursue our own separate goals. We parted most amicably and because we had accumulated virtually no assets, the split-up was easy. We only quarreled for a little while about who would get the black round leather hassock on which we both liked to prop up our feet.

The academic year 1964-65 was an eventful and fast-paced period in my life: I passed my doctoral exams, got married, wrote my dissertation, obtained the Ph.D. degree, got divorced and was ready to move on.

SAGE ADVICE:
Turmoil Can Be Very Destructive. Avoid It At All Costs.

PART III
From Professor to Banker

I became a professor of economics at UCLA just as the Watts Race Riots engulfed the city of Los Angeles. Campus life was disrupted as radical student organizations vied for power and influence. But for me, the time at that great university was transformative, as conservative thinkers like Milton Friedman, Friedrich von Hayek, James Buchanan and Armen Alchian influenced my economic thinking and philosophy.

I journeyed on a quick and adventuresome trip around the world, where I visited a welcoming Japan, wartime Vietnam, contrast-full India and was detained at the Moscow airport. Half a year of teaching at German Universities made me realize that I did not want to return to the Fatherland.

Then I spent a few lazy years teaching at the University of Hawaii and got married on a catamaran off Diamond Head. But I could not stand languishing in paradise forever. So, I took a job as the Chief of the Financial Studies Division of the International Monetary Fund in Washington D.C. just as the entire international monetary system was collapsing. This gave me a front row seat as the debate about the restructuring of the world financial system took place.

During eight years at Bank of America in San Francisco, I learned the corporate way of life. These were exceptionally difficult times for the global economy as the oil price collapsed, the American building boom ended, wide-spread agricultural woes affected farmers, the LDC debt crisis spread around the world and a tight U.S. monetary policy designed to curtail inflation resulted in never-ending financial turmoil and almost broke the back of Bank of America.

13   Seeing the Light at UCLA

After I got my Ph.D. from Berkeley, it was time to get my first "real" job. Berkeley was one of those universities that never hired its own Ph.D. students, so as to avoid the danger of "inbreeding." They figured that everything that the students knew they had learned from someone on the faculty. Consequently, the freshly minted Ph.D. could not possibly contribute anything new and different to the existing knowledgebase of the department. Reluctantly, I agreed with that analysis because it meant that I would have to leave the Bay Area, which I considered paradise on earth.

Hunting for a Job

The job market for economists in 1965 was very good and I was invited to numerous interviews at the American Economic Association convention early in the year. The convention was the traditional first-contact place between the job seeking students and the universities looking for new faculty members. It was generally known as the "meat market." There were no computer-driven job matching services and everything was done in person or by telephone.

Several universities invited me for follow-up interviews on campus. These visits were designed so that both the candidate and the university faculty could get to know each other better. Usually, these visits involved giving a lecture to the students and faculty at the hiring university. This accomplished two goals: it allowed the department to judge the teaching prowess of the candidate as well as to learn more about his or her research capabilities.

While none of the very top economics departments in the country invited me to visit, I got invitations from a nice range of just-below-the-top universities. The elite universities often hired from a very restricted group of their "peers": Harvard would hire from Yale, Princeton, MIT and Chicago — and vice versa. Essentially, it was a closed club and Berkeley was just below that level.

After my interviews at the AEA convention, I got invitations from the University of Wisconsin, Penn State, Maryland, UC Santa Barbara and UCLA to come and visit the campus in person for more interviews and to give the traditional lecture. Visiting the eastern campuses in freezing February weather was no great joy. I remember the chairman at the University of Wisconsin pointing at a fog bank and saying: "There is a very nice lake out there!" But no one could see the lake in the snowy mist. My visits to the University of Maryland and Penn State were similarly troubled. At Penn State the chairman kept telling me that the rural campus was "a great place to raise a family," but raising a family was the last thing on my mind. I was looking for the place with the most parties and the highest concentration of young ladies to date! On top of it, a "Nor'easter" snow blizzard hit as I started to drive to College Park, where the University of Maryland was located. I had rented a huge red Ford Fairlane sedan, which kept slipping and sliding over the icy highway. I was glad to escape alive from the snowy fields of Pennsylvania and Maryland!

It was during that trip to the East Coast that I received a call from Harold Summers, the chairman of the Economics Department at UCLA. He asked me whether I was interested in a position at that university. Upon learning that I was in the middle of a snowstorm in Maryland, he instantly responded that it was a sunny 82 degrees in Los Angeles! When I heard that he also offered the very generous emolument of $8,250 as an annual salary, I accepted without hesitation, in spite of the fact that some of the other universities offered somewhat better salaries. I never regretted my decision, especially in view of the fact that UCLA was clearly the best and most prestigious university among the universities interested in me.

My Dream Job

In the fall of 1965, I started as an Assistant Professor of Economics at UCLA. I was 25 years old and it was 5 years after I had graduated from my high school in Germany. In Germany, it would have taken me a decade or two to become a professor. I felt elated and overjoyed!

I was offered a spacious office on the eighth floor of Bunche Hall, a new faculty office building at the northern edge of the campus. My office window overlooked a tranquil grassy sculpture garden fringed by the library, the theater and the art building. At lunchtime, many students relaxed on the lawn or ate their lunch in the sculpture garden. Nothing could have been more pretty and peaceful, including the female art and theater students who would sun themselves amid the sculptures. What was not to be liked about UCLA?

The university had a quite distinguished Department of Economics. There was Armen Alchian, a brilliant theoretician, who certainly would have deserved a Nobel Prize — if he had not spent most of his time playing golf rather than writing academic articles. Armen was always ready for an intellectual debate. Karl Brunner was our monetary economist and he certainly would have been a candidate for the Nobel Prize as well if he had not died so early. At his time, Karl Brunner was almost the equal to Milton Friedman in his influence on monetary policy in the United States and Europe. Milton Friedman, an actual Nobel Prize winner, also served as a visiting professor at UCLA and I greatly enjoyed our association. James Buchanan became a member of the faculty at UCLA soon after I got there. He later on was awarded a Nobel Prize for his path breaking work in public finance and public choice. Friedrich von Hayek was another Nobel Prize winner who spent a year at UCLA while I was there. He was the author of the classic *"The Road to Serfdom"* as well as many other books on individual liberty and economic freedom. While he was formally attached to the Philosophy Department, he spent much of his time with us in the Economics Department.

I enjoyed the many stimulating discussions with my congenial colleagues that quickly became good friends. Armen Alchian and Bill Allen were constant companions at lunch at the Faculty Club — although Bill was not adverse to occasional excursions to the newly established Playboy Club on Sunset Boulevard in Beverly Hills. One of the great things about UCLA was its location on the West Side of Los Angeles, wedged between Sunset Boulevard on the North and Wilshire Boulevard on the South. Beverly Hills was 15 minutes to the East and the beaches of Santa Monica were nearby to the West. The irony of it all was that the location of UCLA was originally chosen in the 1920's because the land was incredibly cheap and only a few bean farmers eked out a living on that desolate piece of land. No people wanted to live in the no-man's land halfway between downtown Los Angeles and Santa Monica. These facts I learned from Dudley Pegrum, a fellow faculty member who had taught at UCLA since 1927. He was not only the most senior faculty member, but had actually been a member of the original committee that selected the campus site. Usually a bit acerbic, he would regal us with stories about the early days of the now distinguished university. When I knew him, he was well into his seventies, but worked out every day with the UCLA swim team, which was one of the best in the nation. He was a tough competitor.

Riots On and Off-Campus

When I arrived in Los Angeles, the Watts Riots of 1965 were in full swing. From our offices on the eighth floor of Bunche Hall we could see the smoke rising over the downtown section of Los Angeles, where ugly race riots were taking place. Dozens of people were killed; hundreds of buildings burned down and thousands were injured — all over a drunk driving arrest of a black man by a white police officer.

Some time later, the racial tensions also reached the campus. The Black Students Union and the socialistic Students for a Democratic Society held regular protest rallies on campus. Black student issues continued to dominate events on campus. Several black students were killed on campus in a shootout between the two competing black student organizations. At the same time, the self-avowed Communist Angela Davis was first hired and then fired as a professor at UCLA. The atmosphere on campus was hot and divisive.

One day, a few radicals called on Bill Allen, the new chairman of the department, and demanded from him a promise that he would hire several black faculty members soon. Bill Allen, who was a resolute, conservative professor, told them that he would be happy to hire any black faculty member who could also meet the quality standards of the department. But he was unwilling to make any numerical promises.

The next morning, an improvised bomb detonated in front of the department entrance on the second floor of Bunche Hall. The irony was that Ralph Bunche, in whose honor the building was named, grew up in South East Los Angeles, the very same area where the riots were now taking place. He had graduated from UCLA and then gone on to a distinguished academic and diplomatic career as Undersecretary General of the United Nations. Eventually, he was awarded the Nobel Peace Price for his work as the UN mediator who helped to resolve the Arab — Israeli conflict that accompanied the founding of the state of Israel.

The day after the bomb went off, Bill Allen showed up on a local TV station brandishing a huge shotgun and announced that he was ready for all comers. Nothing more happened.

Some time later, Chairman Allen convened a faculty meeting and announced that he had found a distinguished black professor and proposed hiring him: he was Thomas Sowell, who would become one of the most eminent black economists and political thinkers of our time. For a while, Tom Sowell had the office next to me, but I hardly got to know him. He was an intensely private person who kept his own counsel and did not associate much with the other professors or the students. Instead, he spent his time in the research library and wrote book after book. Many of them were erudite treatises on race issues.

Walter Williams was a doctoral student in the department. Walter was an imposing figure and stood about 6 ½ feet tall. While many suspected that he was a Black Panther, he was not a member of the radical group that was bent on revolution. His sympathies were much more in line with the confrontational style of Malcolm X than the "We Shall Overcome" vision of Martin Luther King. But Walter was a diligent graduate student who worked hard and was always open to new ideas. Several of the faculty members, among them most prominently Armen Alchian, challenged his thinking. They worked with him and argued with him until finally Walter saw the light. Eventually, Walter became one of the most conservative economists in the country. A prolific writer and lecturer, he was frequently asked by Rush Limbaugh to substitute for him on his nationwide conservative radio talk show and his influential column is carried by hundreds of newspapers.

Getting Settled and Looking for Fun

My first apartment was in Marina Del Rey, a brand-new yachting community located on the southern fringe of Santa Monica and just north of the Los Angeles airport. As a budding economist, I had done a precise locational analysis of where I should reside in relation to my job on campus, the beaches, recreational opportunities and where the most girls would be. That search led me to Marina Del Rey and I rented a beautiful waterfront apartment at the end of Fiji Way overlooking the sailing channel and the sunsets in the West. I figured that the place should be teeming with like-minded Twenty-Somethings. After moving in, I discovered that I was the only young person in the expensive building overlooking the beaches. Most of the other tenants were retirees. So much for locational economic theory! But eventually, the world caught up with my projections. Marina Del Rey became a thriving metropolis of young people where the parties never stopped. As often in my life, my theory was right, but my timing was way off!

I joined the California Yacht Club, which at that time operated out of a few leased rooms at the Sheraton Hotel in the Marina. Soon, the CYC built a wonderful clubhouse facility at the end of the sailing channel that bordered my apartment. I bought a Schock Santana 22 sailboat and berthed her at the Club. I named the boat *Moonlighter* as I had earned most of the money to buy her from teaching evening courses at the University of Southern California and at Cal State Long Beach. On weekends, I would sail with my friends on Santa Monica Bay or cruise over to Catalina Island and spend the night there. Life was good!

Getting Busy With Teaching and Research

But there was work to be done as well. According to the university rules, my job consisted of teaching, research and university service.

In front of one of my classes at UCLA

Our teaching load consisted of two courses per quarter. As each course consisted of three one-hour lectures, that meant I had to spend only about six hours of each week in the classroom. A pretty light teaching load, I thought.

I loved teaching and taught many different courses: from principles of economics to economic theory and money and banking to graduate courses in international trade and monetary economics. I found it easy to teach my classes during the day and then at night I would write up the lectures to be published as textbooks. In that fashion, I wrote books entitled: *International Trade — Theory and Empirical Evidence, International Monetary Economics* and *The Economic System*. Most of the books were pretty successful and were translated into numerous languages: German, Spanish, Portuguese, Japanese and Arabic. One day, I received what looked like a copy of one of my books and I looked at it in wonderment. I could recognize the graphical reproductions, but I had no idea what language it was written in. Eventually, I discovered the words: Kuala Lumpur at the bottom of the title page and figured that one of my books must have been also translated into *Bahasa Melayu*, the language of Malaysia.

I also got quite a few articles accepted by some of the most prestigious economic journals: The *American Economic Review*, the *Economic Journal*, the *Journal of Political Economy* and the *Quarterly Journal of Economics*. All were renowned refereed academic journals and my publications were enough to earn me tenure and promotion to Associate Professor at the ripe old age of 28. I was a happy camper!

George Hilton, one of my colleagues and a good friend, congratulated me for my achievement by quoting Elizabeth Taylor who apparently snarled at Richard Burton in *Who's Afraid of Virginia Woolf?* "Look at yourself, you flop! What are you? Nothing but a rotten Associate Professor!" Oh well, it was nice to have good and loyal friends, I thought with a grin on my face!

Having Fun Inside and Outside the Classroom

I thought teaching was great fun and I particularly enjoyed giving the large lecture classes. I would pace on the stage of the Royce Hall Auditorium lecture hall in front of 300 or 400 students. I taught principles of economics by using pizza and beer as the illustrative examples to explain the trade-offs faced by consumers. The students loved it and so did I. The only disadvantage was that invariably the class wanted to "surprise" me with a small gift at the end of the course to show their undying gratitude — and inevitably it was a cold pizza and luke-warm beer. While it tasted pretty awful at nine o'clock in the morning, I had to consume it to show my gratitude. Yikes!

Nevertheless, the students seemed to like my lectures. The first time that the Associated Students of UCLA took a survey to evaluate all the instructors on campus, I received a Distinguished Teaching Award. I was quite proud to be accorded that honor.

One of the more embarrassing moments of my teaching career came when I stumbled accidentally off the stage while I was pacing too close to the edge. But perhaps even more embarrassing was the day when I had forgotten where I had left off in the previous lecture in my class on international economics. It was my habit to teach that course with the help of lots of graphs that I would draw with chalk on the blackboard. It was decades before PowerPoint slides became de-rigueur. A young lady by the name of Niva Elpern always sat in the front row, wearing a low-cut summer dress. Prior to coming to UCLA, she had been a Lieutenant in the Israeli Army and so she certainly knew how to take care of herself. She was very bright and also good-looking. That day, she had her notebook with all the graphs from the previous lecture open on her lap. I stepped behind her, looked over her shoulder at her notepad and said loudly: "Do you mind if I take a look at your curves?" The entire class roared with laughter, but neither the Israeli-born Niva nor German-born me knew what they were laughing about. Thus are the perils of English as a Second Language.

Birgitta Hultgren was a very bright graduate student from

Sweden. Some time after Birgitta had finished my international economics class, we started to go out together. One sunny weekend, the two of us went sailing to Catalina Island, which was 24 miles across the sea. A storm had stirred up the Pacific Ocean a few days earlier and big swells continued to abound in the open ocean. The waves would slowly lift our small 22-foot boat and then drop it gently into the next trough, making the LA coastline disappear over the horizon. The waves were not breaking, but they were big. In my opinion, there was no danger at all. But for Birgitta, who was accustomed to sailing on the placid and flat Baltic Sea, the situation was a lot scarier. I tried calming her down by saying that "these waves are just normal swells, like you find them here in the open ocean all the time and there is nothing to be afraid of!" Birgitta was somewhat reassured and we continued to the harbor at the Isthmus of Catalina Island and anchored in the sheltered cove. We rowed our little dinghy to the small bar and restaurant located on the island to get a drink and a bite to eat. Only one "old salt" with a stubbly grey beard and a weathered face sat at the bar drinking his rum. As we sat down near him, he bellowed: "My God, I've been coming to this godforsaken island for decades, and I have never seen waves like these!" And with that, I had lost all my credibility. Birgitta demanded to leave immediately and to return to our homeport at Marina Del Rey. But there was no alternative to sailing back by boat over the dreaded swells and that was the last thing she wanted to do with sunset approaching! She felt trapped and we spent an uncomfortable night in the rocking little boat. We made it back home the next day over much calmer seas.

Eventually, I was forgiven. Birgitta returned home to Sweden, got married and had a life-long career in economics. She made it her mission to keep Sweden out of the Euro-currency area and even helped to establish a new political party to do so.

Michael Mussa was a rather quiet student in my undergraduate international economics class. Very uncharacteristically, he never said a word in class, but turned in an absolutely brilliant final exam, earning him an A+. Later on, he got his Ph.D. in economics from the University of Chicago and had a fine academic career. Our careers crossed a few times in subsequent years. Eventually, President Reagan nominated both of us for high economic posts in his administration. Mike was nominated to the Council of Economic Advisors and I was nominated at the same time for the Federal Reserve Board. The two of us had the honor to appear together in front of the U.S. Senate for our confirmation hearings. After that, he became the Chief Economist for the International Monetary Fund, where I had worked a few years earlier. Unfortunately, Mike Mussa passed away all too early.

Turning Conservative

For me, the time at UCLA was a formative period in my economic and political thinking. In graduate school at Berkeley, Keynesians and left-leaning thinkers had surrounded me. In spite of that, I had a visceral reaction against the student riots and its left-wing intellectual supporters. But I did not see a true alternative intellectual direction.

Now, my association with all these fine intellects and thinkers introduced me for the first time to conservative and libertarian thinking. The association with great minds like Hayek, Friedman, Buchanan, Brunner and Alchian — most of them Nobel Prize winners or worthy thereof — was certainly intellectually exciting. I started to appreciate more and more the role of *freedom for the individual* as the wellspring for liberty and economic growth. By setting free the dynamic forces of the human spirit, imagination and ideas blossom and new inventions can be created and implemented. The freedom to implement one's own ideas in free and unfettered enterprises is a key source for economic growth that generates prosperity as well as jobs for others. Personal freedom goes right along with economic freedom and the two are fundamentally inseparable from each other. One cannot exist without the other.

All that stood in stark contrast to the group-think philosophy of the Leftists and Socialists at Berkeley, who thought that groups were the basic organizational unit of humanity. All too often, that led to one group fighting and arguing with another group. One group would demand that others be taxed so that they could lead a better life at the other people's expense. I was not opposed to charitable giving, done freely, but forcing one group under penalty of law to support another group was an entirely different matter. It was coercion.

In its socialist and communist manifestations admired by many of the intellectual leaders at Berkeley, the individual was not much more than a cog in the machinery. The national-socialistic incarnation of these ideas that I had encountered in my childhood days in Germany was a set of ideas and an ideology that had brought enormous grief and destruction to the world. In my mind, there was not much difference between socialists, national socialists and international socialists or communists. They were all linked to each other by the common belief that the state is more important than the individual. The communist leaders of Eastern Europe and China, exemplified by Stalin and Mao, were little different in their philosophy and destructiveness from Adolf Hitler. It was just socialism in a different guise: Hitler emphasizing a nationalistic, nation-based socialism, while Stalin and Mao wanted to spread it over the entire world. Not that Hitler was any less ambitious in that regard.   The state was all-important and the individual was considered dispensable and counted for little or nothing.

For me it was the reverse: the individual person deserved life, liberty and justice.

Summertime in Hawaii

During the summer of 1969 I got invited to teach at the University of Hawaii. There was a steady stream by faculty members of the UCLA Economics Department to Hawaii. The main reason was that the former chairman of the department at UCLA, Wytze Gorter, had become first the Dean of the Graduate School and then the President of the University of Hawaii. A second reason for the exodus was the attraction of eternal sun, surf and the endless ocean.

That first summer in Hawaii was most enjoyable. I would teach my classes and then spend the rest of the day sitting on the beaches or eating Chinese food and drinking Mai Tai's at one of the numerous Waikiki restaurants. The other faculty members were most congenial, the students laid-back and the climate was like in Paradise. What was there not to like about Hawaii?

Meeting Emily

After that summer, I returned to my regular teaching duties at UCLA. I looked for something new to do and decided to learn how to play tennis. Jim Fox was a graduate student in the Economics Department, who supported himself by teaching tennis on the UCLA courts. I started to take tennis lessons from Jim.

One of the other students in Jim's class was a cute brunette named Emily Mitchell. Emily was a graduate student in Sociology. Emily had dimply cheeks that were always smiling. As was the custom in those days, she wore tiny miniskirts — both on and off the tennis court. It did not take long until I asked her out on a date and pretty soon we were going steady.

Becoming a Citizen

During my last days at UCLA, it was also time to make an important personal decision: whether to become an American citizen. When I first came to the United States in 1960, I came on a student visa to attend Parsons College. I renewed that student visa to study at the University of Minnesota and at UC Berkeley.

When I accepted the teaching position at UCLA in 1965, I had to change from a student visa to a regular immigrant visa. In those days, that was an easy task for a German citizen because immigrants were allowed to come into the country in direct proportion to the population makeup of the United States, as it existed in the 1920s. In essence, the system was designed to maintain the existing ethnic mix of the American population. That favored me because the German quota was large and wide-open for new immigrants. The door to citizenship stood wide open for me.

After I had been a resident in the United States for five years, I went to the Federal Building, filed the required papers, passed the citizenship tests, did the obligatory oral interview and was sworn in as a citizen in March 1970 at the Los Angeles Federal Courthouse. At the same time, I gave up my German citizenship. The die was cast and I was now an American.

SAGE ADVICE:
Individual Freedom is the Cornerstone of Life,
Liberty and Justice

14 A Quick Trip Around The World

During the summer that I spent in Hawaii, I caught the travel-bug and realized that there were places outside of Los Angeles that were exciting and worth visiting. I set out to see more of the world. As a matter of fact, I wanted to travel around the entire globe.

Japan

The opportunity presented itself when a Japanese professor came over to UCLA to do some research together with me. In return for hosting him, the generous Japanese invited me for a return visit to Nagoya City University in Japan. It was 1970 and I had just become a U.S. citizen. I flew over to Nagoya and enjoyed a guided tour of Japan, visiting all the tourist attractions of Tokyo, Kyoto and Mount Fuji. It was an impressive country with a long and cultured history.

As part of the arrangements, I was invited to give a lecture to the civil servants of Nagoya. There must have been over 200 persons that came to hear my lecture. Or, more likely, they were told to do so. As I did not speak any Japanese and they did not understand English, we had a translator who would "consecutively" interpret my English into Japanese. That meant that I would say a sentence in English and then he would translate it into Japanese. There was no flow to the speech and the stop-and-go format made the entire audience drowsy. Soon I noticed that many of them were asleep. When the ordeal was over, I mentioned to one of my hosts that most of the eyes of the listeners were closed. He replied to me most politely: "Ohhh, that's the way Japanese people concentrate — they all close their eyes so to that they can focus better!" I was most grateful to my polite host for that generous interpretation!

In Japan at the Geisha party that the Mayor of Nagoya threw for me

The Mayor of Nagoya gave an elegant reception for me, replete with Geisha Girls. They performed traditional Japanese dances and kept pouring Saki into our cups. When it was time to go home, the mayor left with two Geisha girls on his arms.

At another reception in Japan, I was introduced to the Russian Consul General. We chatted for a while and when he found out that I was travelling around the world, he insisted that I should visit Moscow on that trip so that I could learn about the accomplishments of the great Soviet Union. He offered to trade my PANAM ticket from New Delhi to Stockholm for a ticket on Aeroflot that allowed me to fly from New Delhi to Moscow and then on to Stockholm. To make the proposal more attractive, he also offered three days of lodging and sightseeing in Moscow for free — courtesy of the Russian tourist agency. I think his main goal was to get the U.S. dollar value of the PANAM ticket as the Soviets were short of foreign currency at that time. I thought that there could be no harm in learning more about the Soviet Union. Dumb as I was, I accepted. It was a decision that I was to regret very much.

War Time in Vietnam

But first, my plan was to visit Vietnam. From Japan, I flew to Saigon in South Vietnam. In 1970, the Vietnamese War was still raging and I wanted to see first hand what was happening in that war-torn country. As we approached the Saigon airport, the plane suddenly went into a very tight spiral as it descended towards the airfield. I did not know that Boeing 707's could perform such tricky maneuvers, but I learned that it was standard practice prior to landing in Saigon in those days. The Viet Kong was very close to the city and would regularly shoot at the planes attempting to land at the Saigon airport. As a defensive tactic, the pilots would try to stay over the city itself and descend in a corkscrew pattern towards the airport. We landed safely.

On the ground in Saigon, there were machine gun emplacements protected by sandbags on nearly every street corner. Few cars were on the roads, but there were thousands of little motorcycles with two, three or more Vietnamese riding on them. Maybe a few chickens or ducks were being carried along in a cage as well. It was a fascinating sight, as the small motor scooters would weave through the streets like a swarm of locusts.

I headed towards the Hotel Caravelle, where I had booked a room. The Caravelle was supposed to be the best hotel in the encircled city and all the news crews from ABC, CBS and NBC stayed there. But maybe that made the hotel more of a target for the Viet Kong as well. A short while before my arrival, a bomb had blown up in one of the hotel rooms. When I was there, all windows were taped with strips of masking tape so that the glass shards would not fly around in case of an explosion. I was not sure whether the tape was supposed to protect the hotel residents against

Soldiers standing guard in Saigon

Inside my room at the Hotel Caravelle with its protective stripes
of masking tape

explosions on the outside or to prevent the glass from flying into the street in case a bomb went off inside one of the rooms. I was glad that I never found out.

Suffering a bit from jetlag after my arrival, I slept fitfully and woke up frequently during the night. I noticed what looked like a smoke detector on the ceiling. Every now and then, a highly pitched sound emanated from the small device. I was sure that a microphone was hidden inside the smoke detector and a listener at the other end of the wire would turn up the volume to hear whether anything was going on in the room. I was not surprised to be spied on in a city under siege. Otherwise, the city was pretty peaceful and welcoming to foreigners. But besides watching soldiers behind their machinegun emplacements, there was not much for a tourist to do. After a few days, I had enough of watching the war close-up and I headed to New Delhi in India, the next stop on my journey.

India

New Delhi was another beehive of human activity. People were everywhere. Entire families were sleeping in the trenches alongside the road from the airport to the city. I could not believe the abject poverty of the people in the huts on the side of the road. There were more cars here than in Vietnam, but the driving habits were atrocious. On the wide boulevards of New Delhi, everybody tried to drive in the fast lane. In their eagerness to be the fastest car, most of the drivers were actually driving on the other side of the road and facing the oncoming traffic. Everybody would hold their course until the very last second before giving way. I found it hilarious when an elephant steadfastly marched down the middle of the street and divided the traffic just like Moses had parted the Red Sea.

I was stunned by the poverty around me and I thought that a revolt by the people would be imminent. When I told an Indian that I expected a revolution to happen very soon, he just laughed and said that it had been like that for hundreds of years and would remain the same for centuries to come. He was right.

Trying to Visit Moscow

A few days later, I headed for the airport and boarded the Aeroflot plane to Moscow that the Russian consul in Japan had arranged for me. I got a prized window seat in the first row. I took off my jacket and put it in the open overhead bin. There were no lids on the overhead compartments, like in most American planes. Instead, there was just an open rack that ran the length of the entire airplane. When I tried to store my jacket there, I touched something in the way. It felt like large piece of hard metal. I peeked into the rack and saw that it looked like a submachine gun. These were the days when planes regularly got hijacked all over the world. I was stunned and quietly sat down again. What should I do? Before I could do anything, the plane took off. A few minutes into the flight, the pilot came out of the cockpit, nonchalantly picked up the submachine gun, returned to his cabin and locked the door. Now I knew why no Russian airplanes had ever been hijacked. A few months later, when somebody actually tried to hijack a Russian plane, the pilot shot the hijacker on the spot. The Russians meant business.

When I arrived at the Moscow airport, I joined the long line for tourists trying to enter the country. I did not have a Russian visa, but the consul in Japan had promised that he would take care of everything. He had told me that someone would greet me at the airport and would expedite my entry through customs. A guide would then ferry me to a first-class hotel and give me a private sightseeing tour of the Russian capital. I was looking forward to an exciting adventure.

Instead, the customs officer waved me to the side and told me to wait. Eventually, a hippie with a beard and a guitar slung over his shoulder also joined me in the cordoned-off waiting area. He did not have a visa either. Then, a guard in uniform took both of us into custody and marched us unceremoniously to a barrack near the terminal.

In the barrack, there were two rows of about 10 rooms on each side of a long corridor. At the end of the hallway sat a sturdy

Russian woman in what looked like an army uniform replete with a peaked army dress hat. The epaulets on her shoulders pointed high into the air. She had a stern look on her face and a thick notebook on her desk.

The hippie and I each were assigned very Spartan rooms that looked a lot like jail cells. The furniture consisted of a metal army bed with a blanket. There was no toilet. The bathroom was at the end of the hallway, to be used by all the guests — or should I say inmates? Each time I used the facilities, the Russian guard at the end of the hallway made an entry into her diary.

The guard spoke very little English and I spoke no Russian. I tried to tell her that I was expecting a private chauffeur to drive me to my hotel, but all she said was: "Njet!" She pointed sternly back to my room. It was late and I was tired from the six-hour flight from India. So I gave in and went to bed.

I woke up early in the morning feeling almost totally frozen. While it was early May, there was still snow on the ground outside. There was little or no heat at all in our barracks and the water in the open shower stalls was just above freezing temperature. I had enough! I packed my suitcase and trudged towards the door. When the Russian guard saw me, she kept shouting "Njet! Njet!" as I walked past her. Over my shoulder I yelled back at her: "Airport! Plane leaving!" and kept marching.

The terminal building was only 100 yards away and I quickly headed for the Lufthansa counter. I showed them my around-the-world ticket and told them I wanted to fly to Stockholm on the next flight out. No luck! There were no flights to Stockholm on that day. But I was not going to stay in Russia any longer. So I told them that I would like the next flight out to anywhere. They told me that I could fly to Warsaw and connect there to a flight to Stockholm, which I gladly did. I had enough of cold Russian barracks and broken promises.

Later that day, I landed in Stockholm. I was glad that I had escaped from the unfriendly Soviet Union. My friend Birgitta picked me up at the airport. After receiving her Ph.D. from UCLA, she had returned to Sweden and she showed me around the city. It was nice to be back in a civilized country.

Teaching in Germany

A few days later, I flew on to Germany. I had accepted two guest professorships at the Universities of Göttingen and Saarbrücken in Germany. Emily flew over to Europe as well and together we travelled to Berlin. On her birthday, we got engaged at the Hilton Hotel, overlooking the Berlin Zoo. The next morning, we woke up to the trumpeting of the elephants next door.

We set up our main residence in a faculty-housing apartment at the University of Göttingen. I taught all my classes late in the week. As soon as I was done with the classes, we drove from Göttingen, which was located right next to the border with East Germany, all the way across the country to Cologne near the Belgian border in the West. Then we would spend the weekend with my aunts and visited some of the places I knew from my childhood. On the following Monday, we would drive to Saarbrücken at the French border. I would give my lectures in Saarbrücken and then we would circle back to Göttingen to teach my classes at Göttingen. It was a lot of driving, but also a lot of fun.

Emily took German lessons in Göttingen from Heidi and she can still recite some of the lessons verbatim. "*Schnell, der Zug faehrt gleich ab! Ich kaufe noch schnell eine Zeitung. Ach da steht doch immer derselbe Quatsch darin!*" It meant: "Hurry up! The train is leaving! I will quickly buy a newspaper! Oh, that's always the same nonsense!" That was about all the German she ever learned and she is still waiting for the right moment to apply that dialogue.

At one time, we were invited to a very elegant faculty dinner, with everybody showing up in a dark suit and silver tie. When asked how her German lessons were coming along, she replied: "*Ja, die deutsche Sprache ist sehr schmierig!*" What she wanted to say was: "*Die deutsche Sprache ist sehr schwierig!*" Changing that one little letter in the last word from "*w*" to "*m*" changed the meaning of the sentence from "The German language is very *difficult!*" to "The German language is very *slimy!*" Obviously, everyone broke out in cordial laughter. For Emily, this embarrassment was the end of her attempts to learn that rather difficult and confounding language.

Not that I did all that much better. After giving a lecture at the university in German, one of the students approached me and enquired whether he could ask me a very personal question. Somewhat hesitantly, I agreed. So he asked very politely: "Herr Professor Dr. Heller, are you actually from Cologne or are you from America?" Apparently, my strong regional Cologne accent in German was pretty recognizable.

Germans often wonder why I still speak with a very distinct Cologne accent when I talk German, after having spent most of my life in the United States. The reason is actually very simple: if I had remained in Germany, I would undoubtedly have studied a few years in Munich or spent some time working in Hamburg, Frankfurt or Berlin. Over time, my Cologne accent would have slowly eroded away or completely disappeared. As it is, I still speak the same language as I did when I graduated from high school, and the Cologne accent is preserved in its originality!

Göttingen was close to the heavily fortified East German border, generally referred to as the "Iron Curtain." Our regular radio receiver could intercept the daily broadcasts of the East German Secret Service to their agents in the West: "The brown fox meets with the red rabbit; the smart snake meets with the yellow horse..." and so it went for hours. These were directions by the East Germans to their undercover agents in the West to meet with other agents or to perform certain secret tasks. But in the days before the Internet or satellite communications, all the instructions of the *Stasi* to its spies were broadcast in the open. Of course, nobody really knew who the brown fox was and so it was all pretty much secret and mysterious anyhow.

We travelled a lot through Europe that summer, visiting France, Italy, Spain and Switzerland. But eventually, it was time to return to America.

Travelling with Emily through Europe

The Virgin Islands

On the way back to the United States, Emily and I decided to rent a sailboat in the Virgin Islands. We flew to the tiny island of Tortola and chartered a 30-foot sloop. The trade winds carried us swiftly past Peter Island, Cooper and Ginger Island to Virgin Gorda, the "Fat Virgin." On some of these largely uninhabited little islands, we dropped an anchor and spent the nights alone in a romantic bay. This was 1970, and the hordes of tourists had not yet descended on the then pristine Virgin Islands.

When we reached the end of the island chain, we spent the night in a small cove called "The Bitter End." Yes, it looked like the end of the world. There was only one little shack ashore. When we explored the beach, one of the two inhabitants of the cottage asked us whether we wanted something to eat. Why not, we thought? Accompanied by his German shepherd, he went to the beach and started to pull on a long line. Finally, a lobster cage emerged at the end of the rope. In it were half a dozen thrashing live lobsters. The dog went wild and wanted to get at the crustaceans, but the fellow reprimanded the dog by saying

At anchor in the Virgin Islands

sternly: "No, no, Bowser, this isn't playsie time, this is lobster time!" With that, he grabbed two of the kicking beasties, threw them in a pot with boiling waters and prepared us a most delicious meal. Nowadays, if you should visit the same spot, there is an entire marina, along with hotels and restaurants as well as a sailing school. The idyllic old times are gone!

On the way back to Tortola, we stopped at Jost Van Dyke Island, an inviting place with a well-protected harbor. We anchored our boat and rowed our dinghy ashore to Foxy's Bar and had a few drinks of Pimm's Cup. When we came back to our boat, we noticed to our dismay that our boat's anchor line had wrapped itself several times around one of the coral heads that could be found in the shallow harbor. In vain, we tried to free the boat from the wraps. Eventually, I asked the captain of another boat for help. He answered that there was nothing that he could do to help me, but he recommended that I get Jimmy, who knew how to deal with anchor lines wrapped around coral heads. I asked: "But how can I find Jimmy?" The captain told me: "Just go to Foxy's Bar and you will find him at the end of the bar!" Indeed, there he was at the end of the long bar, a muscular native wearing nothing but a pair of trunks and sipping a beer. When I told him about our predicament, he pulled a long knife out of his pants, put it between his teeth and swam swiftly to our boat. Before I could get back to my boat, he had unwrapped the line and the anchor was free again, ready to be hauled in. I was most grateful, gave him a generous tip and we proceeded on our journey. It was a wonderful week aboard our chartered sailboat in an as yet unspoiled Paradise.

SAGE ADVICE:
No Dictatorship is Worth Experiencing

15 Bliss in Aloha Land

My friend Burnie Campbell, the Chairman of the Economics Department at the University of Hawaii, had kept calling and invited me to spend another semester teaching on the island. The temptation was too great and I decided to accept the invitation to be a guest professor at the university.

In the fall of 1970, Emily and I both flew to Honolulu. We rented a wonderful condominium at the *Ilikai* that overlooked the Waikiki Harbor and the ocean. The Ilikai is a well-known luxury hotel, but there are also a few privately owned condominium units in the building. We rented one of those units for the fall semester. While I was teaching economics, Emily studied for her final M.A. exam in Sociology at UCLA. When the moment came for her to take the tests, she packed an entire suitcase full of books and got on the plane. She hoped to read all those books over the weekend prior to the exams. She was a very diligent student and passed her exams with flying colors!

Getting Married on a Cat

While we were in Hawaii, we decided to get married on that romantic island. But the question was: where? These were the Sixties — well, the Seventies had actually just begun — and weddings on beaches or on mountaintops were definitely in vogue. Because we both liked sailing, we thought it would be fun to get married on a catamaran off Diamond Head. The Hilton Hawaiian Village Hotel next door had the perfect vessel: a 50-foot catamaran that was regularly used for their dinner cruises along with a small ukulele band.

We did not belong to any church and did not know any preacher to help us tie the knot. So I suggested to Emily to go to the social activities desk at the Hilton to make inquiries as to how one could get married in Hawaii on a catamaran. After all, we were planning to rent the vessel from the hotel. The lady at the social desk recommended the Reverend Abraham Akaka, who was a local celebrity preacher. Reverend Akaka was regularly called upon to open new shopping centers or to bless freeways. The Reverend interviewed us for about an hour and upon learning that we wanted to get married on a catamaran, he politely declined, saying that he had did not feel comfortable on a catamaran.

We were back to square one in our search for a minister who would marry us on the high seas. Eventually, we found a Unitarian preacher in the Yellow Pages who also worked as a divorce lawyer. We hired him, the Hilton catamaran and the ukulele band

Getting married on the Hilton Hawaiian Village catamaran off the shores of Waikiki and on December 5, 1970 sailed out towards Diamond Head to get married.

Emily's sister Kathleen was the maid of honor and my best man was Joe Swaffar, whom I knew well from my days at Berkeley and at UCLA. Joe was now teaching at the University of Hawaii in Hilo. Emily's mother and a few relatives flew in from Los Angeles and the other wedding guests consisted mainly of faculty members from the University of Hawaii. There was Armen Alchian and his wife Pauline, who were visiting from UCLA. Another guest was Assibi Abudu. Assibi hailed from Ghana, but I had gotten to know him already at the University of Minnesota, when we both were graduate students there. Now Assibi was teaching together with me at the University of Hawaii.

We exchanged vows on our catamaran next to Diamond Head and tossed the traditional interlinked leis into the water as an eternal memorial to our getting married. After the catamaran got back to the Hilton dock, the guests wanted to know where the reception was. We thought that the ceremony was enough and had not made any further plans. But we could not stay on the catamaran because the boat had to depart soon for the evening cruise. What to do? We invited everyone to our small condo in the Ilikai and ordered room service. Problem solved!

Eventually, the wedding party broke up. Emily and I drove to the Makaha Inn on the Eastern shore of Oahu, where we had planned to spend our honeymoon. Where else to go when you were already in Paradise? When the hostess at the elegant dining room discovered that Emily was wearing only flip-flops instead of proper shoes, she refused to admit us to the dining room — and so it was back to room service, again. As newlyweds, we obviously did not mind as we had more important things in mind!

Shortly after we got married, we went to the popular *Don Ho Show* in Waikiki. Don Ho was a tourist favorite and the audience was always packed with honeymooners from the mainland. When Do Ho asked the obvious questions: "Are there any honeymooners in the audience?" Emily eagerly waived her hand. But instead of asking all the ladies on to the stage, Don Ho asked the newly-wed husbands. After making us dance with the professional hula girls, which was a very demanding and exhausting task indeed, all the guys had to sing a song in order to be permitted to get off the stage again. In honor of Emily, who goes by the nickname of Ducky, I promptly intoned "Rubber Ducky you're the one, making bath time so much fun...." to the roaring applause of the audience. Don Ho got me off the stage very quickly!

Singing "Rubber Ducky you're the one..."
at the Don Ho Show in Waikiki

Our First House in Los Angeles

After the fall semester was over, we both returned to Los Angeles at the end of 1970. Emily continued her studies for her Ph.D. in Sociology, while I resumed teaching. We moved into a house on Lindenwood Lane, which was located at the top of Tigertail Road above Brentwood. The house overlooked the entire Los Angeles basin and on a smog-free day one could see Catalina Island. It was a great location and only a short 10-minute drive over Sunset Boulevard to UCLA. We paid $50,000 for the house, which is now worth over $2 million. The down payment came from the book royalties for my textbooks.

Emily helps to paint our house overlooking the Los Angeles basin

Moving to Koko Head

When the spring term at UCLA was over, we decided to move to Hawaii permanently. Hawaii offered me a full professorship and the future there looked bright. We bought a wonderful house on Koko Head with a Lanai stretching for the entire length of the property. Sitting on the Lanai with a Mai Tai in hand and watching the sunset over Diamond Head was a truly spectacular experience. At first, the sky would turn yellow, then red and eventually a deep purple. We were living in paradise!

We bought a small 14-foot Hobie Cat catamaran and sailed with it along the shore to the Kahala Hilton. There, we would beach the boat and enjoy Sunday brunch with all the folks who had paid hundreds of dollars for their room. We also purchased two Irish Setters: *Baron and Koko*. Baron took his name from the German *Baron von Richthofen*, better known as the Red Baron of World War I fame. What could be a more appropriate name for a

With our first baby: an Irish Setter named "Baron" in Hawaii

red Irish Setter? And Koko was named after Koko Head, where we lived.

The two dogs were totally crazy and frequently got into trouble by running away or peeing on unsuspecting girls who were sunning themselves on the beach. But we loved them anyhow and they were our children. Emily would drive around with the dogs in her little yellow Porsche. One day, Baron jumped out the window as Emily was driving on the only freeway in Hawaii. Fortunately, she had wrapped Baron's leash around the gearshift to restrain him, but he jumped anyhow. After she pulled over to the side of the freeway, she expected to find a dead dog at the end of the leash. But Baron was just hanging there quietly with a sheepish grin on his face.

Another time we took Baron sailing on our Hobie Cat. Again, we restrained him by wrapping his leash around the mast. That did not prevent our stupid dog from jumping overboard anyhow. This time he floated under the trampoline that made up the connecting mid-section of the two pontoons of our catamaran. With Baron gasping for air, we dragged him back on top of the catamaran and he survived yet another unplanned adventure.

On another occasion, Baron and Koko escaped together and Baron returned alone after a few hours. We looked everywhere, but could not find Koko. Baron was not talking! We placed ads in the newspapers and had lost-dog announcements made over a radio station. After 4 or 5 days, a hiker called us. He had found Koko very near to our house, but *inside* the crater that made up the ancient volcano named Koko Head. She was stuck in a ravine and her legs were all covered with blood from her futile attempts to climb the steep volcanic walls. Poor Koko had lost a lot of weight and she never missed a meal again after that experience. Koko became the fattest Irish Setter in the animal kingdom.

Chairing the Economics Department

During our third year in Hawaii, I became the Chairman of the Economics Department. I learned to deal with all the administrative duties of running a department composed of more than two-dozen faculty members. We actually had a pretty congenial group of professors. There was Burnie Campbell, who had recruited me from UCLA. Larry Miller was a somewhat idiosyncratic, but very bright transplant from UCLA. One of the stars of the department was Seiji Naya, who originally came over to the University of Hawaii from his native Japan on a boxing scholarship. After earning a NCAA title in boxing and thereby putting the university on the map, Seiji was a local celebrity. You could go with Seiji into any bar in Honolulu and immediately the party would be treated to free Pupus, delicious Hawaiian hors d'oeuvres, because the proprietor wanted to keep this local sports hero happy. We all benefitted.

The wonderful thing about the University of Hawaii was that nobody would decline an invitation to spend a semester as a visiting professor there. Milton Friedman readily abandoned his perch at the snowy University in Chicago for the winter quarter and taught for several years in a row at the University of Hawaii while I was there. Art Goldberger from Wisconsin and Dan Suits from

Michigan all hailed from Midwestern universities with cold winters and were only to happy to spend the winter semester in Hawaii.

Getting Ready to Leave Paradise

But before long, I missed the bright and challenging students I had known at UCLA. While UCLA students were ready to dispute every word and idea that a professor uttered, the typical students in Hawaii were quiet, relaxed and languid. Many of the local Hawaiian students were young ladies who were studying fashion design and were required to take an economics class. The guys were more interested in surfing than in studying and when someone in the last row yelled: "Surf's Up!" half a dozen students would immediately jump up and head for the beach. First things first!

Most of the foreign students were from Asia and were usually very quiet and reserved. Their English was not always good and they were afraid to ask questions for fear of exposing their ignorance or "losing face." That was a fate worse than death in the Asian culture. Clearly, there were exceptions and there were a few bright and challenging students at the University of Hawaii as well. But for one reason or another, the majority of the students were not as bright as the ones at UCLA or not very much interested in studying. Under these circumstances, teaching was not all that challenging and it got boring pretty fast.

After a few years, Emily and I also knew the island pretty well. Fifty miles wide and fifty miles long, it took two hours to get from one end of Oahu to the other. If one wanted to go for a ride, the main choice was whether to drive clockwise or counterclockwise around the island. Paradise was a small place and it was time to move on.

Because I was always interested in international economics, I focused my job search on the International Monetary Fund in Washington, DC. I contacted a friend at the IMF, Rudi Rhomberg, and asked him whether they would be willing to offer me a visiting position for one year. Soon, the answer came back. They did not have any visiting jobs available, but instead they offered me a job as the Chief of the Financial Studies Division of the IMF. That was an offer I could not turn down.

I have often asked myself whether leaving UCLA and going to Hawaii was the wrong career move. In a sense it was, because I did not like it in Hawaii over the long-term. But if I had never left for Hawaii, I would probably have stayed at UCLA forever, like many of my colleagues did. It would not have been a bad career, but I would have never gotten to the IMF and would not have had the varied and exciting career spanning academia, government and business that I was privileged to enjoy.

SAGE ADVICE:
After a While, Even Paradise Gets Boring

16 At the Center of the Economic World

After leaving Hawaii, I became Chief of the Financial Studies Division of the International Monetary Fund in Washington. The IMF had been founded at the Bretton Woods Conference as part of the post-war effort to provide for a new international economic order. Along with its sister organization, the World Bank, the IMF belonged to the UN family of international organizations. Its employees were drawn from all over the world and traveled on diplomatic passports. Working at the IMF was certainly going to be very different from the relaxed academic environment that I had enjoyed so far.

Working conditions at the IMF were pretty cushy. We all traveled first class on our trips and stayed at fine hotels. The Fund also had its own country club in the leafy Maryland suburbs. It shared the facility with the World Bank and it was aptly called "Bretton Woods." Often, we would spend our weekends swimming and playing tennis at the club.

Settling in Washington

On the home front, things were going to be different as well. Emily and I had spent the summer traveling through Europe and visiting the family in Germany. Emily was pregnant, and our first child was due in October. Emily had gone for a wellness visit in Germany while we were there and the doctor let us listen through a sonogram machine to the little "thump-thump" noises made by the unborn baby. From that day on, we called the as yet nameless baby "Thumper."

We had put our dogs in a kennel in Washington while we were in Europe. When we returned, Baron looked like a skinny skeleton. He had refused to eat because he was lonesome and longed for us. He loved us so much that he would not eat without us. Not so Koko: she had gained a few more pounds as she got to eat Baron's food as well. She was her plump and happy self when we returned!

We rented a house from a gentleman, who worked for the World Bank. The house even had a pool in the backyard. But soon, Emily discovered that the pool had actually been pushed a bit out of the ground by the many frosts that tend to hit Washington in the winter. Consequently, there was a space of two or three inches between the pool and the ground and a small herd of rats had moved in there and called it their home. Emily, who was quite pregnant by that time, was very upset and worried about the rats and what they might do to our future offspring. She insisted on moving to a new house immediately.

We wound up with our two dogs in a nice traditional brick house on Layman Street in McLean, Virginia. The house was located in a leafy neighborhood bordering on a murmuring brook called Pimmit Run. On the other side of the creek was the prestigious Potomac School. Several other IMF couples resided in the area as well. The house was situated on a steep downslope from the street that ended at Pimmit Run. One sunny day, Emily was sitting Hawaiian-style in her bikini in the front yard. She was also eight months pregnant, but she reckoned that the steep slope would shelter her from any unwanted glances. But she had not counted on the mailman, who saw her as he approached our house down the hill. Totally shocked by the sight, he lost his footing and fell down the steep incline. As he tumbled down the hillside, he spilled the contents of his entire mailbag in the process. Emily was as embarrassed as the hapless mailman. I guess it was all caused by the rapid transition from sunny and hang-loose Hawaii to the much more staid and conservative environment of Virginia!

Another fateful accident happened in our own living room. When Koko was in heat for the first time, we put Baron into a kennel, so that the two of them would not get the wrong idea and start a dog family of their own. Soon, Koko was in heat again. As Emily was usually at home, she decided that Baron was now a more mature gentleman-dog and that he could therefore stay at home along with Koko. One day, Emily made a quick trip to the grocery store. When she returned, she found Baron and Koko interlocked on the carpet in the living room.

Nine weeks later, Koko had eight little Irish Setter pups. The first seven were born in the large laundry room that we had prepared for the occasion. We all went to bed, thinking that Koko had had a nice litter of seven. But in the middle of the night, we kept hearing little "miaus" that sounded as if they were coming from a cat in distress. Eventually, I went down to the backyard to investigate and found another puppy, still partially in her birth sack in the backyard. Emily liberated her from the sack and brought her to her mother Koko to nurse. We promptly named her "*Little Orphan Annie*" and Annie quickly became the favorite of all the kids in the neighborhood.

Living next to the CIA

Soon we decided that it was time to have our own house and after a lengthy search, we settled on a house on a quiet cul-de-sac called Duncraig Court in McLean, Virginia. It was an area of fairly new houses that had been built on an old horse farm just inside the Beltway next to the Georgetown Pike. Many of our neighbors worked at the CIA, which was headquartered only a few blocks away.

In those days, nobody was supposed to know where the secret agency was actually located. At various neighborhood parties, it was natural to enquire what the other person did for a living and the answer was invariably: "I work for a government agency and I can't say any more!" I usually replied: "Oh, I guess you have a very convenient commute..." and the typical retort was: "Yes, that's what I love about the job!" Question answered!

I also found out that our very secretive neighbors would tell you all kinds of interesting and often spellbinding stories, as long as you did not ask them how they knew. The CIA mantra was: "Never reveal your sources and methods" and it was a lesson that stood me in good stead later in life as well. Everybody liked to hear a good story, but if you revealed your sources it was not only you, but also your friend that might get into trouble. If you did not reveal your source, all was well!

Our Family Grows

At about the same time, our daughter Kimberly was born. Emily delivered her at Sibley Hospital in the District of Columbia. Sibley was a wonderful hospital and Emily enjoyed being catered to by all the friendly nurses. Thanks to the very generous insurance program for the employees of the IMF, which tried to combine all the best features of the top health care systems in the world, the insurance paid for almost a week in the hospital so that Emily could rest and recover. Emily felt like a queen and enjoyed her first week of motherhood.

We also determined that it was time for Emily to get some help with baby Kimberly and the dogs. We invited Irene Brings, a sister of my cousin's wife, to join us. Irene had just graduated from high school in Germany and she enthusiastically plunged into the American life-style. Irene would eat pizza until she could not walk any more and would go dancing at the local discos until early in the morning. We enjoyed having Irene around and named her our "Disco Kid."

While Irene was with us, our son Christopher was born. Emily delivered him also at Sibley Hospital in the District of Columbia. We had to race across Chain Bridge to the hospital on the other side of the Potomac River, as he was ready to come into this world much faster than Kimberly.

Au Pairs

Irene stayed with us for a year, but eventually she returned to Germany. She was followed by a procession of almost a dozen "*au pairs*" while our kids grew up. There was Uli, a good friend of Irene's, who was a very pretty but also serious theology student. She visited Irene and decided to stay with us when Irene returned home. Next was Leona. She went out every night and hit the bars of Washington, where all kinds of shady characters would hang out. We worried a lot about her safety and welfare, but she always returned with a happy smile on her face. Ruth, who introduced herself to us by saying: "Hi! Please call me Snoopy," had long feathers hanging from her ears and consumed all kinds of "stimulants." Emily had to give her a stern lecture and she shaped up. Alexis was a distant relative of a friend of ours who crashed our family car a few times. She also loved to eat the hors d'oeuvres that Emily prepared for me at the end of the day instead of cleaning up after the kids as she was supposed to. And then there was Lena from Sweden, who always had a dusting cloth in her hand and kept the house cleaner than ever before! Barbara never had a single meal with us for an entire year. But every morning, we would find an empty mayonnaise jar in the trashcan. That was all she ever ate! Then came petite Bettina, who unfortunately got very sick and had to return home early. And then there was Andrea, who loved to date policemen. One of her policemen friends chased my wife Emily down in his police cruiser with blue lights flashing and sirens blaring. On that day, Emily happened to be driving the station wagon usually used by our au pair Andrea. Emily never saw a more red-faced and apologetic policeman than him when she stepped out of our station wagon and the policeman came face to face with her — instead of his girlfriend Andrea.

Virtually all of the girls were involved in one car mishap or another: one young lady took the garage doors off the hinges trying to get the car into our garage; one hit the guard rails along the roadside when she thought a police car was behind her; and one wound up with the car on our lawn when she had the car in reverse instead of forward gear. Emily always claimed that it was like having another teenage daughter to take care of, while I thought that I had magnanimously provided her with additional help. Few of them ever had any kids in later life. I guess that a little foretaste of how much trouble the little ones can create and how much care they require helped them to make the decision not to have kids of their own. Being an au pair was a bit like being inoculated against motherhood!

Work at the Fund

The IMF's Financial Studies Division, which I headed, had fallen into disrepair due to the long absence of a leader. There were only a couple of economists left in the Division when I arrived, while as many as a dozen economists were authorized as staff for the group. Among the three incumbents was Bill White, an older gentleman who had spent his entire career at the Fund. Harvard-trained, Bill was very bright and always ready to argue. He was superb at criticizing and reviewing papers written by the staff, but had a hard time of putting pen to paper and actually finishing his own research papers. There was almost always more work to be done in his judgment.

Mohsin Khan was quite the opposite: young and energetic and always full of initiative, he was a virtual publishing machine who could grind out important research papers in no time at all. We co-authored a few studies and Mohsin went on to a long and successful career at the IMF. Eventually, he became the Director of the Middle Eastern Department, a very prestigious position that put him in charge of many important and challenging countries.

I set out with enthusiasm to recruit new staff members to rebuild the depleted staff. One of the first new recruits was Malcolm Knight, who was then teaching at the prestigious London School of Economics. Malcolm was an extremely bright and energetic economist. Eventually, he became Deputy Governor of the Bank of Canada and the Managing Director of the Bank for International Settlements in Basle, one of the very top jobs in the world of international finance. He and his wife Amy had kids the same age as ours and we spent many days together. Soon our Division was again at full strength of a dozen economists and we started to play an increasingly important part in the research program of the IMF.

When I arrived at the IMF, Andrew Crockett was the Assistant to the Managing Director. This was a very important post that gave a young man an intimate "look behind the scenes" at the very top of the organization. But instead of returning to the Bank of England, where he had worked prior to this posting, Andrew decided to join the regular IMF staff as Chief of the Special Studies Division. His Special Studies Division and my Financial Studies Division were the two main research groups in the Research Department. We cooperated a lot and quickly became good friends. Andrew eventually did return to the Bank of England. This time as Deputy Governor. After that, he was appointed as the Managing Director of the Bank for International Settlements, preceding Malcolm Knight in that position.

In addition to the Knights' and the Crocketts', there were Günter Wittich and Hans Gerhard and their families. They were two wonderful friends that also hailed from Germany and we spent much time together with them in Washington. Günter had been a fellow graduate student at Berkeley and now he worked in the Treasurer's Department. Eventually, he was elevated to be the IMF's Deputy Treasurer and was in charge of the IMF's gold sales. Hans was a former theology student who was always interested in either having a good time or an erudite conversation about the world at large. Hans retired early from the Fund to devote himself to his farm in Virginia and became a quite renowned artist.

One cannot talk about the Research Department of the IMF without focusing on its distinguished leader: Jean Jacques Polak, who had attended the original Bretton Woods conference where the IMF was founded. J.J., as everybody called him, had made many important contributions to the literature of balance of payments adjustment. He was known as the father of the "Monetary

Approach to the Balance of Payments," which also provided the intellectual framework for the IMF missions to countries in payments difficulties. The Monetary Approach to the Balance of Payments provided a simple, yet effective way to estimate the policy measures that a country would have to undertake to get its balance of payments restored to balance. I had the pleasure of editing a book with that title for the IMF. Clearly, Polak should have gotten a Nobel Prize for his contributions to economic science and policy making, but unfortunately he passed away too early.

Jean Jacques Polak, the long-time Director of the IMF's Research Department, myself and Johannes Witteveen, the Managing Director of the IMF.

I had the honor of being asked to write several speeches for Johannes Witteveen, the Managing Director of the IMF. One of them, entitled: "Making the SDR the Central Reserve Asset of the International Monetary System" aroused quite a bit of attention and became a center piece in the discussions of how to reform the international monetary system. Some baby-steps were undertaken in the direction of increasing the importance of the SDR, but the dollar remained king in the international financial arena.

IMF Board Meetings

Attending the IMF Board meetings was always most interesting. It was a privilege to which I was entitled due to my position as a division chief. The Executive Directors representing the largest countries in the world as well as the ED's elected by the various regional constituencies representing the smaller nations would sit around a large horseshoe-shaped conference table. The Managing Director, Johannes Witteveen, who was a former Dutch Finance Minister, presided at the apex of the table. The discussions would center on "mission reports" of visits by IMF delegations to member countries, the world economic outlook and other topics of current interest. During my time, there were lengthy discussions on the reform of the international monetary system, the oil crisis and the problems associated with the recycling of "Petrodollars."

One or two staff members would make a presentation on the topic of the day and then the Executive Directors representing the various member countries of the IMF would have a usually long-winded discussion. Quite often, the opinions varied all over the map and I often wondered how the Managing Director would be able to summarize the quite divergent viewpoints and come to some reasonable conclusion. But Mr. Witteveen was a master at finding common ground and forging a consensus.

Frankly, I always wondered whether the Managing Director's habit to serve plentiful coffee and tea to the delegates during the prolonged discussions contributed to the directors' willingness to agree to his conclusions. Eventually, all directors felt the urgent need to go to the bathroom. That call by nature may have powerfully enhanced their willingness to agree with the Managing Director's conclusions, if only to terminate the seemingly endless discussions and to be free to relieve themselves at last!

Running the IMF Seminars

Mr. Polak asked me to organize the seminar series sponsored by the IMF and I was more than delighted to take on that task. It was my job to invite a prominent economist to give a lecture and then I would chair the presentation given to the entire staff. But beforehand, I had the pleasure of hosting a small intimate luncheon for our guest, which the Managing Director would usually attend. I could invite seven or eight other staff members to lunch with the visiting dignitary. That made me quite popular with the colleagues that I invited because they cherished the opportunity to have lunch with the Managing Director. I invited the best of the best economists, such as the Nobel Laureates Milton Friedman, Bob Mundell, Larry Klein and Wassily Leontief as well as other eminent economists who undoubtedly would have received the coveted prize if they had not passed away too early, such as Harry Johnson.

A Mission to Saudi Arabia

While it was not the major purpose of the research economists in our division to go on country missions to the IMF member countries, we would occasionally be invited to do so. I was asked to participate in the first-ever IMF mission to Saudi Arabia in March of 1975. I remember flying first class on Lufthansa from Washington to Frankfurt and on to Jeddah in Saudi Arabia. As the plane descended to the airport, you could see the endless shimmering Arabian Desert on the left side of the airplane and the calm waters of the Red Sea gleaming under the sun on the right side. I was about to embark on a memorable adventure.

As I started to go through customs, I realized that the German travel brochure that I had casually picked up at the Frankfurt airport also contained a few advertisements for several nudist camps. The pictures of naked bodies were clearly illegal in the conservative Kingdom. But it was too late. There was no way that I could dispose of the brochure easily, now that I was in the entry hall under the eyes of the Saudi airport guards. With a straight face,

I carried the potentially offensive catalogue stealthily though the inspection point. In spite of my diplomatic passport, I probably would have been arrested and flogged in public if somebody had found the pictures of all the nudists.

Our small group of IMF advisors stayed at a hotel in the old part of Jeddah. One morning, I took a brief walk through the neighborhood. I walked for several blocks and saw only Arab men in their white *dishdash* tunics that looked just like white nightgowns. Not feeling too comfortable as I was not seeing any women or men in Western garb, I returned to the hotel and asked the doorman whether it had been safe to walk in that neighborhood. He just laughed and told me that the last time that someone had come to harm in the neighborhood had been a decade ago. The offender was dealt with on the following Friday by being flogged in the public square, where also the regular beheadings took place. Nobody had been bothered since. I felt a bit safer!

I walked to the *souq*, or marketplace, and saw the gold merchants display their wares openly in what looked like converted garages. When the mullahs called for prayers from the minarets, the locals would stream to the mosques to offer their supplications. The gold merchants would leave the doors to their stands wide open and merely string a piece of cord over the entrance as an indication that the shop was closed. All the gold displays were left within easy reach of the pedestrians passing by. But nobody would touch the precious exhibits. If they had, their hand would have been chopped off the following Friday in the marketplace. Justice was severe and swift in Saudi Arabia!

The next day, our IMF delegation called on SAMA, the Saudi Arabian Monetary Agency, for an official visit. After meeting for some time, I asked to go to the bathroom. One of the Saudi officials pointed out the way to me. I tried to follow his directions, but instead of finding the restroom, I found myself in a totally green room. Yes, there were dollar bills stacked from floor to ceiling. I must have wandered inadvertently into one of the safes where SAMA kept its currency reserves. Just like in the gold Souq, there were no closed doors. I turned around and was confronted by a guard holding what looked like a shotgun. I smiled. The guard didn't. I spoke only English and he only Arabic. I started to think about the swift way of Saudi justice. Eventually, my western garments and my gesticulating and the repetition of the mantra "IMF, IMF" over and over again convinced him that I had just lost my way. Ultimately, I found my way to the bathroom. I never felt more relieved in my entire life!

After returning to our hotel, I went to the nice pool area behind the building. There was a small back alley leading from the pool to the regular streets behind the hotel. As I walked down the narrow alley, a black limousine pulled up at the other end. The doors opened and four Arab women in full back *hijabs* emerged from the limo. Hijab's are the traditional Arab black robes for women that cover the entire body, except for a small slit for the eyes allowing them to look out. The ladies took a quick look down the alley, saw only me in my casual Western clothes, and zip-zap, the hijabs were gone. Now they were walking towards the pool area, wearing only the short sundresses that they had worn underneath their black hijabs. Chatting away, they proceeded past me to the swimming pool and hopefully a good time. I wondered what would have happened to them if they had been caught by the morals police or by a mullah out on a stroll.

King Faisal is Murdered.

The following day, our IMF team flew to Riyadh, the capital of Saudi Arabia. Riyadh is located in the middle of the desert and is the traditional seat of the royal family and the government. We had meetings scheduled with the Finance Minister, who was part of the royal family himself.

We were ushered in for our audience, and the minister sat on an elevated stage and waited for us to assemble. Just as we sat down, one of his aides appeared and whispered into his ear. The minister took one look at us and said: "I am afraid, I have to leave. We will have to continue our discussions at some more opportunc time!"

With those words, he got up and hurriedly left the room. Wow, I thought, that was a short meeting!

We went back to our nearby hotel in Riyadh and one member of our group went into the barbershop to get a shave. He was an Egyptian by birth and obviously was totally fluent in Arabic. After a few minutes, he stumbled out of the barbershop. He was not fully shaved and still covered with some white shaving cream around his face. Totally ashen looking, he blurted out: "The King has been killed!"

We were stunned. That obviously was the reason why the Finance Minister had dismissed us. Now we could also hear the roar of helicopters overhead and saw trucks with armed soldiers rumbling through the streets. King Faisal had indeed been murdered and the city was quickly in a total clampdown state. Nobody knew whether this was a conspiracy or even the start of a broader revolution. Everywhere, military and police were in evidence and we hunkered down in our hotel.

Soon, the television stations announced that King Faisal had been killed by his own nephew. It was clear that our mission was essentially over and that there was little chance that we would have any further discussions with governmental officials.

After a brief conversation, we decided to fly back to Jeddah. We were privileged to use the VIP lounge at the airport. As we waited there for our flight, one military or civilian plane after the other arrived at the airport. The disembarking Saudis were obviously high officials and princes assembling to mourn the deceased king. Clad in formal back robes with wide golden embroideries, it was an impressive procession of Saudi Arabia's most important people that filed past us though the VIP lounge. We sat there in wonderment and awe.

The King's own nephew, who had stabbed him to death, was executed just a few weeks later. Justice in Saudi Arabia was swift and sure.

After we made it back to Jeddah, we decided that there was no further work to be done and that we should return home as soon as possible. We rebooked our flights and left the Kingdom.

I still remember asking the Lufthansa stewardess for a drink right after the plane lifted off for our return flight. I really needed it! It was my first drink in a week that had been breathtaking indeed. A glass of gin and tonic never tasted so good early in the morning!

Leaving the IMF

Life at the IMF continued to run its normal course, but I was no longer eager to go on new adventurous missions. Instead, I stuck to my research projects.

After four years at the IMF, I got restless again. Walter Hoadley, the Chief Economist of Bank of America, stopped by frequently at the IMF to visit and to discuss the global economic situation. On one of his visits, he asked me whether I would be interested in moving to the Bank of America in San Francisco. I was happy to entertain that notion, as it always had been my dream to return to the Bay Area ever since I studied at the University of California at Berkeley. Emily also liked the idea of returning to her native California very much. Our two little kids, Kim and Chris, did not get to vote.

> **SAGE ADVICE:**
> Always Stay Friends With Your Colleagues.
> Many of Them May Wind up in Very High Places.
> And: Never Reveal Your Sources

17 Learning the Corporate Way of Life

Ever since being a student at Berkeley, I loved the San Francisco Bay Area. The climate was superb and the scenery spectacular. There were world-class restaurants and cultural amenities as well. Not that Washington was lacking in the latter two categories, but the hot and sticky summers and frosty winters could not compare to California.

Joining the Economics Department

When Walter Hoadley asked me whether I was interested in coming to Bank of America as Director of International Economic Research, I eagerly said yes. Bank of America was at that time the largest bank in the world and had offices all over the globe. John Wilson was the Director of the Economics Department, but both Walter and John let me run the international side of the shop pretty independently. John focused on the domestic U.S. economy and together we produced twice a year the *World Economic Outlook*, which was an important document underpinning the bank's planning process.

I was glad to be back at Bank of America, where I had served as an intern a dozen years earlier. A few of my former colleagues were still there and it was nice to see them again.

A Constrained Giant

With over 1,000 branches all over the state of California, the bank had a formidable retail presence. But due to the restrictive nature of the McFadden Act, which prohibited interstate branching, the bank had virtually no branches in the other states. There were a few so-called Edge Act offices in major cities like New York and Chicago, but they were restricted to dealing only with international transactions. The Glass Steagall Act also prohibited the bank from engaging in substantial investment banking activities. And so you had the anomaly of the world's largest bank's retail presence in the United States being restricted to one state only: California. Compared to the large banks in Europe and Asia, American banks were hobbled by both geographic and functional restrictions.

But then there was the World Banking Division, which had a presence in all the important countries of the world. With offices stretching from Tokyo and Hong Kong in Asia to London and Frankfurt in Europe as well as Buenos Aires in Latin America and Johannesburg in Africa, the World Banking Division truly had a global reach. Furthermore, the bank was not constrained to commercial banking activities in its overseas locations, but could engage in investment banking as well. Abroad, Bank of America was a truly global bank.

The Bank's Leadership

Tom Clausen, the bank's President, ran the organization with an iron fist from the executive suite on the 40th floor of the bank's landmark building in the financial district of San Francisco. The ceilings of the executive offices were almost twenty feet high and Tom occupied a corner office overlooking the entire Bay Area. Leland Prussia was the Chief Financial Officer and he had an office in the opposing corner. Lee had started his career as an economist at the bank and rose to the second highest position in the bank. The heads of the World Banking Division and the California Division, as well as several other department heads, occupied the other offices on the 40th floor. A friendly, but stern executive assistant guarded the empire. No unauthorized person would make it past her desk. It was an imposing executive suite.

The managers of the 1,000 California bank branches were significant figures in their own right. This was true especially in the smaller towns. Along with the mayor, the police chief and the local doctor, they formed the backbone of these small California communities and everybody looked up to them as important community leaders. At one time, a bank consultant took a survey and asked the branch managers to whom they reported. About 90 percent answered proudly: "I report to President Clausen!" The culture of the bank was such that they were largely oblivious to all the Vice Presidents, Senior Vice Presidents and Executive Vice Presidents that formed several bureaucratic layers in between the branch managers and the CEO. In their own minds, they took their lead from the top boss.

Most of the bank's senior executives were homegrown. A typical career path would lead from being a teller in Bakersfield to being a loan officer in Fresno. The next promotion might elevate the person to be an assistant branch manger in San Jose and then be a branch manager in San Diego. Not infrequently, the next stop was an international destination: branch manager in Frankfurt and after that perhaps country manager for France. Many people had extraordinary careers at the bank.

I quickly learned the secret behind these very successful careers: an excellent training program. Not long after I showed up at the bank, our departmental administrator, Lorinda Clemens, showed up and told me: "Bob, it is time for you to take the basic management training course!" I readily agreed in spite of the fact that I had already gotten basic management training at the International Monetary Fund. I always enjoyed leading people and so I did not mind getting further coaching.

Half a year later, there was Lorinda again and said: "Bob, it is time to take credit training!" I weakly protested that I would probably never make an actual loan, but she insisted that I should know what the other people in the bank were doing. And so it was off to credit training. Soon there was a marketing course and some more advanced management training.

The training sessions I enjoyed the most were focused on press and TV coaching. For that purpose, the bank hired my own coach: Jim LaCross, who had anchored the evening news at one of the San Francisco TV stations. Jim had recently retired and the bank hired him to teach me the tricks of the trade and how to do good interviews. He and I spent two full days together in front of the cameras. He would throw all kinds of tough questions at me and I tried to parry them without stuttering or sticking my foot into my own mouth. I was glad that I had lost my basic fear of speaking by teaching the large UCLA lecture classes and that I was accustomed to answer challenging questions from graduate students. Nevertheless, watching your own replays on TV was certainly a humbling experience.

Frank McCormick, Chairman Lee Prussia, Kimi Narita, myself and Emily

The bank put most of us in the Economics Department to good use in front of bank customers and those businessmen that the bank wanted to attract. Gene Conatser would give speeches in cowboy boots in his native Texas drawl to farm audiences in the

Central Valley and the farmers loved his off-color jokes. Eric Thor produced the California forecasts and so did Mike Salkin, who went on to a successful career as a stockbroker at Morgan Stanley. Fred Cannon was another economist who rose later to be Global Director of Research at the renowned investment bank of Keefe, Bruyette and Woods. Kimi Narita would welcome visiting Japanese dignitaries with all the formalities only a Japanese lady could provide. Gabriel Eichler covered Eastern Europe and eventually founded his own investment bank in Prague. Admassu Bezabeh would cover Africa and Hamid Shomali the Middle East. Later on, Hamid became an energy lender in Texas and then went on to become a dean at a well-known university. Frank McCormick, a former Federal Reserve Board staffer, would give talks about monetary policy. John Wilson ran the department and presented our forecasts to the managing committee. And Walter Hoadley, who was a member of the managing committee of the bank, represented the bank to the outside world and gave speeches all over the globe. Unfortunately, Walter's daughter was one of the passengers on United Flight 92 that crashed many years later on 9-11 into the Pennsylvania countryside. After that, Walter's spirits were broken.

International Travels for the Bank

I was very lucky in my out-of-town assignments. In addition to frequent Congressional testimony, I travelled to give speeches and attend conferences all over the world. Being on the international side of the bank, I got to travel to London, Paris and Tokyo — instead of Fresno, Sacramento and Bakersfield.

Because I spoke fluent German, I was invited every year to undertake a speaking tour for the bank through Germany. It was usually the same itinerary: On Monday, we would meet with shipbuilders and exporters in Hamburg; on Tuesday, it would be a speech before industrial customers in Düsseldorf or Cologne; on Wednesday it was Frankfurt to meet with bankers active in the financial center; on Thursday it was Stuttgart for meetings with

Mercedes and Porsche as well as car suppliers like Bosch. And then on Friday, we would meet with BMW and other bank customers in Munich. Sometimes, there would be an extension to Copenhagen, Zurich or Vienna to meet with customers in those branches as well. These speaking tours were always interesting and never boring.

One day, I gave a speech at an opulent farm restaurant in the outskirts of Stuttgart, with both the CFOs of Porsche and Mercedes present. In the middle of my speech, the lady of the house planted herself squarely in front of me, carrying an entire roasted pig on a platter. The pig even had a decorative apple in its snout. And then, the proprietress started to bow, while holding the dead pig in her sturdy arms. She did not stop bowing until I finally interrupted the speech and everybody gave a round of applause for her and the pig, which had paid with his life for this event.

On that occasion, we tried to sell forward foreign currency hedging contracts to the CFOs of Porsche and Mercedes, but they were not interested at all. These were the conservative 1970s and the traditional German manufacturers did not want to engage in what they considered speculative activities. We tried to tell them that covering their foreign exchange exposures from their regular business activities was actually a risk reducing hedging operation and not speculation. But they would have nothing to do with it.

In contrast, when we met with some very prosperous pig farmers a few days later in Aalborg at the northern tip of Denmark, they gladly agreed to become our foreign exchange customers. They were intimately familiar with all the relevant concepts of forward contracts. Whenever they started to raise a litter of new piglets, they sold a few pork-belly contracts in the forward market so as to lock in a fixed price before spending their precious money on fattening the pigs. They were considerably more sophisticated than the CFOs of the largest automobile manufacturers in the world as far as prudent hedging operations were concerned!

Alpbach

Almost every summer, I was invited to speak at the *European Economic Forum* in Alpbach, Austria. The European Forum, which had been formed right after World War II by a group of Austrian resistance fighters, was the granddaddy of all the "mountain-top seminars" like the *World Economic Forum* in Davos and the *Aspen Institute* in Colorado. I usually spoke as part of the Banking Seminar, which attracted many top bankers. Bank of America liked the publicity and I took the family along to enjoy the mountains.

In addition to the bankers, there were many intellectuals, philosophers and scientists in attendance. The famous philosopher Karl Popper, as well as the Nobel Prize winner Konrad Lorenz, were among the regular attendees. Our kids liked to hear the stories about Lorenz' research on how little ducklings were imprinted by the first moving object that they encountered. After meeting them, our kids debated who was "the smartest man in the world." Even high politicians like the President of Austria, Kurt Waldheim, attended the meetings and we got to eat our meals with them.

The village of Alpbach offered a small "passport" to the children of the conference attendees. If they collected a dozen stamps that were placed on various mountaintops and other hiking destinations, the kids would get a medal as a reward for their accomplishments. Like eager little goats, they would ascend a new mountain every day to collect their prized stamps. At the end of the vacation, the medal was their well-earned reward. A little bribery sometimes works wonders!

The Alpbach Forum was always held in August, the same time that our little son Chris celebrated his birthday. One year, the festive opening of the Forum fell on the very same day as his birthday. We usually stayed at the *Hotel Böglerhof* in the center of the charming alpine village. I told Chris that in honor of his birthday, the town band would appear and play a melody for him. After that, he would have to lead the band up the mountain to the conference hall. He was a bit suspicious, but when the entire village marching band in their Tyrolean costumes showed up in front of

With Kimberly and
Christopher hiking
in the Austrian Alps
at Alpbach

our hotel room balcony and started to play oompah-pah melodies, he started to believe me. He ran down to the band, placed himself in front of the drum major, and marched in front of the Alpine music band up the mountain. Pretty brave for an eight year old boy!

My Dad Does the Comics for Bank of America

Little Chris was not all that impressed by all the speechmaking that his dad did for the bank. One day, I overheard him talking with one of his friends. His friend wanted to know what I did for a living. Chris answered: "Oh, my dad, he does the *comics* for Bank of America!" Maybe "economics" was too difficult a word for a little boy. But after Chris' pronouncement, my prestige among his friends seemed to increase enormously!

Participating in the Management of the Bank

To my delight, the bank appointed me to several strategic committees that were running substantial parts of the bank.

I was appointed as a member of the International Money Policy Committee, a group that determined all the risk management limits for the bank's international exposures. It was the international counterpart to the all-important Money and Loan Policy Committee that guided the financial affairs of the bank on the domestic side.

I also became a member of the Trust Investment Policy Committee, which was responsible for the independently run trust activities of the bank. Larry Nerheim was in charge of the Trust Department and he frequently asked me to give speeches to his customers. On one occasion, he asked me to give a speech to some of his clients in New York. In order to squeeze the speech into my tight schedule, I took a red-eye overnight flight from San Francisco to New York. I arrived around 7 o'clock in the morning and asked Larry whether I could come to his suite at the Waldorf Astoria Hotel to take a quick shower to freshen up for the speech. In order to save money, he agreed and the bank did not have to rent a separate room just for me to have a shower. Just when I stepped out of the shower, a waiter arrived with coffee and some breakfast rolls that Larry had ordered for the two of us. You should have seen the eyes of the waiter when he saw two men from San Francisco in the room that had been booked for single occupancy. He almost dropped his coffee and bread tray right on the floor. Of course, this was over 40 years ago and long before the days when male cohabitation was generally accepted.

I also ran the foreign exchange research activities of the bank. We initiated a comprehensive foreign exchange forecast for the most significant countries in the world. Proudly, I made a presentation of our new product to the Managing Committee of the bank. After I had finished, someone asked: "Well, what are we going to do with this new forecast?" There was silence around the table. Eventually, Paul Verburgt, who ran the huge International

Financial Center in London where much of the foreign exchange trading of the bank was concentrated, piped up: "I don't give a hoot what you do with the forecasts, as long as you don't give them to my foreign exchange traders!" Now the entire group was stunned. Why should the foreign exchange traders not have these forecasts? Wasn't that their daily business? But Paul opined: "Well, if your forecasts are wrong, and they loose money, they will blame the forecasts! But I want to hold them to be personally responsible for their actions and not to have an excuse!" So that was that. Our forecasts became quite popular with the bank's customers, although I quickly learned that making accurate foreign exchange forecasts is a very difficult and treacherous business, indeed.

Another group, the Country Limit Committee set the international country exposure limits of the bank. These were the maximum amounts that the bank's officers could commit to lend in any particular country. In turn, the country risk ratings were a key ingredient into setting these lending limits. When the country risk went up, the lending limits were generally reduced. Obviously, lending was the lifeblood for the various country officers in the World Banking Division. Without open limits they could not lend any more funds.

Our economics group, in conjunction with economists stationed around the world, determined the country risk ratings. These were the late 1970s, and countries in Latin America as well as in Asia and Africa were in frequent payment difficulties. This was largely due to the second oil crisis and the political and economic troubles in Iran that resulted from the fall of the Shah. We reduced the risk ratings for many of the developing countries to reflect the increased economic and political risks. Consequently, the lending limits came under downward pressure as well. Especially the officers in the Latin American Division took umbrage and they started a virtual war against our ratings. One senior officer threateningly told me: "First, we will go after your ratings. If you don't give us the ratings we want, we will try to change the system. And if we don't get the system changed, then we will come after you!" It was war and not very pretty.

Bank of America Gets Into Trouble

In 1982, Mexico defaulted on its debt, just as our models had predicted. Soon, Brazil and several smaller Latin American countries followed. The so-called "Latin American Debt Crisis" was in full swing! Now the officers in the Latin America Division were in trouble. But no one in the bank ever gave us credit for having been spot-on with our risk assessments. Instead, the lending officers were mad at us because now they had egg in their face. I ran an analysis of our forecasts and the results showed that out of 100 countries, we had gotten 97 forecasts right. And two of the three erroneous predictions were wrong only because the U.S. government gave generous foreign aid to Egypt and Ghana, while we had predicted on the basis of our strictly economic models and quantitative analysis that they would default along with the others. We were pretty proud, but kept our mouths shut. There were no victory celebrations while the bank was in deep trouble.

Not only the loans to the developing countries were in default. The United States itself experienced a severe recession in the early 1980s as well. The U.S. economy still suffered from the sharp oil price increase engineered by the oil-exporting countries. In addition, many labor strikes added fuel to the inflationary fires. The wage-price spiral started to accelerate.

The Chairman of the Fed, Arthur Burns, argued that the Fed was powerless against the wage-push inflation that gripped the country and inflation as well as interest rates were inexorably on the rise. The country was experiencing "stagflation": stagnation and inflation at the same time. Eventually, President Jimmy Carter appointed Paul Volcker as Chairman of the Fed and he set out to get inflation under control again. He drove the interest rates on Fed Funds to a record 20 percent in 1981. Promptly, a double-dip recession gripped the country. Many firms and households defaulted on their loans and the entire savings and loan industry was in turmoil.

Bank of America was also in deep trouble as many domestic and international loans went into default. On top of it all, the bank was also a large agricultural lender and the falling commodity prices hit the bank's loan portfolio very hard. While most banks battled losses in their international, energy and commercial loan portfolios, Bank of America was also struck by the enormous losses in the agricultural sector. An ill wind was impacting the loan portfolio of the bank and threatened to sink the institution.

At the peak of the crisis, President Carter selected Tom Clausen to be the President of the World Bank in Washington and he accepted. Sam Armacost was chosen as his successor at Bank of America, but many people argued that Sam was not the peer of Tom Clausen. Friendly, gregarious and jovial, Sam was the antithesis of the austere and determined Clausen.

While Clausen ran the bank with an iron fist, Armacost sought to lead by consensus and *Kumbayah*. On one occasion, Tom Clausen invited me to give a presentation before the Management Council, which comprised the top 50 officers of the bank. The meeting was held in the boardroom atop of the Bank of America headquarters building. Tom Clausen's assistant informed me that the boss wanted to loosen up the meeting a bit by having the staff ask several questions. So, he asked me to approach a few of my friends and to tell them that they should ask me a question or two after my presentation. I did so and they all agreed. I went so far as to suggest what questions they might ask. When I finished the speech, Tom Clausen with a stern eye asked from his chair: "Well, are there any questions?" I looked desperately at the appointed interrogators, but all their eyes were fixed firmly on their hands in front of them. Silence. There was not a single question. Nobody wanted to look stupid in front of the demanding boss. And that's the way it was under Tom Clausen. The bank ran like a well-oiled clock, with the President firmly in control.

That was not what Sam Armacost wanted. At the very peak of the banking crisis, he hired a management consultant named Ichak

Adizes. Adizes had developed his own management processes, which centered on organizing all the employees into small "pods." The bank staff was divided into hundreds of pods, whose members were to discuss the problems of the bank and to find solutions. Typically, the pods would comprise a completely heterogeneous group of people. An Executive Vice President might sit together with a loan officer and a teller in a pod. The meetings dragged on for weeks and months and nobody was focused on the real problems of the bank, like bad loans and how to manage in an environment of highly volatile interest rates. The bank's problems grew and intensified while precious time was frittered away in endless pod discussions.

Eventually, the stock price dropped below $5 per share and the regulators told Armacost that the bank had insufficient capital. No money could be raised in the capital markets and the bank was forced to sell its iconic headquarters building at 555 California Street in San Francisco. The bank also jettisoned many of its prized financial assets. To the great consternation of Claire Giannini Hoffman, the daughter of the original founder of the bank, Banca d'America e d'Italia, which had branches all over Italy, was sold to Deutsche Bank; Finance America was unloaded to Chrysler; and the Schwab subsidiary was sold back to its founder Charles Schwab.

The Fed Calls

Let me jump a little bit ahead to finish the story about Bank of America.

It was at this desperate time for the bank in 1986 that I received a call from President Reagan's office asking whether I was interested in becoming a Governor of the Federal Reserve Board. I felt like I had won the Big Prize and been offered a helping hand off a sinking ship.

Just after I was ensconced at the Federal Reserve Board in October 1986, Paul Volcker called me to his office. That was a rare event and I figured that something important must be up. He got right to the point and asked me: "Who should be the President of

Bank of America?" I was dumbfounded because Sam Armacost was still the President. After collecting my thoughts and surmising that a change was in the works, I said: "There are not many people in the country who could run such a complex institution in these difficult circumstances. The only person whose name I could suggest is John Reed, the new CEO of Citibank, but obviously he is not available!"

Paul Volcker took a few puffs on his ever present cigar and asked: "How about Tom Clausen?" I instantly replied: "Well, that would be great! Of course he can run Bank of America, because he has done so successfully for many decades!" Volcker said nothing and just smiled at me. But two days later, the board of directors of Bank of America installed Tom Clausen as President and Chief Executive Officer for the second time. I figured that someone at the Fed must have a hand in that important appointment that rescued Bank of America from the abyss.

Tom Clausen and I stayed friends ever since, although it probably took twenty years before I told him about the small role that I played in his reappointment. After I moved back to the San Francisco area, we would see each other regularly either at a club or at his home in Hillsborough, where Tom and his wife Helen would throw large birthday parties for his group of friends that he called the "Hillsborough Mafia." Tom always presided over stimulating dinner discussions and he would often throw out one word or a phrase and have everybody around the table debate: "What is love?"

SAGE ADVICE:
Anybody Can Make it to the Top Once —
   But if You Do it Twice, it is a Sign of Genius!

PART IV

At The Federal Reserve

Being appointed by President Reagan as a Member of the Board of Governors of the Federal Reserve System was undoubtedly the highlight of my professional career. I was privileged to sit in the boardroom alongside Chairmen Volcker and Greenspan and participated in the monetary policy decisions that helped to set the country on a course towards price stability and sustained prosperity.

The regulatory decisions that we made during that period were also of enormous importance as they helped to eliminate the barriers separating commercial and investment banking and helped to create a modern universal banking system.

As chairman of the Committee on Bank Supervision and Regulation, I participated in the Fed's supervisory and judicial functions, holding bankers accountable for their actions or inactions. During my time, a record number of banks failed and we were responsible for making sure that it was all done in an orderly manner and without damage to the financial system as a whole. I also learned how some political actors bilked the system for their own benefit by reaping rich payoffs for their opposition or acquiescence to regulatory actions by the Federal Reserve Board.

18 The Oval Office Calls

Preston Martin, the Vice Chairman of the Federal Reserve Board, resigned unexpectedly at the end of April 1986 after a confrontation with Chairman Paul Volcker over interest rate decisions. Together with three fairly new board members, Wayne Angell, Manley Johnson and Martha Seger, Pres Martin wanted to vote to lower the discount rate in February. Volcker was opposed and caught by surprise. He thought that the chairman should never be outvoted on a monetary policy matter and asked whether the other Board members wanted him to resign. They did not want to start a major confrontation and the vote was postponed to give Volcker time for policy-coordination discussions with the German and Japanese central banks. Eventually, Volcker joined the entire Board in a unanimous vote to lower the discount rate.

But bad blood had been spilled and soon thereafter Preston Martin was on a speaking trip in Japan, when Paul Volcker called his remarks "incomprehensible." Thus challenged, Martin sought backing from the Reagan White House and even tried to elicit a promise to make him the Chairman when Volcker's term was up in the following year. The White House refused to make such a commitment and Pres Martin resigned in April, thereby creating not only a vacancy to a Governorship on the Federal Reserve Board, but leaving also the position of Vice Chairman open.

The White House Calls

I was on a Bank of America business trip to Japan in early 1986 when the phone rang in the middle of the night. Don Regan, President Reagan's Chief of Staff was on the line and quickly came to the point: Would I be interested in being considered for the Federal Reserve Board?

In spite of the fact that I was half asleep, I quickly answered: "Yes, Sir! It would be a great honor!" Don Regan thanked me and hung up. I rubbed my eyes — was this for real or was one of my friends trying to play a trick on me? It was the middle of the night in Japan and therefore early afternoon in Washington D.C. But how did Don Regan know my hotel phone number in Japan? I was a bit suspicious, but later learned that the White House "has its ways" to track down people.

When I returned to my job at Bank of America a few days later, there were more requests from Don Regan's staff for a biography and other background information. I began to realize that this might be for real.

Difficult Decisions

I loved my job at Bank of America with its multi-faceted responsibilities in the economic and banking arena that had me travelling the globe. It also brought me in contact with interesting economists and banking leaders around the world. But the Fed job would offer even bigger challenges and opportunities.

On the negative side, there would be a big drop in salary and I had a young family to take care of. We had built a nice new house on Strawberry Point in Marin County, the kids were settled in their schools, and Emily liked the community. I had already taken her from her native Los Angeles to Hawaii and Washington D.C. — and now another move back to Washington? Wasn't that a bit much? But she was game and the fact that we still had good friends there from our days at the IMF made a large difference in both our minds. Also, if we moved during the coming summer, both of our kids would enter a new grade anyhow. Kimberly was leaving grade school and about to enter sixth grade in middle school. Our son Christopher was ready for third grade. The kids still had a few friends back east that they could reconnect with and that would make the transition for them easier.

I went to my boss and mentor, Walter Hoadley, and told him in confidence that I might be considered for the Federal Reserve Board. He was delighted and told me that "the brass ring comes around only once in life and you better grab it!"

Walter had served at the Chairman of the Board of the Federal Reserve Bank of Philadelphia and also as the Chairman of the Conference of Chairmen of the Federal Reserve System. Consequently, he had full appreciation and knowledge of what the job would entail and what a big honor it was to be considered. He urged me to accept the nomination and counseled that such an important job prospect might never present itself again. Walter was experienced and wise and realized that this was an once-in-a-lifetime opportunity.

Sam Armacost, the bank's President and CEO, was a bit less committal. He propped up his feet on his desk, folded his hands behind his head, congratulated me and told me that I should just make up my own mind. Well, I could hardly expect that he would implore me to stay or tell me to get out of here. A simple economist was certainly not indispensible to the bank and it might not be bad at all for him to have a friend in Washington.

Getting Qualified for the Board

How did I get this prestigious invitation that would change my career path and greatly influence the future life of our entire family?

Several of my friends and acquaintances had joined the first Reagan administration after he was elected President in 1980. Early in the Reagan administration, I had gotten a few informal feelers whether I was interested in being the Deputy Assistant Secretary of the Treasury for International Affairs or the Executive Director at the World Bank. The first job would have buried me at a mid-level position of the Treasury bureaucracy and the second position would have been largely that of an order taker and spokesman for the Treasury at the World Bank. Given my prior experience at the IMF, this would not have been all that challenging and new. Also, I really liked my job at Bank of America and the day-to-day involvement with the affairs of the bank. In addition, any one of these assignments would have cut my salary almost in half — and I did not want to do that to my family, which was happily settled in our nice new house on Strawberry Point north of the Golden Gate Bridge. So I demurred.

But the Fed job was different. Being a Governor of the Federal Reserve System would be the capstone of the career of any economist interested in monetary policy, banking and international affairs. It was one of only seven positions that offered a significant opportunity to make important policy decisions in the economic arena combined with responsibilities in the banking sector. In my eyes, only the position of Secretary of the Treasury would be more important and challenging than being a Governor of the Federal Reserve System. Besides, there were only 65 persons in U.S. history that had served as a Governor of the Federal Reserve. I would be in select company indeed. Not bad for a kid who grew up during World War II in Germany. I would be an unlikely Governor.

The Federal Reserve Act specifies that the seven Governors of the Federal Reserve System be nominated by the President and confirmed by the Senate. There is one additional qualification that is written into the Federal Reserve Act. It states that each one of the seven Governors has to come from a different Federal Reserve District. This was part of a careful balancing act by the framers of the Federal Reserve System. According to the legislation, the country is divided into twelve Federal Reserve Districts, each of which has a Federal Reserve Bank located in it. These Federal Reserve Banks are formally incorporated as private banks, with a board composed in equal parts of three bankers elected by the shareholding banks, three public representatives also elected by the banks and three public representatives selected by the Federal

Reserve. But all directors have to be confirmed by the Board of Governors. These rather complex arrangements are designed to provide for balance between federal and regional interests; between the public and the private sector; and between bankers and non-bankers. While sometimes criticized, this structure has served the country amazingly well over the last 100 years, and nobody has been able to come up with a more appropriate organization.

I was lucky that Pres Martin had been a representative of the San Francisco Federal Reserve District as this opened up an automatic vacancy for this district. While the future nominee did not *have* to come specifically from the San Francisco District, the new Governor could *not* come from any of the six other districts already represented on the Board. This fortunate happenstance removed one potential hurdle for my nomination. After I left the Board, the San Francisco District was left without representation for quite a few years until eventually Janet Yellen, the future Fed Chair, was nominated to represent the district again. But we are jumping ahead in time — first I had to be nominated.

My Supporters

While I knew numerous people in the administration, there were three people who were particularly crucial in getting me considered by the Reagan White House. They were Beryl Sprinkel, Robert Mundell and Jude Wanniski. The three belonged to very different ideological camps.

Beryl Sprinkel was the recently appointed Chairman of the President's Council of Economic Advisors. He had a Ph.D. from the University of Chicago and was a stout Monetarist and disciple of Milton Friedman. I had gotten to know Beryl through the network of bank economists that met regularly at conferences and meetings. Beryl represented the Harris Trust Company from Chicago in these forums. Over time, we had become quite friendly and we respected each other's views.

Bob Mundell and I had met frequently during my days at the IMF. Bob had worked a few years earlier in the Research

Department and he still visited the IMF regularly. In 1976, Bob Mundell and Jean Jacques Polak, the Director of the Research Department, convened a conference on "The New International Monetary System." The conference discussed what the new international monetary order, which was to succeed the old Bretton Woods System established after World War II, should look like. As Chief of the Financial Studies Division, I helped to organize the conference and to edit the resulting book with the same title.

Polak and Mundell were also known as the fathers of the "Monetary Approach to the Balance of Payments," which gave an elegantly simple prescription of how to correct balance of payments imbalances under a system of fixed exchange rates. Here, too, I had the honor of editing a book by the same title that presented the relevant research done by the staff of the IMF. This policy prescription became the standard recipe for the IMF to counsel countries in payments difficulties. Consequently, Bob Mundell and I got to know each quite well and we remained in contact over the years.

Mundell also did path-breaking work on "optimum currency areas" which was instrumental in getting the Euro currency off the ground. As a result, he was often referred to as the "Father of the Euro." Eventually, he was awarded the Nobel Prize for his path breaking work.

Jude Wanniski had been an editor at the Wall Street Journal and authored many of its editorials. He is often credited with coining the phrase "Supply Side Economics," which advocates low tax rates as the key to economic growth. In his book *The Way the World Works*, Jude laid out the reasons why low rates of taxation are the fundamental driver of economic growth and prosperity. This policy prescription became one of the hallmarks of the Reagan administration and one with which I readily agreed.

While the Monetarists and Supply Siders often fought pitched battles in the political arena, I believed that both theories had much to commend themselves and saw nothing contradictory in them. Instead, I saw them as supplementary to each other: the Monetarists should run monetary policy and the Supply Siders the fiscal arena. Couple that with the international financial theories espoused by Bob Mundell to solve any balance of payments problems and you had a recipe to address all major economic issues of the day. It was a triple play. I believed that all three postulates were essentially correct, each one in its own realm of applicability.

Maybe that made me attractive to all the diverse factions in the Reagan administration and allowed me to enjoy the support of the various camps. Some of the newspapers reporting on my nomination called me a "pragmatist." As I had never engaged actively in the political arena, I was *tabula rasa* in the political minefield. This was also a distinct advantage in the upcoming Senate confirmation hearings.

White House Interviews

Soon, I was invited to Washington for a round of interviews at the White House. Beryl Sprinkel, the Chairman of the President's Council of Economic Advisors, received me in his cavernous office in the Old Executive Office Building next door to the White House. As Beryl was a friend and one of my sponsors, this was more of a conversation among friends than a hard-nosed job interview. In a way, it was surprising that we were good friends as Beryl had been a tank commander during the Battle of the Bulge while I was hiding in a cave from the advancing American troops. But all went well and the conversation was over in a half hour.

Shortly, I was on my way to the White House. I was chaperoned through the small pathway from the Old Executive Office Building to the side entrance of the White House used by the President's staff. Entering the White House through the basement was not a very impressive affair, but I was too excited to notice the cramped staff quarters in the White House basement. Don Regan's office was in the West Wing overlooking the Washington Monument, down the hall from the Oval Office of the President.

Don Regan, the President's Chief of Staff, and Jim Baker, the Secretary of the Treasury, were already waiting for me. Don Regan was a tall and imposing man with broad shoulders. Jim Baker looked equally impressive. Both of them had been Marines and it showed. The two had traded their jobs at the beginning of President Reagan's second term and it was clear that they were most comfortable with each other.

Jim Baker wanted to know whether there were any skeletons in my closet that nobody knew about. I replied that my wife was a Democrat. He just laughed, saying: "Quite a few of us have that problem!" Don Regan asked whether I wanted to be Vice Chairman of the Federal Reserve Board. Of course, I would have loved to be Vice Chairman, but I did not want to make that a precondition for accepting the Governor's position. So I tried to answer as diplomatically as possible: "Yes, of course that would be wonderful, but that just being a Governor would be a great honor!" The rest of the conversation was a pretty amicable discussion of the economic situation and the independence of the Federal Reserve. Pretty soon, the conversation was over and I was on my way out. This time I was escorted out through the front entrance, with the two Marine guards saluting smartly.

That was it. I took a taxi back to my hotel and then caught a plane home to San Francisco.

White House Leaks

Pretty soon, the intention to nominate me to the Federal Reserve Board was "leaked" by the White House to the press. This was standard procedure for all the important Presidential appointments, so that the news reports would smoke out any detrimental information or political opposition that might cause the nomination to be derailed and cause the White House potential embarrassment.

A few days later, President Reagan announced my nomination to be a Governor of the Federal Reserve Board. He also announced the elevation of Governor Manley Johnson to Vice Chairman of the Board.

The FBI Calls

With the formal nomination by the President, the vetting process started for real. It was late May 1986 and I started to fill out the voluminous and complicated background information forms required by the administration and the Senate. I was required to list every job or appointment that I had held and every foreign trip that I had ever taken. In addition, the financial information about my income, as well as all assets and liabilities, had to be documented in a detailed but somewhat archaic fashion.

This background information was then turned over to the FBI and they verified every statement, all former residences and my numerous foreign trips. FBI agents also visited my former employers and our neighbors in person. Not all the neighbors were pleased. We lived in a Marin County area known as Strawberry Point. The area was settled for the most part in the late Seventies — not long after the fall of the Shah of Iran forced many Persians to flee their home country. Quite a few of them bought houses on Strawberry Point, an area that was often referred to as "Iranian Hill" by people in the neighborhood. When the FBI agents knocked on their doors and wanted to know what they knew about me, several of them got very suspicious. They thought that the FBI was really trying to find out things about these immigrants themselves — a practice that they were accustomed to from the secret police in their home country. Afterwards, they would come by our house and reveal to me in a whisper that the FBI was after me. When I told them that I was delighted to hear that, they shook their heads in utter disbelief. It was clear that they did not quite understand the customs of the new world that they had moved to. How could a person nominated to a high government post be subject to a governmental investigation himself? That would never have happened in Iran!

A few weeks after the FBI investigation was closed, I got a follow-up phone call from the agent that I had dealt with. He wanted to come by and ask me one more question: "Did I ever participate in the *Oh pah eher Program*"? At first, I had no idea what he was talking about, but then it dawned upon me that he was talking about the "*Au-Pair Program.*" Well, formally, we had never participated in that program, but we had been host to several young ladies from Europe who helped us with the kids. The first one was actually my own niece, Irene Brings, who had come over on a 6-month tourist visa to help with the kids just at the time when our son Chris was born. She renewed her visa for another six months and then returned home. And then followed a chain of other young ladies. Were they "Au-Pairs," the FBI agent wanted to know? I told them they were family friends and friends of friends and that every single one of them had returned to Europe. This was certainly true and seemed to satisfy him. In any case, I never heard from the FBI again.

Senate Confirmation Hearings

Soon, I was asked to make the rounds at the Senate to get acquainted with the Senators on the Banking Committee, which would be responsible for my confirmation hearings. Senator Pete Wilson of California graciously agreed to be my official sponsor and to introduce me to the Senate Banking Committee.

When it was time to travel to Washington for the confirmation hearings, my two children did not want to come along and watch the proceedings. They claimed that they had listened to Dad talk too much already! So it was just Emily who accompanied me. We packed our bags and flew to Washington.

I appeared on a hot August 5, 1986 before the Senate Committee on Banking, Housing and Urban Affairs for my confirmation hearings. After a short introduction by Senator Wilson, I stated: "If confirmed, I will do my best to support monetary policies that will encourage economic growth and employment within a framework of price stability. I also look forward to participating in the design and implementation of market-oriented regulatory and supervisory policies that will be supportive of a strong and vigorous financial system."

I think that I pretty well stuck to these principles throughout

S. HRG. 99–815

NOMINATIONS OF H. ROBERT HELLER AND MICHAEL L. MUSSA

HEARING

BEFORE THE

COMMITTEE ON
BANKING, HOUSING, AND URBAN AFFAIRS
UNITED STATES SENATE

NINETY-NINTH CONGRESS

SECOND SESSION

ON

THE NOMINATIONS OF

H. ROBERT HELLER, OF CALIFORNIA, TO BE A MEMBER OF THE BOARD OF GOVERNORS OF THE FEDERAL RESERVE SYSTEM FOR THE UNEX-PIRED TERM OF 14 YEARS FROM FEBRUARY 1, 1982, VICE PRESTON MARTIN, RESIGNED

AND

MICHAEL L. MUSSA, OF ILLINOIS, TO BE A MEMBER OF THE COUNCIL OF ECONOMIC ADVISERS, VICE WILLIAM POOLE VII, RESIGNED

AUGUST 5, 1986

Printed for the use of the Committee on Banking, Housing, and Urban Affairs

U.S. GOVERNMENT PRINTING OFFICE

63–040 O   WASHINGTON : 1986

For sale by the Superintendent of Documents, Congressional Sales Office
U.S. Government Printing Office, Washington, DC 20402

my career at the Fed and still believe that this is the way the Fed's priorities should be ordered. While Congress has tasked the Fed with the attainment of stable prices as well as maximum growth and employment, the Fed has only one monetary policy tool at its disposal. Every economist knows that you cannot achieve two different and sometimes conflicting targets simultaneously when you have only one policy tool at your disposal.

I believe that the primary target has to be a stable price level. Consequently, the top priority has to be stable prices. In turn, the absence of inflation will be conducive to foster maximum economic growth and employment. If instead one were to give priority to economic growth and employment, there would be the danger of ever accelerating inflation that eventually would get out of hand. This is what we had witnessed only a few years earlier in the late 1970s, when both stagnation and inflation together beset the country — an episode that became known as *Stagflation*. Nobody on the Federal Reserve Board wanted to risk a return to those conditions.

I also believe that a healthy financial sector needs a light, but firm regulatory and supervisory hand, with as few rules as possible. A few simple rules, including a strong capital base, are more important than micromanagement of the banks by the regulators. Complex regulations lead to huge compliance departments that just add a dead-weight bureaucracy to the financial system. Better to invest in higher capital levels that present a true and reliable cushion against adverse circumstances. Ever more complex regulations and a myriad of regulators and overlapping regulatory jurisdictions do not make the financial system more safe and sound.

When the questioning started, Chairman Jake Garn wanted to know right off the bat whether I had sold all of my Bank of America stocks. The answer was yes — and unfortunately I had done so at a big loss.

The progressive Senator Proxmire wanted to know what to do about the "colossal deficits" of the federal government, which were running at about $200 billion at that time. Such an amount would be considered modest by today's standards, when federal deficits sometimes exceeded a trillion dollars. As a good supply sider, I answered that tax and spending cuts would rejuvenate economic growth and thereby reduce and eventually eliminate the deficits. Senator Proxmire also got me into a spirited debate on the capital adequacy of banks and their role in the LDC debt crisis.

The discussion ranged pretty far. Chairman Garn wanted to know whether I would favor a "farmers seat" on the Federal Reserve Board. I deftly reflected the question by arguing that Governor Wayne Angell, who was already on the Federal Reserve Board, was actually a farmer and that no further action was needed.

At one point in the discussion about the long 14-year terms that the Fed Governors enjoyed, we even started to discuss the Supreme Court. Senator Garn promptly cited the court for its "independence and arrogance." I decided better not to follow up on that comment.

Senator Heinz asked what to do about the current short-term interest rates of 6 to 7 percent in an environment of very low inflation. Financial market participants still remembered the high inflation years that we had experienced only a few years before. Once inflationary expectations become embedded, markets continue to demand a high inflation premium for credit. I agreed with him that a cut in the discount rate from its current level of 6 percent might well be called for.

Eventually, the questioning was over and the Senators turned to the confirmation of Michael Mussa to be on the President's Council of Economic Advisors. Mike had been a student of mine at UCLA, where he took an international economics class and got an A+. I was glad to see that now both of us were headed for high office.

A few days later, on August 16, 1986 the entire U.S. Senate unanimously confirmed my nomination. It was one of the few times that there was a unanimous vote in favor of a Federal Reserve Board nominee.

I was a very happy man.

The Press Covers My Departure

When it was time for my departure for Washington, *Business Week* wanted to run a story about my appointment to the Federal Reserve Board. They decided that a picture of me under the fog-shrouded Golden Gate Bridge should accompany the article. When the Business Week photographer and I drove to the bridge, a few private security guards stopped us. "You can not proceed any further!" they bellowed. When the reporter objected and immediately invoked the freedom of the press, they told us that Kim Novak was there to film a remake of *Vertigo*, the famous movie. Now we really wanted to see what was going on. Eventually, the guards relented and they let our crew shoot a picture of me with the bridge in the back-ground — but no Kim Novak! I was very disappointed!

A cartoonist for the *San Francisco Chronicle*, Phil Frank, honored me by devoting his Cartoon of the Day to my Fed appointment. He copied the previous day's headline from another

Phil Frank's cartoon about my appointment published in the San Francisco Chronicle

local newspaper, the *Marin Independent Journal*, which read: "Marin man gets Fed Post." Under it, he drew me in a hospital bed and being fed a small wooden post by a nurse.

A few days later, a local radio station called and they wanted to do an interview with me. The show was *Whalen in the Morning* and was a somewhat irreverent combination of news, flippant political commentary and country western music. I listened to the show frequently and was familiar with its format. Before the interview began, I told Mr. Whalen to ask me at the end of the program whether I ever listened to his show. At the end of the interview, he asked the last question: "So, Mr. Heller, do you ever listen to *Whalen in the Morning*?" I responded: "Of course, it's the greatest show on earth!" And with that, he concluded: "Oh, my God! This guy actually listens to us! Head for the hills! Sell dollars and buy Pesos!" Everyone had fun!

SAGE ADVICE:
The Brass Ring Comes Along Only Once —
When It Does, Grab It!

Walter Hoadley

19 Getting Settled at the Fed

"**I** do solemnly swear that I will support and defend the Constitution of the United States..." I had my hand on the bible and stood with Emily, Kim and Chris in front of Paul Volcker in his ornate office at the Federal Reserve, taking the official oath of office. It was Tuesday, August 19, 1986 and a few minutes before 9 o'clock in the morning. Over the weekend, we had flown out from San Francisco to begin our new life in Washington.

A minute later, Paul Volcker opened a door right behind his office desk and the two of us stepped into the cavernous Boardroom of the Federal Reserve. The entire Federal Open Market Committee composed of the other Governors and the Federal Reserve Bank Presidents rose and gave a round of applause. It was an impressive, and yet, somewhat scary moment. It was almost overwhelming!

Chairman Volcker sat down, lit a cigar, and called the FOMC meeting to order. I found my seat — it was the last one of the Governors seats to the right of the chairman and was always assigned to the most junior Governor. A brass name plaque engraved with my name was already affixed to the back of the seat. The Fed's staff was pretty efficient!

Paul Volcker congratulates our family after the official oath
of office *(Federal Reserve photo)*

My First Vote

The FOMC meeting began with several housekeeping items, such
as the approval of the minutes from the previous session and the
ratification of the actions taken by the Open Market Desk of the
Federal Reserve Bank of New York in the period since the last
meeting. Then, the staff began with the "Green Book"
presentation, which presented an overview of the current economic
situation. Consumer spending was robust, but investment sluggish;
total payroll employment grew strongly, but manufacturing
employment dropped somewhat; retail sales were up, but car sales
were weak; construction spending expanded, but investment was
down; the producer price index was down sharply, but consumer
prices were up; the monetary aggregates grew significantly and the

dollar was down. It was certainly a very mixed economic picture that the members of the committee faced on that hot August day.

After the staff was finished, all the Governors and the Reserve Bank Presidents offered their comments on the economic situation. Many of the Reserve Bank Presidents focused on developments in their own Districts. These largely anecdotal reports were just as conflicting as the staff report about the conditions in the country at large.

Then the staff focused on the financial conditions in the country as detailed in the "Blue Book." Another round of discussion ensued. Again, there was a litany of positive and negative developments. Then the FOMC adjourned for lunch in a private dining room atop the Fed's Martin Building, which offered a fabulous view of the Capitol, the Washington Monument and the Lincoln Memorial. The view impressed upon us the grave responsibilities we had for the entire country.

After lunch, the staff presented their monetary policy recommendations. These were also finely balanced. As the discussion coursed around the table, it occurred to me that the views of the FOMC members were very much divided. I suddenly realized that there might well be a tied vote. What if I had to cast the deciding vote? I was certainly not prepared to assume that level of responsibility.

I think it was one of the few occasions in my entire life that I was truly apprehensive about what to do. I started to perspire and to fidget while thinking about my responsibilities. What had I gotten myself into? Here I was at my very first FOMC meeting. Could it be that I would have to cast the deciding vote about the future direction of monetary policy for the entire country? That was a scary thought indeed!

But then, Paul Volcker presented a monetary policy directive that called for a slight decrease in pressure on reserve positions, but allowed for somewhat greater or lesser reserve restraint based on the growth of the monetary aggregates, economic conditions, the foreign exchange market, progress against inflation and changes in the credit markets. It meant that essentially anything might happen. Everybody seemed to be mollified and in agreement. Ten members of the committee voted for that largely open-ended compromise, which represented a slight easing of monetary conditions, but also allowed for a potential firming if the conditions should warrant it. I did the same. Two members dissented: Governor Henry Wallich and St. Louis Fed President Tom Melzer voted against the directive and preferred to keep the current more hawkish policy stance to further combat inflation. As far as Fed decisions went, two dissents represented a rather divided vote that reflected the uncertainties in the imbalanced economic outlook.

Phew — that was a load off my shoulders. I did not have to cast the deciding vote after all! I was greatly relieved.

The vote also showed the skill of Paul Volcker in forging a broad consensus that called for an immediate slight easing, but allowed for virtually any eventuality in the period up to the next FOMC meeting.

I noted that several members of the FOMC had stated during the discussion that the economic outlook at the present time was unusually uncertain and difficult to discern. I think that someone made a similar statement at every single meeting that I ever attended in the years to come. How could that be? Upon reflection, I realized that this would generally be true as long as the committee had done a good job in setting the right policy at the last meeting. If the Fed had made the right decision, the economy would have been nudged into the direction of balance and stability, so that the chances of positive or negative deviations from the expected economic outcome were pretty evenly balanced. For me, this observation was an important insight into the policymaking process. But it also would assure the same high degree of tension in the decision-making process at future meetings that I had witnessed during this meeting.

Getting Settled on Constitution Avenue

My first job was to pick my own office. Ascending the giant staircase from the atrium to the second floor of the Federal Reserve building on Constitution Avenue, one reaches the Boardroom floor. The Boardroom is located right in the center of the building and it overlooks Constitution Avenue.

Next to the Boardroom are eight large Governors offices: four on each side of the building. The first one on the right, with its connecting door to the Boardroom, is the Chairman's office. The other Governors are free to pick their own offices and do so traditionally in order of their seniority. There is one spare office. I was lucky that the last office to the left, the corner office on Constitution and 20th Street was vacant and so I decided on this magnificent office with a head-on view of the iconic Washington Monument. At least it offered an unobstructed view during the wintertime, after the trees had lost their leaves. During the rest of the year the tree leaves slightly obscured the view of this Washington landmark.

Each office also had a nice anteroom for the governor's assistant as well as a private toilet — heaven forbid that a Governor would be seen using a public commode!

While the office had a fabulous view, the interior was completely empty. There was no furniture whatsoever. Bob Frazier, the Board's Director of Support Services, stopped by to explain. Bob was a stout retired army colonel who had commanded a tank battalion. You could see his proud army heritage in his ramrod-straight bearing. He told me that it was a tradition for the senior staff to raid the office whenever a Governor left and to drag all the nice furniture to their own offices, which were otherwise furnished by government-issued grey steel desks and bookshelves. Every new Governor, in turn, was given a $15,000 furniture allowance to furnish his own office. Bob Frazier was ready to go shopping.

$15,000 was a princely sum to buy a desk and a few chairs plus a sitting couch for visitors. I splurged and bought a Persian carpet that Bob Frazier knew how to get at a good price. I also found a historic portrait of Alexander Hamilton, the first Secretary of the Treasury, in the Board's art collection for my wall. When I left a few years later, Alan Greenspan selected this important picture for his own office. Everything was passed on in typical Fed tradition.

A few weeks later, Bob Frazier came by and wanted to know whether I liked my new office. I told him that it looked splendid and thanked him for all his help. But he kept hanging around and asked: "Governor, is there anything else that I can do for you? Do you have any further wishes? Any unfulfilled needs?" I sensed that I would have to ask for something else so that he would feel useful and I said: "Ok, why don't you get me an American flag as well as some of those other flags like Chairman Volcker has behind his desk!" "Yes, Sir, I will be glad to get you an American flag" he replied, "But I cannot obtain any of those other flags for you. These are the Chairman's personal flags from his service as Assistant Secretary of the Treasury, Deputy Undersecretary of the Treasury, and as Undersecretary of the Treasury! I am sorry, but I cannot get these flags!" "Oh well, then get me a Federal Reserve flag to go along with the American flag," I replied. "Sir, I cannot do that either, because there is no Federal Reserve flag!" he said. I was disappointed, but got an idea in my mind to remedy that situation if the opportunity should present itself in the future. More about that later!

My First Encounter With The Chairman

While I was still at Bank of America, I had agreed to address the German Foreign Exchange Dealers Association in Frankfurt. Of course, the Germans were delighted to hear that I was now at the Federal Reserve Board, as they would now have a real life Governor on the podium instead a mere Bank of America economist.

Word had also gotten to the German Bundesbank that I was going to speak on their home turf in Frankfurt. The President of the Bundesbank, Karl Otto Poehl, and his Deputy Helmut Schlesinger invited me to the Bundesbank to have lunch with their entire Board of Directors. I had known Helmut Schlesinger for many years, while he was the head of the Economics Department of the Bundesbank and I was looking forward to seeing him and his colleagues. Of course, they were also delighted that a German-born Governor was now a member of the Federal Reserve Board.

A week or two before the planned speech I went to see Paul Volcker and to ask him whether there were any messages he wanted me to convey or any topics I should stay clear of. These were the days when the exchange rate between the dollar and the Deutsche Mark was an important topic discussed in all the newspapers and I did not want to commit any faux pas by saying the wrong things. After puffing on his ever-present cigar, Paul wanted to know why I had not informed him earlier of this impending speech. I told him that the speech had been listed for several weeks on the regularly circulated list showing all future speaking engagements of the Board members. He said that he had not seen it and I surmised that he must not have looked at that paper for quite a while. Hence his surprise.

After a long period of quiet and several more puffs on his cigar, Volcker intoned in his deep voice: "Cancel the speech!" I was shocked and retorted: "I do not think that is possible, as there are several hundred people already invited and I made a firm commitment to give that speech a long time ago." He continued: "Then don't say anything! It's a minefield out there!" And with that, I almost started to laugh — how could I give a speech and not say anything??? How could anybody do that?

We talked for quite a while about the situation in the foreign exchange markets and the need to coordinate exchange rate policies and I promised to show him the entire draft of my speech. Eventually, he was mollified and after a few more puffs on his cigar, he gave me one more piece of fatherly advice: "Obfuscate!!!"

Obviously, he was a master at that. In any case, I gave the speech and it did not cause a ripple in the markets. All was well.

The luncheon at the Bundesbank was a festive affair and it began a long and friendly time of close relationships between the leaders of the Bundesbank and me. I would meet the Bundesbank

President Karl Otto Poehl at various international meetings and conferences. Helmut Schlesinger, his Deputy and eventual successor, was a regular delegate to the OECD meetings in Paris that I would attend on behalf of the Federal Reserve.

I thought that I was going to like my life at the Fed.

Life in Washington

On the home front, we bought a nice house on Spring Hill Lane in McLean, Virginia. It was not far from the house that we had lived in during our time at the International Monetary Fund. The kids loved the little yellow school buses that would pick them up right in front of our house every morning. Koko, the Irish Setter, was also still with us; but Baron had died earlier in California. When a neighbor's cat had a litter of kittens, China and Dusty joined our family.

We also reconnected with many of our old friends from IMF days: Hans Gerhard now owned a farm in Culpeper, Virginia and Gunter Wittich and his family were living in nearby Maryland. Malcolm Knight and his family were also frequent companions as they had children the same age as ours.

Our social life was considerably different from the San Francisco Bay Area. In San Francisco, people departed the bank after work and almost everyone had to cross a bridge to get back home: the Golden Gate Bridge to Marin County, where we lived, or the Bay Bridge to Oakland and the East Bay region. Others would drive down the Peninsula to Hillsborough or San Mateo. They would seldom return for dinner in the city, and people socialized in their own neighborhoods.

Life in Washington was very different: after work, people drove home, but they would return for dinner or a theater performance to the District of Columbia. There were numerous formal dinner parties at foreign embassies or elegant social events at the State Department to which we were invited. The White House Correspondents Dinner was always a fun affair where the President would poke fun at himself. Emily, however, did not enjoy

Our family in front of the Federal Reserve building on
Constitution Avenue.

the formality of these occasions and never got used to entering the
venues walking behind me. That was due to the diplomatic custom
that "The Principal Always Goes First." But we had fun anyhow!

Daughter Kim quickly settled into her new middle school
routine, but Chris' reading was not quite up to the exacting
standards of the East. His first report card in reading was not very
good. We explained to the teacher that he would do much better
if she would hold the book upside down and played music in the
background — just like his teachers had done for him at the private
Marin Country Day School. Oh, what they would do to coddle the
kids in Marvelous Marin! Once Chris realized that his new teachers
would not do this for him in the staid and no-nonsense Virginia

public schools, he quickly shaped up and within a few weeks he could read the entire *Washington Post*!

The first big snowstorm was a great adventure that the kids had not experienced in California. Schools were closed for a whole week, as Washington and its suburbs are notoriously inefficient at snow removal. Koko, the dog, bounced through the snow banks and the kids loved sledding in their own backyard.

In the middle of the storm, I had an important Federal Reserve Board meeting to attend, but my car could not get me to the Fed over the slippery roads. So, the Board sent a truck with four-wheel drive and chains to transport me to the meeting. All the roads were completely deserted and we had the George Washington Parkway to ourselves. All government offices were officially closed. So were the Fed dining rooms. When it came to lunchtime, we sent the same truck to get us hamburgers and sandwiches and we ate them during the board meeting. It was quite an adventure, but we got our work done!

Given our tight budget situation, Emily decided to look for a job to help us maintain the lifestyle to which we had become accustomed. She found a very fulfilling job as Secretary of the Academic Senate at the University of Maryland. She loved and cherished that job during our entire time in Washington. Given Emily's contribution, we were all set to enjoy the good life in Washington.

SAGE ADVICE:
If you don't want to say anything, but must: Obfuscate!
Paul Volcker

20 Inside the Boardroom

The Board Members

After I settled in at the Fed, I got to know my colleagues. Paul Volcker was the Chairman and he tended to rule with a firm hand and determination. He knew what he wanted and how to accomplish it.

Paul was always very congenial, polite and diplomatic. He could also work a room filled with people like a political pro. Typically, he would enter the room after most of the other guests had already arrived. Everyone immediately noticed his towering 6½-foot presence. Then he would make the rounds, spending a minute or two with each person before swiftly moving on. It is a skill that not many people have.

At board meetings, he always gave everyone plenty of time to speak and was scrupulously fair in presenting a balanced summary of all the arguments presented.

None of the other board members believed that he knew where our offices were and certainly he never visited any of us. If he wanted to see us, his assistant, Catherine Mallardi, would call up with the stringent command: "The Chairman wants to see you *now!*" We would dutifully trot to his office and often there was trouble waiting for us. Typically, there were stacks of books or his briefcase on the chairs in front of his desk. Consequently, you had to stand like a little schoolboy in front of the principal and hear what he had to say. Usually, it was something we had done wrong. Most of us referred to these audiences as "being taken to the woodshed."

One day, I was ordered to Volcker's office and he immediately stated: "You made the stock market crash!" I was dumbfounded, as I had not heard anything about the market crashing. But he had observed the market going down on this day and he claimed that a speech I had given that morning had been the cause for the drop of the market. Virtually all of my speeches were coauthored or edited by the staff and for the most part they faithfully represented our current monetary policy stance. But I was guilty nevertheless. There must have been some reason for the market to fall, and so it was my speech. I never knew that I was that powerful.

When I joined the Board in the summer of 1986, Henry Wallich was the most senior board member. He had served on the Board for about a dozen years and the two of us had very similar backgrounds: both of us were born in Germany; we both had an academic career before coming to the Fed; both of us had worked in the financial service industry; and both of us had a particular interest in international economics. Henry was also an inflation hawk. Just like my family, his had lived through the German hyperinflation and experienced its devastating consequences. He frequently declared that inflation was the same as burglary in that it deprived people of the value of their hard-earned assets. He even went so far as to advocate that special taxes be imposed upon companies that raised their wages too much — a position that stands certainly in stark contrast to current views that wages are too low and that companies should be forced to pay higher minimum wages!

Unfortunately, Henry Wallich suffered from a brain tumor and had to resign from the Board in December 1986, only a few months after I joined the Board. I would have enjoyed being his colleague for a much longer time.

Emmett Rice was the only black Board member during the time that I was there. He was a very quiet man and kept largely to himself. But my children always thought that he was the friendliest Board member of them all. Emmett Rice resigned from the board in the same month as Henry Wallich, in December 1986.

Manley Johnson became Vice Chairman at the same time that I joined the Board. He had previously served as Assistant Secretary to the Treasury and consequently he personally knew many of the officials in the White House and the Treasury. Manley hailed from Alabama and like many Southern gentlemen, he was the ultimate politician. He was always courteous and cordial and my wife Emily was sure that he would eventually become a U.S. Senator from Alabama. Unfortunately, he never even tried to run for public office. He would have made a great Senator!

Prior to coming to the Fed, Wayne Angell had waged an unsuccessful campaign to be a Senator from Kansas. During that time, he got to know the other Republican Senator from Kansas, Bob Dole. The two became friends and Bob Dole had a hand in him being appointed to the Federal Reserve Board. Wayne still owned his large farm in Kansas and would fly there in his own airplane. As far as monetary policy is concerned, he advocated using gold and commodity prices as early inflation indicators. While I would not advocate targeting the price of gold, or a return to the Gold Standard, I did find changes in the price of gold very useful as an early indicator of inflationary pressures.

Martha Seger rounded out the Board when I got there. She was an eclectic economist from Michigan, who had also been a bank regulator in that state. Moreover, she had been active in Republican Party politics. She was very much in favor of giving banks more powers as far as interstate branching and entry into investment banking was concerned. I agreed with these views as well. But she was somewhat burdened by the fact that after a very contentious Senate Banking Committee hearing, President Reagan had given her a so-called "recess appointment" to the Board while the Senate was not in session. Volcker looked somewhat askance at that and assigned her an empty office without allowing her to spend the prized $15,000 furniture allowance because she was there only "temporarily." She was upset and retaliated by decorating her office most lavishly after she finally won the official confirmation.

Martha was also a confirmed non-smoker and after the resignation of Henry Wallich and Emmett Rice, she was the most senior Governor. With that came the privilege to sit immediately next to the Chairman, who loved to light up his cigars in Board meetings. Whenever he did, Martha would grab a large piece of paper and waved the smoke clouds back at Volcker. And so, the mini-warfare continued between the two. But Martha was not intimidated and valiantly stood her ground. She was also the most frequent dissenter on the Board and at the FOMC during my time there.

In the spring of 1987, Edward Kelley joined the Board. He was a congenial Texan, whom everyone called "Mike." He was a retired businessman and brought much common sense and good humor to the Board.

The "Volcker Board" towards the end of his term. Seated in front are Vice Chairman Manley Johnson, Chairman Paul Volcker and Martha Seger. Standing in back are myself, Edward 'Mike' Kelley and Wayne Angell. *(Federal Reserve photo)*

Most of the Governors were not all that well known. One day, the New York Times quipped about the Federal Reserve Board: "Everyone knows that Paul Volcker is the Chairman of the Fed; if you can name two of the other Governors, you are economically literate; if you know all of them, you are probably one of them!" That put it all into perspective.

Peggy O'Brien, my faithful and efficient Administrative Assistant, usually listed my name on the airline tickets as "Governor Heller." One day, a flight attendant asked me: "Governor Heller, what state are you a Governor of?" I was so embarrassed that I told Peggy never to do that again. From that moment on, I was always plain Mr. Heller. But all the Board staff members always addressed you politely as "Governor." Rank had its privileges.

Giving Speeches for the Fed is No Joking Matter

At Bank of America, I had given many speeches on behalf of the organization. The bank liked for all the economists to have lots of public exposure, which typically generated free publicity and good public relations for the bank. I had learned to start my speeches with a good joke. That would not only "break the ice," but would also help to get the attention of the audience and establish a good rapport with the people in front of me.

After arriving at the Fed, I continued that tradition. But it did not take me long to notice that very few people in the audience ever laughed at my introductory jokes. The jokes were often the same ones that had elicited a very hearty laugh when I was at Bank of America. "What is wrong?" I asked myself. I quickly realized that the audience did not really want to see a jokester at the Fed. After all, the Federal Reserve Board is in charge of the nation's money and that carried with it a grave responsibility. Consequently, I discontinued the introductory jokes and started my speeches with a statement that conveyed more gravitas.

Work at the Fed

During my time at the Fed, the Board typically met Mondays, Wednesdays and, if necessary, also on Fridays. Tuesdays and Thursdays were reserved for Committee meetings and to do the voluminous reading necessary to be prepared for the Board meetings. Some people believed that the Board met only every couple of weeks, like corporate boards of directors tend to do, and that board service was therefore pretty leisurely and cushy. This mistaken view was also enhanced by the fact that the monetary policy-making body, the Federal Open Market Committee, which includes the Presidents of the twelve Federal Reserve Banks, typically meets only eight times a year. While the monetary policy decisions of the FOMC garnered most of the public interest, the board was busy virtually every day either in formal Board meetings or in Committees gatherings.

Much of the Board work was done through its Committees. In these Board Committees two or three Governors worked with the staff to review issues and cases before they were brought up for a final Board discussion and vote. In essence, the Committees were there to resolve potentially troublesome issues ahead of time and to smooth the final Board discussions.

The two most important Committees were probably the Committee on Bank Supervision and Regulation and the Committee on Reserve Bank Operations. Wayne Angell was the Chairman of Reserve Bank Operations, a position he cherished as he had served on the Board of Directors of the Federal Reserve Bank of Kansas City. I was appointed as Chairman of the Committee on Bank Supervision and Regulation. I assume it was because I had a banking background. But given the terrible shape of the American banking system in the late 1980's, that assignment was a hot seat, indeed.

With the resignations of Henry Wallich and Emmett Rice, the Board had shrunk to only five members by the end of the year 1986. When one of the board members was on a trip, the Board was down to four, which was the minimum required for a quorum. If one of us should catch a cold, the Federal Reserve Board no longer had a quorum and the Fed was paralyzed! It was not a pleasant situation that the nation's central bank found itself in. It also made Committee work pretty difficult as the individual Governors were spread pretty thin.

One day, the Chairman called me into his office. That is, his assistant Catherine Mallardi did so. Of course, I was searching my brain whether I had again committed some faux pas, but Paul wanted to ask me for a favor. Would I agree to serve on the Consumer Affairs Committee? He badly needed someone on this committee as it consisted only of Martha Seger at that time. I said that I was already a member of every single other committee — probably five of them — but I had lost count. Volcker offered a compromise: I would have to show up only if a meeting was scheduled and Martha was not there. I agreed. I do not think that I ever attended a single meeting of the Consumer Affairs Committee as Martha was very devoted to her duties and would never miss a meeting.

Becoming the Administrative Governor

When I got appointed to the Board, Emmett Rice served as the Administrative Governor. In those days, the Administrative Governor position was generally assigned to the most junior Board member. This situation changed radically in later years, when this position was suddenly considered much more important and prestigious. In these later years, the Vice Chairman was often given the honor to be the Administrative Governor. I was delighted to accept the position. Running the administration of the entire Federal Reserve Board would be an important and challenging responsibility!

Human Resources, Legal, Support Services, Security and Information Resources — we call it nowadays Information and Technology or simply IT — all reported to me. The Legal Department had a special status, so that the Chairman could get his confidential advice from the General Counsel. Consequently,

Legal Affairs reported to the Chairman on a substantive or functional basis, but to me regarding the everyday mundane housekeeping decisions.

One day, David Frost, the Staff Director for Management, came by to see me. As a retired Admiral of the U.S. Navy, David had a ramrod-straight bearing. Always polite, he would never sit down as long as someone else was still standing. Admiral Frost was somewhat embarrassed, but he quickly come to the point: he needed $85,000 dollars to fix a few leaks in the roof of the Federal Reserve building before winter set in. I said: "No problem! This is important and you will get your money, but let me first clear it with the Chairman!" I trotted over to Volcker's office and put forth the request. "Oh, $85,000 is an awful lot of money — let me think about it!" was his answer. After two weeks had passed and the rainy season was beginning, I returned to the Chairman's office and reminded him that the roof needed to be fixed urgently. For emphasis, I added that the buckets on the top floor of the building were filling with rainwater. "Do we really have to spend all that money?" Volcker wondered aloud. He clearly was in no mood to authorize the expenditure, and so I implored him: "Paul, if we don't do it now, it will cost us two or three times that much if the rain causes extensive damage inside the building!" I encouraged him to make a quick decision. He kept evading an answer for a while, but finally relented and authorized the expenditure.

A similar dialogue ensued when the Fed's tennis court developed holes big enough to make people stumble. While the tennis court was on Federal Reserve property, it was officially a public court and accessible to everyone. But nobody knew about it and so only Wayne Angell and later on Alan Greenspan, as well as a few staffers, got to play on it. While Paul Volcker was a determined and forceful monetary policy maker, he did not like to make the small decisions — and he hated to spend money even more! But eventually, the tennis court was repaired.

The Board Gets A Flag

During my first days at the Federal Reserve Board, I had requested a Federal Reserve flag for my office and discovered that the Fed had no official flag. Now, that I was the Administrative Governor, I figured that I could do something about that. Every other government agency had a flag and I thought the Fed should have one as well.

I called in Bob Frazier, the head of Support Services, and told him about my plan. "Governor, what kind of flag do you have in mind?" he asked politely. I told him that I liked the flag on top of the State Department next door and maybe he could obtain a sample for us to look at. A few days later he was back without a flag. He stated somewhat sheepishly: "The State department does not have a flag either!" Incredulous, I asked: "Then what is that thing flying on top of their building?" He replied: "Sir, the Department of State displays its seal on cloth!" "Well, then let us do the same!" I replied. At that moment I had a great idea.

I thought that the very attractive official seal of the Federal Reserve could be the centerpiece for an absolutely beautiful and impressive looking flag. But what would be the right colors for the flag? Being a bit colorblind myself, I decided to turn the job over to my children. I made a few Xerox copies of the outline of the official seal of the Federal Reserve System and took them home. Daughter Kimberly was thirteen years old at that time and Christopher was nine. I got them a couple of crayons and they went to work.

My son Chris came up with a design that placed the Federal Reserve seal on a stark black background surrounded by a bright red border. Everybody would have immediately recognized it as a pirate flag. Pirates clearly played an important role in his fantasy, and so he came up with an appropriately looking flag. I probably should have been grateful that his flag did not sport a skull and crossbones design!

Daughter Kimberly came up with a very appealing design. There was the Federal Reserve seal, all colored in with a brown eagle holding a shield showing the red white and blue American colors. The shield was bordered by green laurel and oak leaves and surrounded by the legend: Board of Governors of the Federal Reserve System. Fifty golden stars representing the 50 states of the Union surrounded the circle. All that was set on a bright Navy blue background and framed by a golden tasseled border. It was a truly impressive and classic, timeless design. Not bad for a thirteen year old and a proud father.

My children Kimberly and Christopher proudly holding up the new Federal Reserve flag which they helped to design.

Next, I had the Board staff prepare a professional drawing based upon that design. It looked even prettier. I showed it to Volcker and all the other Governors, one person at a time. They all liked it very much and pledged their support for the design.

I prepared an official Board memorandum and requested Board approval for the official flag. I also recommended the purchase of a supply of large flags that could fly atop the Federal Reserve building, in the Boardroom, and at other appropriate places.

On June 9, 1987, I presented the resolution to the Board and the official Board vote was taken. It passed with the enthusiastic support of all the Governors, but Chairman Volcker did not vote for it. Somewhat surprised, I went to see him in his office and asked: "Paul, I thought you like the flag — so why did you not vote for it?" He leaned back and said in his sonorous voice: "Oh, I really like the flag, but $12,000 for a couple of flags is an awful lot of money!" I should have known that the tight-fisted Chairman would not approve of any unnecessary expenditure.

But when Paul Volcker retired from office a few months later after having served two full four-year terms as Chairman, he truly beamed when he was given the official flag of the Federal Reserve as a good-bye present and a memento for his years of outstanding service.

Representing the Fed Abroad

Henry Wallich was the Governor who represented the Federal Reserve at many international organizations and conferences when I joined the Board. After he resigned due to ill health a few months after my arrival, that area of responsibility was unattended. Much of my work at UCLA, the International Monetary Fund and at Bank of America had involved international economic and financial matters, and so it was no surprise that I was asked to represent the Federal Reserve in the international arena as well. My two standard international assignments were to attend the Economic Policy Committee and the Working Party 3 meetings at the Organization for Economic Cooperation and Development in Paris.

Paris was always a breathtaking city to visit. Flying to France in the supersonic Concorde half a dozen times a year was certainly no hardship duty. But at that time, certain terrorist groups were very active in Europe. To provide for safe passage and to protect me, I would be picked up at the Paris airport in a small armored car. These official cars were not air-conditioned and the glass windows were reinforced with thick plastic bulletproof panels that were bolted inside the window frames. Consequently, there was no way to open the windows, and riding in these hermetically sealed cars in the middle of the summer felt like being in an incubator.

The French drivers were on duty from nine to five, but our meetings at the OECD often lasted well past five o'clock. Then we would return to the official offices of the U.S. delegation to discuss the day's events. Around seven o'clock in the evening, I usually would be ready to return to my hotel. But by that time, the drivers and their armored cars would long ago have departed for home. When I inquired how I could find a taxi, I was advised that it was much simpler and faster to walk two blocks to the left and then two blocks to the right and to catch the Metro subway at the Porte de Saint-Cloud. So much for tight security!

My friend Beryl Sprinkel chaired the Economic Policy Committee meetings in his capacity as the Chairman of the President's Council of Economic Advisors. The EPC meetings were always interesting, but somewhat formal comparisons of the economic situations in the various countries. In contrast, the Working Party 3 meetings, which focused on the balance of payments situation, were more informal and lively. Jean Claude Trichet chaired these WP3 meetings. At that time, he served at the French Treasury Department, but later became the Chairman of the Banque de France and then President of the European Central Bank. Other participants included Helmut Schlesinger from the German Bundesbank as well as Hans Tietmeyer from the German Ministry of Finance. Both of them would serve later on as Presidents of the Bundesbank. It was a very interesting and powerful group indeed and the discussions are always fascinating. It was amazing to me to see these life-long civil servants go to work and pick apart the U.S. position, which was often presented by inexperienced short-term political appointees like me.

Greenspan Comes on Board

In June 1987, President Reagan nominated Alan Greenspan as Paul Volcker's successor in office. Greenspan was well known as an economic forecaster and was also in favor of deregulation of the banking system — an objective that was dear to the President's heart.

It was my job as the Administrative Governor to brief Greenspan on the procedures to get him installed as Chairman of the Board. I flew up to New York and met him in his offices at Townsend Greenspan, the economic consulting firm that he was leading. He listened most graciously when I took him through all the bureaucratic procedures. But when I told him that from now on he would have guards from the Federal Reserve protecting him wherever he went, he demurred. "No, I will not have any of that" he insisted with a strong voice. There was none of that circuitous and elaborate reasoning that he was famous for. It was a simple "No"!

As politely as I could, I told him that there was no real choice in the matter and that the protection came with the job. In the early 1980s, when the economy was in sharp recession, angry farmers and construction works had protested with a big tractor parade in Washington against the Federal Reserve policies. The Chairman had received several threats that made this protection necessary. One day, I had experienced a bit of that lingering public anger myself when I was walking with Paul Volcker to a luncheon on Massachusetts Avenue. A man suddenly accosted the very tall and instantly recognizable Chairman. The fellow screamed at Volcker: "The blood of the world is on your hands!" It was not a comfortable situation for either one of us. The protection of the second-most powerful person in the country was well justified. Greenspan relented after I recounted all the reasons for this security protection that came with the job.

On August 11, 1987, Alan Greenspan was sworn in at the White House as the new Chairman of the Board of Governors. Paul Volcker was there as well. President Reagan did the honors and welcomed Greenspan to his new position. He also thanked Volcker for his many years of service to the nation.

Our entire family was invited to the formal White House swearing-in ceremony. As a Governor, I was permitted to sit in the front row to witness the ceremony with my wife Emily and our two

At the White House for Alan Greenspan's swearing in as the new Chairman. From the left: myself, Wayne Angell, Manley Johnson, Vice President Bush, President Reagan, Alan Greenspan, Martha Seger and Edward Kelley. *(White House photo)*

children Christopher and Kimberly. They were all dressed up for the occasion. Son Chris, who was by now almost ten years old, had his favorite three-piece suit on. He was fascinated by the fact that there were foot markers made out of paper placed on the low stage right in front of him that read: "The President," "Mr. Volcker" and "Mr. Greenspan." They were arranged such that the principals would know precisely where to stand and all the cameras could record the event perfectly. When the ceremony was over and the principals had departed, little Chris took one high leap, clambered upon the stage and retrieved the paper marker that read "The President." It was a prized possession of his and I would not be surprised if he still owns that cherished piece of paper to this day.

While Volcker had generally remained a bit aloof and distant from us Governors, Greenspan struck us as a much more congenial personality. Usually, Volcker seemed to have already made up his mind on most issues and merely wanted us to go along. Instead, Greenspan solicited our views and ran the Board meetings in a more collegial fashion. For us Governors, there was no more "going to the woodshed."

Although political views never entered the discussions, I sometimes wondered whether Volcker's perceived distance was due to the fact that a Board composed entirely of Reagan appointees surrounded him. Some of them had rebelled against him just prior to my coming aboard. And yet, this was at a time after he himself had received his second appointment as Chairman from President Reagan. He obviously enjoyed the President's blessings. Frankly, I never fully understood the reason for this perceived difference, as Volcker was certainly more gregarious in social situations than the somewhat shy Alan Greenspan.

When I reflect upon my experience several decades later, I recognize that both Volcker and Greenspan were excellent Chairmen. Volcker had clearly been dealt a tougher hand, inheriting a high-inflation economy and he needed to put the country through a painful double recession to wring the inflationary forces out of the system. Greenspan was able to build on the progress made by Volcker in reducing the inflation rate and led the Federal Reserve during a long period of prosperity and low interest rates. After that long and difficult battle against inflation, I find it somewhat incongruous that nowadays there are some Federal Reserve Board members that actually argue for higher inflation rates instead of basking proudly in the low-inflation environment.

Getting Ready For World War III

One of my duties as the Administrative Governor was to make sure that the Federal Reserve was ready for all potential emergencies — including World War III. To that end, the ever-present Bob Frazier informed me that it was one of my duties to inspect the Fed's Emergency Evacuation Facility. I readily agreed as he promised that a helicopter would pick us up and fly us to Culpeper in the Virginia countryside, where the facility was located.

Boarding a military helicopter for the flight to the secret Fed
Emergency Evacuation Facility near Culpeper in Virginia.

We took an exciting helicopter ride flying over the Virginia
scenery until we landed on Mount Pony. But there were no ponies
in sight. Instead, there was a peaceful herd of Holstein cows grazing
on the undulating hills. One of the hills looked like it had been slit
open on the side and an enormous glass window covered the oblong
opening. We marched to the opening and entered a hidden gateway
while the cows looked on.

Inside the mountain, there was a cavernous hall with desks, all
covered with see-through plastic sheets. I could discern desk
markers that read: FDIC and Comptroller of the Currency. "What
are these desks for?" I inquired. "They are for the liaison officers
from the other regulatory agencies and will be occupied by officers
from these institutions in case of a national emergency!" was the
answer. Underground below Pony Mountain there was a replica of
the entire regulatory and monetary policy making apparatus
covered with plastic sheets. There was also a huge vault stashed
with currency in case the government needed spending money after
the start of World War III. It was all very impressive.

There was even a suite of small bedrooms and bathroom facilities, one suite for each Governor. I was informed that the Governors could bring their spouses into the facility during World War III, but that staff members would have to come alone. As a matter of fact, they might have to hot bunk around the clock, as there were more staffers than beds! Poor fellows!

There was also plenty of frozen food for all of us and — very comforting — a morgue and an incinerator to take care of dead bodies. They had thought of everything!

As I walked through the facility, I noticed that it looked a lot like the cave that my mother and I had hidden in at the end of World War II. But our cave certainly had a much thicker rock cover overhead. Also, the facility was not as well fortified as the former air raid shelter in our house in Cologne, which had thicker walls and a better-supported ceiling. I meekly offered my observations to the officer on duty. I told him that as a child, I had probably been better protected during World War II. Taken aback, he offered that the facility was not designed to withstand actual bombs, but would primarily serve as a fallout shelter in case of nuclear attack. That was not too comforting, as the Russians certainly knew how to target their weapons.

It is my understanding that the Federal Reserve's Culpeper facility has long been abandoned and that it now is used to store old movies for the Library of Congress. I am hoping that I am not revealing any deep national security secrets and would have to be punished for doing so. But I am happy that our cultural heritage of Hollywood movies might survive World War III intact.

Life at the Fed was always interesting!

SAGE ADVICE:
When You Are in High Office,
Always Set a Good Example and Count Your Pennies.

Making Monetary Policy

The Federal Reserve System fulfills three important functions: formulating and implementing the nation's monetary policy, serving as a supervisor and regulator for the banking system and providing the backbone of the nation's payments system.

Most people would agree that making monetary policy is a central mission of the Federal Reserve. Many books have been written about the Fed and monetary policy and there is no need to recount that voluminous material. Instead, let me set out how I looked at the monetary policy making process during my time on the Federal Reserve Board.

The Board and the FOMC

There are two distinct bodies involved in setting monetary policy: for one, there is the Federal Reserve Board composed of the seven Governors. It is responsible for setting the discount rate at which banks can borrow money from the Fed at the discount window when they need additional liquidity. It is a rate that is truly administered or precisely controlled by the Fed. Second, there is the Federal Open Market Committee, which is composed of the seven Governors and five of the twelve Reserve Bank Presidents, who serve on a rotating basis. The Chairman of the Board usually serves as the Chair of the FOMC and the President of the Federal Reserve Bank of New York serves as the Vice Chairman.

All twelve Reserve Bank Presidents speak freely at the FOMC meetings, but just five of them get to vote. Alan Greenspan was once asked in Congress to name the five Presidents of the Federal Reserve Banks that were current voting members of the FOMC. He could not remember their names on the spot. It may have been a bit embarrassing for him, but it also showed that everyone around the table was considered an equal. All were colleagues whose views were valued and fully taken into account in the policy discussions around the table — regardless of the fact whether that person was entitled to a vote in that particular year or not.

The FOMC meets normally eight times a year. It concludes its meetings with a Monetary Policy Directive that determines U.S. monetary policy until the next meeting. In it, the FOMC gives instructions to the Open Market Desk of the New York Federal Reserve Bank on how to conduct its open market operations that influence the interest rates in financial markets.

Unbeknownst to the Board members at the time that I was there, the Secretary of the Board also recorded the discussions. He relied on these recordings to prepare the official minutes of the Board meetings for later publication. But those tapes were never erased. Several years later, the existence of these tapes was revealed and it is no surprise that someone asked the tapes to be made public under the Freedom of Information Act. As a consequence, we now have detailed transcripts of all the meetings publicly available. If we had known about this practice, some of us might have told a few less jokes than we actually did!

Controlling the Money Supply

I had frequently encountered Milton Friedman during my academic career. Just like him, I believe that the money supply occupies the central role in the monetary policy making process. The demand for money by the private sector defines the relationship between interest rates and the quantity of money demanded by the public. The Federal Reserve in turn controls the supply of money. Together, the money supply and money demand determine the prevailing short-term interest rate, which is the price for holding money.

If the Federal Reserve increases the money supply, this will lower short-term interest rates and the economy will grow faster than it otherwise would. But it is also likely to increase inflationary pressures. If the Fed lowers the money supply, money becomes dearer and interest rates will rise. Consequently, the economy will slow down.

Getting Inflation Under Control

When I arrived at the Fed, Paul Volcker and the other sitting Board members were very much focused on reducing the rate of inflation by keeping the money supply under tight control. They followed Milton Friedman's famous dictum that "inflation is always and everywhere a monetary phenomenon."

Under Volcker's leadership, the Fed used tight control of the money supply during the 1980s to bring down the inflation rate. Prior to that, inflation had been running at double-digit rates. At the time when I joined the Board, inflation had been brought down to about three percent. Of course, bringing down inflation had not been without significant costs as evidenced by the "double-dip recession" of the early 1980s, during which unemployment soared to almost 11 percent.

Looking at the Future

Monetary growth influences inflation only with a long and often variable lag. In essence, the Fed has to steer the economy towards a goal that lies a year or two in the future. Consequently, it is useful to analyze a range of leading indicators to discern where inflation is headed. In particular, I find it very helpful to look at the entire inflationary process and inflationary expectations as evidenced in financial and commodity markets.

Gold is an asset that has served monetary purposes over the centuries and its price is very sensitive to inflationary expectations.

If investors expect inflation to rise in the future, they will buy gold, driving up its price. Other commodity markets are also sensitive to future price expectations.

Similarly, if people expect that inflation will increase, they will ask for higher interest rates on money that they lend to others in the credit markets so as to make up for the expected erosion in their purchasing power. Rising long-term interest rates in bond and credit markets are therefore often a harbinger of future inflation.

Once commodity prices rise, these increased input prices will influence producer prices and wages. From there, the rising prices find their way into intermediate goods and eventually into final goods and the prices paid by consumers. This chain may look a bit like the proverbial snake that is devouring a rabbit. The rabbit produces a bulge as is transcends the body of the snake to its ultimate destiny. The same holds true for prices as they manifest themselves sequentially through the production process.

Therefore, I watched not only the money supply and the entire term-structure of interest rates with great care, but also kept an eye on gold and commodity prices, producer prices and wages as well as final consumer prices. Together with the unemployment figures and capacity utilization rates, these indicators gave me a pretty good picture of the inflationary or deflationary pressures as they were transmitted throughout the economy.

Of course, I also used much more sophisticated analytical methods to discern the appropriateness of our monetary policy. The Federal Reserve model of the economy at that time was a largely Keynesian macroeconomic model. While it offered much detailed information, I did not find it very useful to analyze the effects of money supply changes on the economy. Consequently, I hired my own research assistant, Kal Wajid, a bright young man whom I knew from my days at Bank of America. I then subscribed to the macroeconomic forecasting model that Laurence Meyer had developed at Washington University in St. Louis. This econometric model made it easy to analyze the effects of changes in the money supply on the economy. With the help of the Meyer model, Kal and I produced our own economic forecasts and we were also able to model the effects of contemplated monetary policy changes on the economy. In later years, Larry Meyer himself became a member of the Federal Reserve Board.

As a sailor, I always thought that the monetary policy making process was similar to steering a sailing vessel. First, you set a long-term goal as to where you want to wind up. Then you analyze the wind and current patterns ahead of you and set the rudder and trim of the sails such that it will get you to your intended destination. Every now and then, you increase or decrease the pressure on the rudder, but it is the totality of the ever changing environmental conditions and your actions that will determine whether or not you reach your goal. Sailing and making monetary policy is part science and part art and an experienced skipper will be able to reach the intended goal.

Price Stability — The Central Goal of Monetary Policy

In the Federal Reserve Act of 1977, Congress tasked the Federal Reserve with three broad objectives: namely to "maintain long run growth of the monetary and credit aggregates commensurate with the economy's long run potential to increase production, so as to promote effectively the goals of maximum employment, stable prices and moderate long-term interest rates."

In order to accomplish these three potentially conflicting objectives, my colleagues and I generally interpreted this sentence to mean that we should provide first of all for stable prices. In turn, this price stability would provide an environment that would be conducive to maximum economic growth. It was clear to all of us that the economy will only prosper in the long-term if prices are in fact stable.

Stable prices will also result in moderate long-term interest rates as the inflationary premium inherent in interest rates will be reduced and hopefully even eliminated. The term-structure of interest rates will then only reflect the time-preference for money and not an additional inflationary premium, thus fulfilling the often-overlooked Congressional mandate of moderate long-term interest rates.

In the 1970s and early 1980s, the country had experienced first hand what happens if prices accelerate and inflation takes hold. Stopping that inflation resulted in a double-dip recession that was accompanied by many business failures and high unemployment rates. Interest rates also skyrocketed to double-digit levels as markets incorporated high future inflationary expectations into long-term interest rates.

The lesson learned was that high inflation negates all the other goals specified in the Federal Reserve Act. Low or no inflation is the prerequisite for sustained economic growth, maximum employment and moderate interest rates. Fighting inflation was therefore our central goal, the accomplishment of which would enable the economy to more readily achieve the other two objectives as well. I believe that all of my colleagues were in general agreement with that objective.

The German Hyperinflation Lesson

The enormous costs of ever increasing inflation and eventual hyper-inflation are probably more deeply etched into my own mind than in that of the average American, because the United States never experienced very high inflation rates. In the Germany of my parents and grandparents, the inflation rate hit truly astronomical levels. In 1921, one U.S. Dollar bought 60 Marks, but by 1923, one dollar fetched 4,000,000,000,000 Marks. You do the math! The result was economic turmoil and political chaos in Germany that probably helped to bring radicals like Adolf Hitler to power.

Preserving the Value and the Role of the Dollar

I find it therefore somewhat incongruous that these days the Federal Reserve argues that two percent inflation constitutes "price stability" and calls for a more stimulative monetary policy as long as inflation is below that "target." In fact, with two percent inflation, a dollar will lose half of its value every 35 years. After a lifetime of 70 years, a dollar is worth less than a quarter and will have lost 75 percent of its original value. That does not constitute "price stability" in my opinion.

Of course, it is true that deflation is not desirable either. But let us not forget that some of the most dynamic sectors of the U.S. economy, such as information technology and computer production, have experienced continuing price declines for many decades. "Moore's Law" argues that productivity in the computing industry doubles roughly every 18 months. Falling prices are a result of these technological improvements and this has certainly not led to stagnation, falling wages and unemployment in the technology sector. Maybe the fears that some people have of falling prices are a bit overblown.

Consequently, for the nation's central bank to establish a formal inflation target of 2 percent and to argue that this is good for the economy is not constructive in my mind. It is also not in congruence with the Congressional mandate to the Federal Reserve to maintain "stable prices."

Higher inflation not only threatens domestic price stability, but also endangers the preeminent role of the dollar as the key currency of the international financial system. This key currency role of the dollar is also jeopardized when the Fed buys up large quantities of Treasuries and other securities to keep interest rates close to zero. Who wants to hold U.S. dollars when that asset is not only depreciating annually by two percent, but earns close to nothing — resulting in negative real or inflation-adjusted interest rates? Why should the Federal Reserve make the dollar less attractive as an international reserve asset and thereby foster the substitution of Euros and even Chinese Yuan for the once almighty dollar? One has to seriously question whether this policy is in the national interest of the United States.

The Financial World Changes

Of course, monetary policy depends on a stable and reliable empirical relationship between the money supply and the level of economic activity. If that relationship breaks down, monetary policy makers are in potential trouble. At the very least, they have to compromise and improvise to adapt to the changing circumstances.

In the 1980s the U.S. financial system was undergoing vast structural changes and consequently the relationship between the money supply and economic activity started to change as well. This found its expression in a change in the velocity or the rate of turnover of money. Increase the velocity of money and economic activity will speed up; decrease its velocity and the economy will slow down — as long as the other factors remain unchanged.

For instance, in the early 1980s Money Market Deposit Accounts became widely used for the first time. These MMDA accounts actually paid interest to their holders, while paying interest on demand deposits at banks was still prohibited by the government. As a result, there was an enormous flow from demand deposits into money market accounts. Accordingly, the relationship between the narrowly defined money supply M1, which focused on cash and demand deposits, and the important macro-economic variables changed as well.

At the same time, many savings and loan institutions were under extremely great pressure to pay higher interest rates to their depositors. However, these institutions were earning only 5 or 6 percent on the fixed-rate long-term mortgages that they were holding. As a result, over 1,000 S&L's went out of business in the 1980s and eventually the entire industry was decimated. As deposits in these savings institutions disappeared, the broader definitions of the money supply were affected as well. Again, adjustments had to be made in monetary policy to allow for these deposit shifts, which found their expression in velocity changes of the various monetary aggregates.

As the world changed, monetary policy had to change with it. Eventually, the Fed decided to focus more on interest rates, i.e. the price of money, rather than on the monetary aggregates themselves. Nevertheless, there is very important informational value in the monetary aggregates and any central banker will ignore the monetary aggregates at his or her own peril. Seeing the money supply (M1) double between 2008 and 2014 certainly bears watching!

Monetary Policy Making in the Open or Behind Closed Doors?

During the Volcker years, when I served at the Fed, monetary policy decisions were tightly guarded secrets. Wall Street employed a large stable of "Fed Watchers," who earned a good living by divining the state of current monetary policy. Reading the tea leaves for any evidence as to what the Fed was up to was a lucrative profession.

When asked about how he made monetary policy, Paul Volcker once jokingly explained that he had three envelopes in his desk drawer. One of the papers inside the envelopes said "Tighten"; a second one stated "Ease"; and a third one said "Do Nothing." Every morning, he would open one of the envelopes and see what the paper inside said. If it read: "Tighten," he would call the New York Open Market Desk and tell them to do so. If the markets reacted positively, he would stick to that policy and all would be well. If, instead, the markets went wild, he would tell the Open Market Desk to reverse course — and all would be well again. The market watchers simply figured that they had read the tea leaves the wrong way. Policy was flexible and surrounded by mystery. Paul Volcker was a master at keeping them all guessing.

There remains the serious question whether the Federal Reserve, and especially the FOMC, should conduct its business in the open or behind closed doors. The key issue is whether greater openness will reduce uncertainty and thereby lead to more stable financial markets and possibly higher economic growth or whether it might actually increase uncertainty and be harmful.

Consider the case where the Fed works behind closed doors and makes essentially no announcements of its policy — except for changes in administered rates, such as the discount rate. Market participants will try to read the "tea leaves" and attempt to discern from the Fed's actions what monetary policy course it is pursuing.

At the other extreme, by announcing even its future intentions, the Fed essentially commits itself to a predetermined course. If conditions should change due to external circumstances that force the Fed to change its policy direction, the Fed may lose credibility. But maintaining credibility is extremely important for any central bank. Hence, the Fed may loose the flexibility to react to changing circumstances. It takes years to build credibility, but it can be lost with one erroneous pronouncement. Why risk the Fed's credibility for very little potential gain?

I believe that the middle ground of immediately publicly announcing any policy actions that have been actually taken, but refraining from pronouncements regarding planned future policy actions, is the most effective, consistent and trust-building approach for a central bank.

Snugging Up

I was sitting in my office one day in late April 1987 when the phone rang. To my great surprise, it was James Baker, the Secretary of the Treasury. I had never received a phone call from him before and I guessed that something important was up. The dollar had been under pressure and had drifted down a bit in the foreign currency markets during the last few days. The value of the dollar is the responsibility of the Treasury. So I was eager to hear what he had to say.

The Secretary wanted to know whether we had changed monetary policy, as short-term interest rates were moving upwards in the markets. He wanted to know whether we had taken this action to support the dollar, which was the responsibility of the Treasury Department. I told him that we had voted in favor of a slight tightening bias at our FOMC meeting a few days earlier, but not made any actual decision to raise rates at that meeting. Baker was not happy. He suggested that we should take action to support the dollar by raising interest rates *only* if the Germans and the Japanese would agree to lower their rates at the same time. When I insisted that somewhat higher interest rates might be appropriate just for domestic purposes, as the money supply had been growing rather rapidly recently, he was not convinced. Baker was the ultimate politician and dealmaker. Whenever we did something in the United States that would affect the foreign exchange market, he wanted to get something in return from our foreign partners. In his view, we had missed a golden opportunity to extract a concession from the Germans and the Japanese in return for our own policy action.

At the next Board meeting, Chairman Volcker opened the session by intoning in his sonorous voice: "While there has been no overt change in policy, we have been erring on the side of restraint!" Baker's hunch had been right — we actually had changed our posture in the Fed Funds market at the behest of the Chairman. It was clear that Volcker had that latitude in accordance with the FOMC policy statement that we all had voted on. But even as a Board member, I had no idea that he had actually acted on that authority and had implemented a change in the Fed's monetary policy stance.

A few days later, during a Congressional testimony, Volcker confirmed that the Fed had been "snugging up a bit" on interest rates in response to the weak dollar. I was dumbfounded again — what was "snugging up" on interest rates? As I looked in Webster's Dictionary, I was humiliated to read that "snugging up" meant to tighten the lines on a ship. For a sailor like me, it was an embarrassment not to know what "snugging up" meant. In any case, the newspapers soon came to call these discretionary actions by the Chairman as the "snugging-up episode" of the Fed.

Never mind that according to Webster's "snugging up" also means: "getting cozy in bed with." And we had certainly not gotten cozy in bed with the Germans and Japanese, which was why Jim Baker was so upset. Oh well, making monetary policy is not always easy to explain!

Option B is Always Right

The staff always presented the monetary policy options open to the Board in the form of three alternatives in the so-called "Blue Book" that laid out the monetary policy options for the Board. Option A provided for an easing of monetary policy, Option B represented the central position and Option C called for a more restrictive policy. At one meeting, it was fairly clear that nobody would be in favor of an easing of policy. Consequently, there were only two options: do nothing or tighten. Curiously, in the Board briefing book these two alternatives were labeled as Options B and C. Somebody asked the staff why there was no Option A, but only B and C. While some of us were quite perplexed, someone else offered the following explanation: "Oh, that is easy! When Henry Kissinger was President Nixon's National Security Advisor, he always presented very long and complex decision memoranda to the President that enumerated many alternatives: A, B, C, D and so on. Kissinger was always afraid that the President might not pick the answer that he considered to be the "correct" answer, and so he labeled the preferred alternative always as Option "B." So, the staff thinks that B is always the right answer!" Everyone had a good laugh!

Smooth Sailing

Most of my time at the Fed it was pretty smooth sailing. We aimed to control the monetary aggregates by influencing the reserve positions of the nation's banks. If we supplied more reserves, then the money supply would grow faster. If we did the reverse, the money supply growth would be more restrained. Over the years, we aimed at approximately 6 percent growth in the broader monetary aggregates. When inflation rose slightly in 1988, we immediately tightened policy. As a result, the annual growth rate of the broad money stock M 2 declined from about 8 percent to about 3 percent. Promptly, the Fed Funds rate increased to 9 ¾ percent in early 1989. We did not want to endanger the hard-won battle against inflation, after having gotten the rate of price increase down from the double-digit range at the beginning of the 1980s to about half that level by the end of the decade. Fighting inflation was Job Number One in our mind.

Paul Volcker used to warn us against allowing even a small increase in inflation without taking corrective actions. One of his favorite admonishments regarding inflation was: "Once the toothpaste is out of the tube, it's very difficult to get it back in again!" Right he was!

Black Monday and Program Trading

There was one major disruption to the smooth sailing paradigm during my days at the Federal Reserve: Black Monday of October 19, 1987. Alan Greenspan had become Chairman of the Board only two months earlier.

Alan boarded a plane in Washington on the morning of that fateful day. He was bound for Dallas, where he was supposed to give a keynote speech at the annual convention of the American Bankers Association. As he boarded the plane, he heard that the Dow Jones Average was down about 100 points.

As the Chairman landed in Dallas, a delegate from the Dallas Fed picked him up. Greenspan inquired: "How is the market doing?" The Dallas staffer told him: "Down 5-0-8." Greenspan was nonplussed and opined: "Oh, that's not too bad!" He was thinking that the Dow Jones index had recovered and was down only 5.08 points. When he heard that the market was actually down a record-setting 508 points or by almost 25 percent of its entire value, he cancelled his ABA speech and boarded a military jet back to Washington.

What was going on?

The stock market had risen nicely during 1986. When Iranian vessels attacked several U.S. tankers in the Persian Gulf in mid-October, U.S. warships shelled an Iranian oilrig in retaliation. Needless to say, markets got nervous and some people started to sell stocks as a precautionary move. Pretty soon, trading programs that were designed to minimize losses by selling securities when the market dropped did kick in. The computer driven programs started to sell securities in ever-larger volume. As the markets dropped, numerous participants started to face margin calls that further exacerbated the downward spiral as individuals and institutions were forced to liquidate their positions to raise cash. It was that interaction of destructive forces: the Iranian attacks on the oil supply, the program trading and the ensuing margin calls that led to the catastrophic and self-reinforcing downward spiral of the markets.

Back at the Board in Washington, Vice Chairman Manley Johnson had taken charge, and we started to formulate our policy reactions. On Tuesday morning, the Board met and we issued a one-sentence statement that assured the financial markets that the Fed was ready "to serve as a source of liquidity to support the economic and financial system." That simple statement, along with an injection of reserves into the system, calmed the markets considerably.

In addition, the New York Fed called the major commercial banks and told them to lend freely to the investment bankers, securities firms and brokers. That was an action that I did not like very much. Essentially, we were putting the banks on the hook to assure the liquidity needs of the securities industry. If something had gone wrong and one or several of these securities firms had failed, who would have absorbed the losses of the banks who were lending at our behest?

I thought that the Fed ran the danger of increasing the circle of institutions that might be affected by the market crash and thereby endanger the entire banking system. Rather than acting indirectly through the banks, I would have preferred that the Fed would have acted directly by supporting the stock market itself or by directly lending to the securities firms. In fact, during the 2008 crisis, the Fed undertook the latter action to rescue some of the failing investment banks, while other investment banks changed their charter to those of commercial banks so that they became formally eligible for Fed assistance.

While I was at the Fed, I did not want to upset the consensus and formally dissent — especially not at such a precarious moment in the nation's financial markets. But shortly after leaving the Fed,

I wrote an op-ed piece for the October 27, 1989 issue of the *Wall Street Journal*. It was entitled: *"Have Fed Support Stock Market, Too."* In it, I argued that if the Fed wanted to support the market and the investment banks, it should take on that responsibility onto itself and not to act indirectly through the commercial banking system. I suggested that the Fed might want to buy broad market indices or futures in order to provide liquidity and stability to the markets in extraordinary circumstances instead of telling the commercial banks to support their investment banking brethren. Later, such operations were nicknamed as being the responsibility of the *"Plunge Protection Team."*

In a way, my suggestion was akin to the Fed's "Quantitative Easing" programs undertaken a quarter of a century later, when the Fed bought massive amounts of Treasury bonds and mortgage-backed securities. But I had intended my suggestion to provide only immediate *liquidity* support for the markets, instead of becoming a long-term support measure that essentially amounted to a new source of financing for Treasury debt and the mortgage market. These programs came very close to "credit allocation" by the Fed to the housing market and to the government itself. I believe that supporting just one sector, like housing, in preference to other sectors is not an appropriate use of the monetary policy instrument. That is why I would have preferred to spread the action over the entire economy, such as by a purchase of a very broad index fund. In the end, the result was probably similar, as the "Quantitative Easing" programs resulted in a huge surge of the stock market itself.

In a similar action, the Bank of Japan engaged in massive buying of stocks in 2013. This policy measure essentially implemented my original idea of supporting the stock market directly. But here again, I had thought of the program as I initially conceived it only as a short-term liquidity-support measure for markets in turmoil and not as a long-term support measure designed to prop up the market and the economy over long periods of time.

The Black Monday episode also instilled in me a sound skepticism against computerized program trading. Once these program trades kick in, there is no stopping them and they easily degenerate into a self-perpetuating trading loop that might exacerbate any already dangerous situation. Computerized flash-trading programs may offer the possibility of a gain to individual traders by executing an action faster than a human can, but they can also be a source of enormous instability and impose large costs on the financial system and the economy at large.

Several years later, I wrote an article on the creation of a *"Prudent Investor's Exchange"* (*San Francisco Chronicle*, Insight Magazine, front page, January 11, 2009) in which I argued that it should be up to each company whether to permit trading in derivatives for its own stock. I proposed a three-pronged approach: One, to implement a minimum holding period of two or three days for stocks to prevent computerized flash trading. Two, to permit companies to disallow put, call, options and derivatives trading in their own stock. Three, to end uncovered short or margin trading. All that would make the markets safer for regular, long-term investors. I still think it is a good idea, whose time will eventually come.

A Grave Responsibility

While I was on the Federal Reserve Board, we voted 13 times at the FOMC to increase the Fed Funds rate, but only 5 times to decrease this important policy rate. Changing the rate was generally done in very small and cautious steps.

Nevertheless, changing the Fed Funds rate was never easy for me — especially if it entailed an increase in the rate. I remember flying over the country soon after a rate decision and looking down on all the small villages and farms. I asked myself: "What have we just done to all the people living down there?" If we had increased the Fed Funds rate by a mere ¼ percent or 25 basis points, a person with a mortgage of $400,000 and a flexible interest rate provision would soon receive a letter from his bank informing him or her that the bank now expected an additional $1,000 in interest payments per year. We might undertake such a policy tightening several times in a year. That would quickly add up to thousands of dollars taken out of the family's budget. For people wanting to buy a new house that could mean an additional burden or even that they could not afford to buy the house at all.

During my entire time at the Fed, we raised the Fed Funds rate from 6.5 percent to 9.5 percent. For an adjustable-rate mortgage holder with a $400,000 mortgage this increase amounted to an additional $12,000 in annual mortgage payments. If Congress had voted that much of a tax increase of the same magnitude, people would have been very upset. Nevertheless, raising the Fed Funds rate was an action we had to undertake to further work towards the goal of price stability, so that the economy could prosper for several more decades.

I realized that the Fed was a very powerful institution, indeed.

SAGE ADVICE:
Providing for a Stable Price Level Is the All-Important Policy Function of a Central Bank

Supervising and Regulating the Nation's Banks

W hen I arrived at the Fed, I was obviously intrigued by the task of helping to shape the nation's monetary policy. Most of my academic and professional background had been focused on macroeconomics and I looked very much forward to participating in the monetary policy decision-making process.

To my great surprise and delight, the microeconomic tasks of supervising and regulating the country's banks also proved to be a most interesting and fascinating challenge. Of course, I had worked for many years at Bank of America and become familiar with the interactions between the banks and their regulators. While my formal employment there was as an economist, I had been a member of many of the bank's policy-making committees and had a great opportunity to learn banking by osmosis and through on-the-job training.

I was not alone with that background on the Board. Paul Volcker had also been a bank economist at Chase Manhattan Bank, and Wayne Angell had been an economics professor as well as a banker. Nevertheless, I was somewhat astonished when Paul Volcker appointed me as the Chairman of the Committee on Bank Supervision and Regulation. That meant that I was going to play an important role in the oversight of the nation's banking system.

Our Complex Regulatory Structure

While the Federal Reserve plays a significant role in supervising and regulating the banking system, there are many other agencies that share that responsibility. There is the Office of the Comptroller of the Currency in the Treasury Department, that charters and supervises the national banks with a federal charter; the Federal Deposit Insurance Corporation insures and examines all federally insured banks; and each state has a Superintendent of Banking or a similar office that charters and regulates the state chartered banks. Furthermore, there is the Office of Thrift Supervision, which is in charge of the nation's thrift institutions and the National Credit Union Administration that looks after the credit unions. More recently, the Consumer Financial Protection Bureau has been added to the long list of supervisory agencies.

Moreover, there is the Securities and Exchange Commission, which supervises all public companies, including the banks. The Commodities Futures Trading Commission rides herd on the futures markets. In addition, there are all the various state and federal law enforcement agencies that watch out for infringements of the commercial and criminal codes. Thus, there are plenty of regulators and supervisory agencies that have some jurisdiction over the nation's banks. If you total them all up, there are well over 100 bank regulators in the country!

Many banks have five or even more agencies looking over their shoulder. It is little wonder that compliance officers for banks are vastly increasing in number.

Given the myriad agencies with overlapping jurisdictions, there is also an official inter-agency group, the FFIEC, which tries to coordinate the activities of many the agencies mentioned above. After all, somebody has got to harmonize and ride herd over all these regulators! Thanks to my position as the Chair of the Federal Reserve System's Committee on Bank Supervision and Regulation, I was also a member of the FFIEC. We used to joke that if you knew what FFIEC stood for, you were probably a member of this august body: the Federal Financial Institutions Examination Council.

As an example showing that new laws only create more agencies and never abolish any existing regulatory functions, consider that even after the U.S. Congress created the Consumer Financial Protection Bureau in 2010, the Fed's own Division of Consumer and Community Affairs continues to exist. This is true in spite of the fact that both agencies are financed off-budget through the Federal Reserve System. Is there really any good reason not to consolidate these two agencies?

I believe that it is high time to greatly simplify this excessively complex regulatory structure. In most countries, there is only one bank supervisor — a situation that provides for clarity and reduces cost. All the costs on both the regulatory side and on the bank side have to be borne eventually by the consumer.

Record Bank Failures

When I joined the Fed in 1986, the country was faced with a record number of bank failures. There were many economic events that combined to produce a perfect storm for the banks and caused many of them to get into serious difficulties. In the early 1980's, oil prices collapsed — largely due to the Iran-Iraq war. Moreover, commercial real estate prices fell some 40 percent and prices for most major commodities declined. More than a dozen developing countries could not pay their debts. In addition to these problems, most banks and all savings and loan associations had huge investments in fixed rate mortgages. Typically, these mortgages carried only five percent interest rates. In this environment, the Fed drove interest rates up to the double-digit range to break the back of inflation. This resulted in a high negative spread for many bank loans and the banks experienced increasing losses. Consequently, both large and small banks as well as most Savings and Loan Associations were in severe trouble.

In 1980, over 14,000 FDIC-insured banks were in existence in the United States. In the following years, between 250 and 350 banks failed every single year. But entrepreneurs had not yet learned their lesson and just as many new banks were being formed. As a consequence, the number of banks was virtually unchanged when I arrived at the Federal Reserve Board in 1986.

From that moment on, however, the number of new bank formations dropped abruptly from 217 in 1986 to only 40 in 1992. At the same time, the number of bank failures started to rise precipitously, reaching a peak of over 800 failures in 1988. That's when I was the Chair of Bank Supervision and Regulation. During my three-year tenure at the Fed, over 2,000 banks went out of existence — either through outright failure or via an FDIC-assisted merger. This is an all-time record of which I am not very proud.

Every Thursday, a Green Sheet would be circulated among the Board members. It carried the ominous heading: "The Following Banks are Scheduled to Fail This Week." It listed about half a dozen banks every week. The FDIC was so overwhelmed by the number of bank failures that they kept a waiting list for banks to be closed. They just did not have enough staff to handle all the cases.

The FDIC would select the most urgent cases, and every Friday afternoon their staff would descend upon the banks that were scheduled to be taken over. The FDIC would immediately announce to the public that it was now in charge of the bank. After a busy weekend, the FDIC staff would declare on Monday morning that the same bank was now open as an FDIC-controlled institution. For the customers, there was virtually no visible change. This was the regular weekly scenario while I was at the Fed. The only exceptions were the two weeks of Thanksgiving and Christmas, when the entire travelling staff of the FDIC was on vacation and no bank failures occurred. I guess that was the FDIC's holiday present to the banking community.

All these bank failures were resolved in an orderly fashion and there was no turmoil or panic in financial markets. While a very large number of banks failed in the Eighties, their bigger brethren absorbed many others through mergers and acquisitions. For instance, in 1988, there were 600 unassisted mergers of banks. In virtually all cases, this involved the purchase of a small bank by a larger institution. By the end of 2013, the total number of banks in the U.S. had shrunk by 40 percent from over 14,000 in 1980 to a much more reasonable level of 5,880 banks.

Legalized Extortion

Having come from Bank of America, I naturally watched with keen interest how the Fed handled these mergers and acquisitions. My position as Chairman of the Committee on Bank Supervision and Regulation gave me the perfect perch from which to follow the action.

When two banks agreed upon a merger, they had to get the permission of the regulators to consummate the transaction. As part of that process, the Fed staff would analyze whether the merger would result in an undue concentration of market share. Frequently, the staff asked that some branches would be closed or sold off to a competitor as a condition of the acquisition.

Another important requirement was that the banks should serve "the needs of the community." That generally meant that they would grant a fair share of their loans to underserved or minority communities. That was certainly a reasonable requirement, but it also could lead to the extension of loans to very marginal borrowers. Often these borrowers got into financial difficulties because they could not really afford to make the loan payments. Sometimes, they had to declare bankruptcy — the very opposite of the intent of the legislation.

If all the legal requirements were met and there were no protests to the merger, the Fed had 60 days to act on the merger. Sometimes I noticed that an application lingered for many months on the Fed's calendar. When I enquired why no action had been taken, the typical answer by the staff was that a community organization had protested the merger and that public hearings were to be held. Obviously, that would postpone the merger by several months and would usually be very costly to the banks involved. Customers might leave the bank for a competitor and employees might look for other opportunities and resign. The carefully laid merger plans might be seriously disrupted.

I was just as surprised when I suddenly noticed that the staff now recommended approval of an application, but there had been no public hearings. When I asked the staff why the application had suddenly moved forward, the typical answer was that the community organization had withdrawn its protest. Therefore, there was no further obstacle to the merger and the Board could take final action immediately.

Something smelled fishy to me. When I did not relent with my inquiries, I was often told that the bank had given a substantial donation or grant to the community organization prior to them withdrawing their protest. I told the staff that that sounded like extortion to me, but the staff demurred and said that it was all perfectly legal. The law required that public comments be solicited. Then, if there was a protest, there would be a hearing and considerable delay. But if the protest was withdrawn, the merger could proceed swiftly. The fact that the bank made a donation to the community organization was an entirely different and separate matter. I was stunned. It sounded to me like the community organizers actually had a monetary incentive to file a protest and then collect a "donation" from the bank. In essence, the bank was paying off the protesting community organization. That entire procedure did not sound just and fair to me, but there was nothing that could be done! It was all perfectly legal and that was the way the game was played. Nevertheless, I found it outrageous and it looked like legalized extortion to me.

Fairness Before the Federal Reserve Board

There was one other matter that irked me during my time at the Fed: it was the manner in which the Board dealt with infractions of the Federal Reserve Act and other banking regulations. Congress has tasked the Federal Reserve with several important supervisory and regulatory responsibilities. First of all, the Fed is in charge of writing many of the rules and regulations governing the conduct of banks and bank holding companies. Second, the Fed has to supervise the banks' actual adherence to these regulations. Third, the Fed has the responsibility of administering justice to those who have infringed against any of its rules. That is, the Fed makes the rules, monitors adherence to the rules and also punished infractions of the rules. I wondered whatever happened to the principle of separation of powers?

Just think what our country would look like if the local police department would make the laws, monitor compliance with the laws and then determine punishment as well. Would this still be a democracy?

The division of powers enshrined in the Constitution delegates the legislative function to Congress, the enforcement function to the executive branch of the government and the judicial function to the nation's courts. This is the very bedrock of our democratic system. It is designed to prevent a concentration of too much power in any one institution and thereby acts as a bulwark against tyranny and injustice.

Yet, with respect to the banking system, the Federal Reserve essentially combines all three functions under one roof.

What is more, any person accused of a misdeed typically does not even get to appear before the Federal Reserve Board itself to defend himself and to present his or her case in person. Instead, the Fed's staff investigates the matter and then negotiates an agreement with the presumed perpetrator. If the banker consents, the Fed staff will then present both sides of the argument along with its own recommendation for punishment to the Federal Reserve Board. Typically, the accused is not even invited to be present during this presentation. During my entire time on the Board, I never once saw a single occasion where a defendant actually made an appearance.

While the staff presentations were usually very serious and somber, there were occasions when they bordered on the hilarious and comical. I remember one staff presentation, in which the staff reported about its investigation into an inappropriate diversion of banking funds that went roughly as follows:

Federal Reserve Staff: "Mr. President, have you ever used bank funds for non-bank purposes or private gain?"

Banker: "Of course not! I have never done such a thing!"

Staff: "Did, in fact, the bank pay for your daughter's wedding last June?"

Banker: "No, of course not!"

Staff: "Well, did the bank sponsor a reception and dinner for about 200 persons last June 15?"

Banker: "Oh, I think on that day we had one of our regular community affairs dinners. We have an important community event like this every year!"

Staff: "Did your daughter wear a white dress on that occasion?"

Banker: "Yes, Jennifer always dresses very well!"

Staff: "And was a large white cake served to the group?"

Banker: "Of course! I already told you that we served dinner."

Staff: "Well, was the local minister also present on that occasion?"

Banker: "We customarily invite prominent community leaders to our functions. That is just part of our regular PR!"

Staff: "Did in fact the preacher perform a wedding ceremony on that occasion?"

Banker: "Yes, yes — we always provide for some sort of entertainment at these gatherings!"

Staff: "So, did in fact the bank pay for the wedding of your daughter?"

Banker: "Of course not! Her wedding was just incidental to one of our regular community affairs functions! What's wrong with that? Everybody liked it and it generated lots of goodwill for our bank!"

The Board members were barely able to suppress their laughter and quickly approved the official order forcing the community banker to pay a considerable fine and to resign from his office.

In spite of the comedy of this situation, the basic principle is an important one. Namely, everybody accused of a violation of the rules and regulations of the Federal Reserve should have the opportunity to appear in person before the Board to present their case. Of course, nobody is forced to agree to the Consent Decree and can go to an Administrative Court as an alternative, but I still do not like the process.

In my mind, it would be better if one institution, such as the Federal Reserve Board, would write the banking rules and regulations; the Comptroller of the Currency or a state banking agency would supervise the banks and check on infringements; and an impartial third party, such as an administrative law judge, would render a judgment on guilt or innocence and impose an appropriate penalty. Division of power is an important concept that prevents abuse.

Beginning to Tear Down the Glass Steagall Act

Ever since 1933, the Glass Steagall Act has prohibited commercial banks from engaging in investment-banking activities and vice versa. Specifically, the Act prohibited commercial banks from issuing and dealing in non-governmental securities and conversely barred investment banks from taking deposits from the public.

To me, this separation of commercial and investment banking never made much sense. In Europe, where I grew up, so-called "universal banks" were able to engage freely in commercial and investment activities. Many of these institutions prospered for centuries. Swiss banks were generally considered the epitome of safe and sound banking.

Furthermore, if underwriting a security for a firm and thereby incurring an exposure for a few weeks or months was such a dangerous activity for a bank, then why would that same bank be allowed to make a 20-year loan to that same enterprise? That was certainly a much more risky proposition in my mind.

As a result of these two considerations, I was never a supporter of the separation of commercial and investment banking brought about by the Glass Steagall Act. For America's banks to be strong and to be able to compete with European banks, the Glass Steagall barriers needed to come down so that the institutions could diversify their earnings streams and their overall risk profile. To me, that was the basic lesson that everybody learned in Finance 101.

During my term at the Fed, the Board was asked to interpret the meaning of the rule that commercial banks should not be "principally engaged" in securities activities. The proposal before the Board was to allow up to ten percent of the bank's revenues to derive from these otherwise prohibited securities activities. Deriving ten percent of a bank's revenues from securities activities certainly did not mean that the bank was "principally engaged" in securities activities. Instead, it was a sideline and an ancillary activity to the bank's main business, which was commercial lending. The proposal passed by a vote of 4 to 2, with Paul Volcker and Wayne Angell voting against the proposal.

After the vote was taken, a very senior Fed official approached me with raised eyebrows: "Bob, do you know what you just did? The Board has considered this matter over a dozen times before and never passed it. You just punched a hole into the Glass Steagall Act!" I demurred and said that the proposal passed by a rather solid 4 to 2 majority. I was only one of the four "yes" votes, so it could not possibly have been me alone who was responsible for this outcome. He countered: "That is true, but if you had voted "no," the vote would have been tied at 3 to 3 — and a tied vote does not carry the motion. So you did it!" I was not sure whether I should be proud or chagrined. I quickly decided to be proud, as I had helped to spearhead the drive to make the American banking system a bit more competitive and also safer.

A decade later, Congress finally abolished the anachronistic separation of commercial and investment banking by enacting the Gramm-Leach-Bliley Act and President Clinton signed the legislation.

There has been considerable debate whether the elimination of the Glass Steagall barriers was a positive or negative development for the safety and soundness of the American banking system. The fact is that during the financial turmoil of 2007 and 2008 all major investment banks either merged with commercial banks (such as Bank of America acquiring Merrill Lynch or J. P. Morgan buying Bear Stearns) or took out commercial banking charters, like Goldman Sachs and Morgan Stanley did. These actions allowed the Fed to render direct support to these important institutions. Without this assistance, the investment banks would probably have failed and further exacerbated the financial crisis.

In my view, the combination of commercial and investment banking activities under one roof also deals with my concern that the Fed should not lean on commercial banks in times of distress and ask them to extend liberal credit facilities to their brethren in the investment-banking business. Instead, the Fed can now offer appropriate liquidity assistance to these former investment banks directly. Thereby the unpalatable possibility that the indirect assistance route might put commercial banks in danger is eliminated.

In spite of some voices to the contrary, I believe that by eliminating the Glass Steagall barriers, the American banking system has become safer, more competitive and more diversified across product lines.

Interstate Banking

The repeal of the McFadden Act prohibitions against interstate banking in 1994 made it possible for banks to branch across the entire country instead of being restricted to the geography of only one state. Just like the interstate commerce clause in the Constitution allows for the free flow of commerce across state lines, the abolition of the McFadden Act allowed banks to operate on a nationwide basis, thereby allowing for greater geographic diversification. Again, greater geographic diversification of income streams and asset portfolios should foster greater safety and soundness to the banking system through broader diversification.

Furthermore, nationwide corporations like IBM, Chevron and United Airlines, need to be served by nationwide banks. Companies operating in all 50 states need banks that can serve their financial needs across the country. It would be highly inefficient or impossible for corporations to deal with 50 separate state banks on a day-to-day basis.

Both the broader product spectrum and the geographic expansion allow for better diversification and thereby help to reduce the overall risk profile of banking institutions. This enhanced diversification makes American banks more stable and able to weather financial storms. It also allows American banks to compete on a more level playing field with their foreign competitors, many of which have been universal banks all along. In addition, more financial institutions are now able to rely on direct liquidity assistance from the Federal Reserve in times of need.

Are Banks Too Big?

Not surprisingly, the abolition of these artificial barriers resulted in a large merger wave and consequent growth of the most successful banks. At the time of this writing in 2015, four American banks have over $1 trillion in assets: Bank of America, Citibank, J.P. Morgan Chase and Wells Fargo Bank. Given the size of the U.S. banking system with about $14 trillion in total assets — roughly equal to the GDP of the country — the concentration is high, but not overwhelmingly so. In most advanced countries, we also find that three or four banks are dominant in size.

In many other economic activities, we also observe that three or four companies dominate any specific market. There are three large U.S. car manufacturing companies: GM, Ford and Chrysler; four large phone companies: ATT, Comcast, Sprint and T-Mobile; four big accounting firms: Ernst & Young, KPMG, Deloitte and PricewaterhouseCoopers; four national airlines: American, Delta, United and Southwest; and the list goes on. Thus, the structure of the banking system is not unique, but quite normal.

In addition to the four large national banks, there are quite a few big regional banks and a multitude of community banks. This makes for a vibrant and competitive banking system overall.

What worries me most about the future of the American banking system is that the increased amount of regulation has led to a virtual cessation of the formation of new banks in recent years. Ever since the passage of the Dodd Frank Act of 2010 with its vastly increased regulatory burden, the number of new bank charters granted has come to a virtual standstill. Only one single new bank has been formed in the three years from 2011 to 2013. This is certainly not a sign of a vibrant industry, but of an industry strangulated by overregulation. That is a development that is worrisome, indeed!

SAGE ADVICE:
Overregulation Is the Deathknell For Any Industry

23   An Early Departure

In the summer of 1989 Jim Wiesler, a former Bank of America colleague, approached me and inquired whether I might be interested in joining VISA, the credit card company. Jim had been the Vice Chairman for retail operations of Bank of America and also represented the bank on the VISA governing board. While Jim was now retired, he was still well connected. VISA was reorganizing and undergoing a split between its domestic and international functions and needed to staff up rapidly the two organizations.

Temptations

While I had no intentions to leave the Federal Reserve after having served only slightly more than three years out of my ten-year term, I was tempted. There were several reasons for this.

For one, our family really liked living in the San Francisco Bay Area and had only reluctantly agreed to move back to Washington DC. Here was an opportunity to return to all our old friends in California. Furthermore, there would be no major disruption in the kid's school routine. Daughter Kim was just turning 15 and about to enter High School. Son Chris was 12 years old and was ready to enter Middle School. Both of them had to switch schools anyhow. As far as the kids were concerned, this was the ideal time to move. If not now, we would probably have to stay through their high school years so as not to disrupt their education unduly.

Second, while my wife Emily liked her interesting job as Executive Secretary to the Academic Senate at the University of Maryland, she was a true native Californian at heart and liked that state better than all others. Going back to California was a very attractive proposition to her.

Third, I loved the San Francisco Bay Area ever since I had been a graduate student at the University of California at Berkeley. The eight years that I had spent at Bank of America only deepened that affection for California. I had been reluctant to leave San Francisco for the Fed, knowing that the prospect of returning to the Bay Area was slim indeed. But now, the job inquiry from VISA presented just that opportunity.

Fourth, our salaries at the Fed were a just bit more than $80,000 per year and just that summer Congress had refused to increase our pay. Before joining the Fed, my salary at Bank of America had been $125,000 plus bonuses and some stock options that unfortunately proved to be worthless. I also remembered vividly a conversation with my fellow-board member Emmett Rice soon after I joined the Board. Emmett had told me that his take-home pay at the Fed was less than the combined college expenses for his son at Yale and his daughter at Stanford University. Yes, his daughter Susan Rice was later to become Ambassador to the United Nations and the National Security Advisor in the Obama administration. I figured that my kids would soon be ready for college as well, and I did want my family to be well provided for.

Fifth, the Federal Reserve Act contains a provision that prohibits Governors from taking a job at any bank supervised by the Fed for two years after resigning from the Board. Consequently, joining a bank in the next few years was essentially ruled out. I would have to work for a non-banking institution, and VISA— while owned by many banks — was not a banking organization. Thus, there was no formal barrier to me joining that company.

And yet, I was very reluctant to leave the Board after just three years. So I studied the pattern of service by previous Board members. To my great surprise, I found out that the average tenure of Board members was only about four years — in spite of the very generous 14-year terms provided for in the Federal Reserve Act.

What was the cause of this short tenure? First of all, Governors that were appointed to fill the unexpired term of another Board member would get to serve only for the remaining term of that Governor. In my case, that was a generous 10 years because my predecessor Preston Martin had served only four years out of his full 14-year term. But for my successor, there was going to be less than 7 years remaining in my unexpired term. Successively, the actual terms got smaller and smaller.

I also noticed another pattern: most Board members appointed in mid-career realized that their term would not stretch out to their retirement. So they had to plan on another job after their Fed term expired, and few companies would hire somebody in his sixties. Maybe they also had a young family to take care of financially. In addition, many of the Fed Board appointees came from academic institutions. After having been on leave for two years, they typically had to return to their professorships or resign their tenured positions that carried a lifetime guarantee of employment. Faced with that choice, many returned to their academic institutions after serving only two years. Alan Blinder, Randy Krozner, Fred Mishkin and Jeremy Stein are recent examples of that pattern.

Matters were different for older people near their retirement age. These professors or businessmen found the Fed a convenient place to serve out their working life and they often stayed for a decade or longer. They were happy long-time Governors, indeed. As a matter of fact, the Board salary might even provide them with a second income in addition to the pension from their previous job. Henry Wallich, Wayne Angell, Mike Kelley and John LaWare were good examples for that pattern during my days at the Fed. In a sense, I envied them. But I was too young to fully retire after the expiration of my own term. I would have been only 56 years old at that time and getting another good career job at that age might have proven to be difficult. So, my incentive to leave for another career was great when the VISA opportunity presented itself.

As I weighed the pros and cons of accepting the position at VISA, it seemed more and more like an exceptional opportunity to me, and so I accepted the position offered to me by VISA.

Saying Good Bye to the Fed

When I told Alan Greenspan of my decision to leave, he was more than surprised. I was the first Governor to resign on his watch. So, this was a novel experience for him as well.

After sharing with him the various reasons why I had chosen to leave, the two of us agreed that I would mention prominently the fact that the Board salaries were not really adequate. This was a hot topic as Congress had just turned down a general salary request increase for all Federal executives. Hopefully, my mentioning this reason might help to persuade Congress of the need to improve salaries for all.

After I sent my resignation letter to President George H. W. Bush, I invited all the reporters that had very diligently covered my tenure at the Fed to a luncheon at the Federal Reserve dining room. About a dozen of them showed up. They were just as surprised as Greenspan was about my decision. As intended, the press highlighted the need for higher salaries at the Fed in their articles covering my resignation. Mission accomplished!

The Federal Reserve Board sponsored a dignified farewell reception for me. Chairman Greenspan presented me with the official Federal Reserve flag that I had helped to create. I was very proud of that. I was also presented with the chair that I had occupied at the Board table. It was one of the few remaining original Board chairs and represented a wonderful memento of the many hours that I had spent sitting at the Board table. In addition, my FOMC colleagues presented me with a large wall plaque that displayed the official calling cards of all the other Governors and Federal Reserve Bank Presidents as well as a collection of hand-autographed one-dollar bills issued by each of the twelve Federal Reserve districts. This was a truly unique memorial of my service on the Board.

President George H. W. Bush saying good-bye to Christopher, Kimberly, myself and my wife Emily in the Oval Office of the White House. *(White House photo)*

President Bush invited our entire family to the White House to say good-bye and gave me a nice note accepting my resignation. In it he commented: "Your role in sustaining the economic vitality of our country during the last few years was a significant one, in which you can justifiably take pride." He concluded the letter by writing: "I wish you all success in your endeavors in the private sector, and Barbara joins me in wishing you and your family all happiness in your California homeland."

All these were treasured mementos of my service at the Fed that I will cherish forever.

Our family packed up, we sold our house in McLean, Virginia, and we moved back to California just in time for the beginning of the school year.

SAGE ADVICE:
Nothing Lasts Forever and You Have to be Ready to Leave — Even if You Have a Good Time

PART V

The Corporate World

After leaving the Federal Reserve Board, I joined VISA. The founder, Dee Hock, proudly called it a *chaordic* organization, combing elements of *chaos* and *order* at the same time. And chaordic it was! While there was constant infighting and turmoil at the company, the basic business model was extremely strong and helped VISA to attain a preeminent position in the retail payments world. During my time at the helm of VISA U.S.A., we developed the VISA Debit Card and began to dominate that sector as well. But eventually, the cultural conflicts within the company became too great and I had to depart.

Fair Isaac, the company that pioneered credit scoring, was next and offered many challenges. Changes in corporate leadership put the company's strong corporate culture to the test, but the company continued to expand its dominant position in its markets.

This segment of the book concludes with two chapters distilling a lifetime of experience in management and leadership as well as in corporate governance. I explore why excellent managers will not always become outstanding leaders because leading an enterprise demands very different skills from those learned in many years of management.

Eventually, I became a member of many boards, helping institutions to navigate through the ever-changing waters of an uncertain world. Having a properly constituted board to help the leadership of a company to navigate though internal and external challenges is most important to the success of any organization.

24 VISA – The Chaordic Organization

Finding a Place to Live

As the family moved back to California, it was house-hunting time again. We all wanted to get the job done quickly, so that the family could settle in and the children could start to attend their new schools soon. Consequently, we all decided that we would make the decision about which house to buy within one week.

We also determined that we could not afford to pay more than a million dollars for the new house. With the help of a realtor, we began the search near VISA's headquarters in San Mateo on the San Francisco Peninsula. As we searched in the leafy suburbs of Hillsborough, San Mateo, Menlo Park, Woodside and Palo Alto, it became quickly evident that we could afford only an old run-down house in a nice location or a nice new home in a not-so-desirable neighborhood, where old pick-up trucks were parked on the neighbor's lawns. Not much has changed with that picture since then, but the houses have become even pricier in the heart of Silicon Valley!

Disappointed by the available housing supply on the San Francisco Peninsula, we returned to our neighborhood in Marin County across the Golden Gate Bridge. Quickly, we found a wonderful home on the Tiburon hillside that we all liked. In addition, the location had the advantage that we would be returning to our former community. Kimberly and Christopher would be

Our family on the balcony of our new house in Marin:
Christopher, Emily, Kimberly and myself.

able to reconnect with the same playmates that they knew from our
time at Bank of America. Emily and I would also be able to join up
with many old friends. We were also still members of the San
Francisco Yacht Club, which had been at the center of our social
and recreational life before we moved to Washington. All that was
wonderful.

But when I remarked that Tiburon was 40 miles away from
my new job in San Mateo and that it would take me over one hour
in each direction to commute to work, our 12-year old son Chris
piped up and opined: "Dad, you made us move all the way across
the country — now you can drive a little!" That settled the
argument. We moved right back to our old neighborhood in Marin.

Actually, I did not mind the long drive very much as the hour-
long morning commute gave me an opportunity to make business
calls to banks on the East Coast and during the return drive I
listened to my favorite Country Western radio stations. I was a
happy camper and looked forward to my new job at VISA!

The Birth of VISA and the Chaordic Organization

Everyone knows what a VISA card is, but few people know that VISA had its origins in 1958 when Bank of America first started to issue credit cards under the *BankAmericard* label. Later on, Bank of America issued franchise licenses to several banks in the U.S. and abroad, thereby allowing for national and international acceptance of the card and creating a truly global retail payments network.

In 1970, Dee Hock, who worked for the National Bank of Commerce of Seattle, was one of the leaders of a revolt of the franchisees against the mother company. Hock and his supporters threatened to leave BankAmericard unless the banks were given equitable ownership rights in the organization. After a contentious debate, Bank of America consented to their demands and eventually two associations were formed: one for the United States and one as an international umbrella organization. Now, all the member banks issuing the cards had ownership rights in the associations. Dee Hock was a unique individual, who was just as much interested in reading Cicero and Machiavelli as he was in running a credit card organization. He was rewarded with the presidency of the new organizations and he led them with a grand vision and an iron hand.

Many of the banks both in the U.S. and abroad did not particularly like to issue BankAmericards, as they were effectively advertising the name of a competitor. For instance, Barclay's Bank in the U.K. always called its card the Barclaycard.

Clearly, a unifying name was needed, but what should it be? Dee Hock asked the staff to come up with a new, catchy and descriptive name to replace the BankAmericard appellation. Generously, he offered a grand prize of fifty dollars to the person who would come up with the best name. In the end, it turned out that several people had suggested the name VISA, but noone could remember who had suggested the name first. So, Dee decided that nobody could claim the rich prize of fifty dollars. He certainly knew how to run a tight budget!

After that, the member bank association formally changed its name to VISA International Service Association. Note that the first letters of that rather long name spell out V-I-S-A as well. According to some researchers, the brand name VISA is now worth over fifty billion dollars!

After leaving VISA, Dee Hock wrote a book entitled *The Chaordic Organization*, in which he details his own personal history and that of VISA. Dee himself coined the word chaordic out of the two words chaos and order, both of which he wanted to incorporate into the VISA organization. And chaos and order it was — but few people could tell which one dominated the organization.

Decentralizing the Organization

The central question was how to run the new association, which was conceived to be a global payments organization. The creative mind of Dee Hock solved the situation by decentralizing much of the company. Dee's plan established five regional organizations, each one of which had its own local or regional board of directors. In turn, the five regional groupings owned VISA International, which was an umbrella organization, holding the five regions together.

In addition to VISA International, there were the five regional entities: VISA U.S.A., VISA Canada, VISA Latin America, VISA Asia as well as VISA Europe, Middle East and Africa (EMEA). A decade later, a further split occurred between Europe and the new Eastern Europe, Middle East and Africa Division, bringing the total number of regions to six.

All were member-bank owned associations with their own boards of directors. Just to add to the complexity, VISA U.S.A. and VISA Canada were separately incorporated, while the other regional groups were divisions of the VISA International organization. Chaordic it was!

After much acrimonious debate, everybody signed on to the reorganization and Dee Hock came up with the convivial slogan: "*Think Globally — Act Locally!*" Everybody was mollified.

As Dee implemented his plans for the new global organization, he also decided that this grand enterprise needed impressive headquarter facilities. Without telling his board of directors, Dee leased space in the elegant and brand-new 101 California Street building overlooking the San Francisco Bay. He furnished the offices with graceful and costly furniture befitting his vision of the global organization.

When the directors saw the fabulously expensive new headquarters, they were aghast. Most of them were in charge of the credit card divisions at their respective banks — and many had rather modest offices furnished with plain wooden furniture or austere steel desks. They toiled in the "backrooms" of their banks and thought that Hock was spending their money lavishly and unwisely. They rebelled. Soon, Dee Hock was on the way to early retirement.

Chuck Russell Takes Over

After Dee Hock retired as President and CEO, Chuck Russell, his long-time deputy and COO, took over the helm. But with the founder gone, things at VISA quickly got more chaotic. Dee's genius was able to hold the "chaordic" organization that he had created together and to impose "order" when there was a need for it. His brilliant mind could win most any debate with questioning bank directors. But Chuck Russell was challenged to do that, and some thought that the balance was tipping more and more in the direction of "chaos." While Dee had been an inspiring leader, Chuck had spent his entire career as a manager — and there is a big difference!

Chuck Russell had spent his military service in an Army marching band playing the trombone and felt comfortable when someone else was holding the baton. He would happily tell anybody willing to listen that he had started his banking career at Pittsburg National Bank by pure accident. As he told the story, he was walking through Pittsburg looking for a job when a heavy rain shower surprised him. He took refuge in a doorway, which happened to be the entrance to PNB. As he was stuck there, he thought that he might as well go inside and inquire whether they had any job openings. To his own surprise, he was hired and soon assigned to the newly formed credit card division.

With a broad grin on his face, he loved to tell the story about how they beat the emerging competition from MasterCard. The bank would issue its credit cards with a hole in the middle of the card. It would also issue the ubiquitous credit card impression machines, generally called Zip-Zap machines, with a sharp spike in the middle. Russell and his colleagues would tell the merchants that the spike made the placement of the credit card more accurate and prevented the card from sliding around in the machine. But when the merchant placed another card into the machine and moved the sliding lever, the spike would punch a hole into the competitor's card and render it unusable. Mission accomplished!

Eventually, Chuck Russell rose to be head of operations at the PNB bankcard division. Soon after Dee Hock wrestled control of the Bankamericard organization from the founding bank, Chuck joined the credit card company as Dee Hock's number two in command. While Dee dealt with the board of directors and determined the grand strategy, Chuck was in charge of the nitty-gritty of operations. He excelled at that job.

The first thing that Chuck Russell did after his promotion to President of VISA was to cancel the lease at 101 California. Instead, he moved the headquarters to San Mateo on the San Francisco Peninsula, where the computers of the VISA data center were already located. That set the right tone and Chuck was comfortable leading the troops from what used to be the back office.

Instead of driving the 50 miles from his home in Bel Marin Keys in Marin County to the VISA compound in San Mateo, Chuck commuted via a whole range of conveyances. He would begin the trip by riding one of his many Harley Davidson motorcycles from his home to the nearby Marin County Airport. There, he would board his private plane and pilot it himself high over the jammed Golden Gate Bridge to San Carlos Airport just south of VISA's new headquarters. Then he would drive an old dilapidated Ford Thunderbird with a Landau roof that was literally falling apart to the VISA campus right next to the College of San Mateo. Motorcycle, airplane and car — Chuck enjoyed them all!

Chuck Russell on one of his beloved Harley Davidson motorcycles. (Visa photo)

Staffing Up VISA International

As VISA expanded around the globe, the same individuals staffed VISA International and VISA U.S.A. Thus, the General Counsel, the Treasurer and all the other top officers held dual positions in both organizations. Eventually, the non-U.S. members demurred as the staff would tell them one day that they represented their interests in VISA International and the next day told them that they could not do something because it was contrary to the desires of VISA U.S.A. The situation became confusing and eventually untenable.

To solve the problem, it was decided to separate the staff of VISA U.S.A. from the staff of VISA International. Consequently, there was a sudden need for many new employees as the newly separate organizations had to rapidly increase their executive staffs in a short period of time.

My job offer was part of that hiring process. Chuck Russell

offered me a position as Executive Vice President of VISA International. I was to be in charge of all the administrative functions, including global risk management, security, audit, and property management. All that would very much build on my experience as the Administrative Governor at the Fed and so I thought it was a great fit for me. I found the VISA offer professionally and financially very attractive and accepted.

Welcome to the Chaos

As in many organizations undergoing a radical organizational change, there was much turf-fighting going on. Everybody wanted to grab as much of the territory as possible. Chuck was challenged to lead the troops under him with the same iron will as Dee had done. Consequently, frequent arguments and fights would break out among the employees. Everyone would defend his own turf against all others and try to gain an advantage over the fellow next door. The *chaos* part of the chaordic organization began to dominate the *order* part.

Soon after I joined VISA, we had a meeting of the Executive Committee. The group was comprised of the senior management of the entire VISA organization and included, in addition to the President and CEO Chuck Russell, the Executive Vice Presidents of VISA International and the Presidents of the five regional associations.

The meeting was held at the Waikoloa Resort on the Big Island of Hawaii. This was one of the benefits of working for the global VISA organization: all meetings were held in exciting locations somewhere around the globe, such as London, Hong Kong, Barcelona, Carmel or Cannes. We all would travel there via first-class — and of course, our spouses were invited as well.

As this first meeting that I attended progressed, an argument broke out between some of the Regional Presidents. Soon, they were not just yelling at each other, but grabbing fruits from plates that offered abundant snacks meant for a different purpose. Oranges and macadamia nuts were flying through the air as the

Presidents and EVP's pelted each other with fruits. It was like a fraternity party that had gotten out of control. The last time that I witnessed such a food fight was in college when immature students started to throw whole plates of food at each other. But these were grown men, in charge of a global financial organization!

Eventually, calm settled in again and I started to think: What have I done? Leaving the genteel and refined world of the Federal Reserve Board for such a juvenile, raucous and chaordic organization? Oh, here was that word again!

Actually, many of the people working with me were fabulous colleagues. But it was not easy to overcome the infighting between the international group and the various regional organizations. At VISA, the battles were not directed against external competitors, like American Express and MasterCard, but were fought against the guy in the office next door!

Legend had it that the founder Dee Hock would often assign the same project to several people with the admonition not to tell anybody else about the assignment. So, three or four persons would spend several weeks doing their best to develop the project in isolation. When they were finished, Dee would call all of them into a room and have them present their solutions — and they would argue with each other until the best concept would win. Maybe that was not an altogether bad way to come up with the best idea, but the competitive atmosphere did little to build team spirit, cooperation, trust and a congenial work atmosphere.

One time, Dee Hock thought that one of the executives in a management meeting was talking too much. So, he ordered the perpetrator to stand in a corner facing the wall with a pencil in his mouth. Quiet was restored.

Just like a good kindergarten teacher, Dee could control his underlings. But once he departed, the inmates ran the asylum! It was my observation that once such a culture is firmly embedded in the DNA of an organization, it is exceedingly difficult to change that culture again.

My First Assignment: Resolving The Petra Bank Mess

I joined VISA International in August of 1989, and was soon told that the Jordanian government had just closed Petra Bank. I had never heard of Petra Bank. But because I was responsible for risk management and security, it would soon consume much of my attention.

Ahmed Chalabi had founded Petra Bank a decade earlier. Chalabi was an Iraqi who had left Iraq as a young child and was opposed to Saddam Hussein. He went on to earn a B.A. degree from MIT and then topped it off with a Ph.D. in mathematics from the University of Chicago. Obviously, he was a brilliant man. He also had a reputation as a most engaging and charming person. Most important for me in my new job, he was also on the VISA International Board of Directors.

In early August 1989, the Jordanian government closed down Petra Bank as the bank did not comply with a new requirement to deposit 30 percent of its foreign exchange holdings at the Central Bank of Jordan. In addition, many loans were in default and eventually the government had to cover over $200 million in losses. Obviously, Chalabi had to leave Petra Bank and also had to resign his position on the board of VISA International. All that happened at exactly the same time that I joined the VISA organization and I never had the chance to meet him.

According to the news reports, Chalabi fled Jordan and was put on trial and eventually convicted in absentia. He claimed that Saddam Hussein was behind a plot to depose him at the bank — but the truth of that claim has never been established. Later on, Chalabi was one of the founders of the Iraqi National Congress Party, the group that allegedly found the evidence for Saddam's hidden weapons of mass destruction. After the fall of Saddam, Chalabi returned to Iraq and tried to become President of that country. That effort was ultimately unsuccessful.

But back to the VISA story. Among its various overseas subsidiaries, Petra Bank owned a London-based merchant bank that signed up merchants for VISA cards. Given Chalabi's prominence in the VISA organization, that small merchant bank managed to become the exclusive bank for all Russian merchants accepting VISA cards. When the parent bank in Jordan went out of business, the London-based subsidiary did not pay to the Russian merchants the money that was owed to them. Obviously, the Russians did not like that at all.

The now defunct Petra Bank and its London subsidiary owed Russian merchants some $30 million for goods and services that they had provided mostly to foreign tourists prior to the time that Petra Bank was shut down. When we told the Russians that the merchants' contract was with the Petra Bank subsidiary and that VISA itself owed them nothing, they were not pleased. The Russian government made it known that if the $30 million owed to the Russian merchants was not paid promptly, they would make sure that no VISA card was ever going to be accepted in Russia again. As usual, the Russians meant it.

But where were we going to come up with the $30 million for the Russians? VISA's total capital in those days amounted to a paltry $40 million and paying out the $30 million demanded by the Russians would stretch the resources of the company to the limit.

Eventually, we worked out a deal to pay the Russians the money owed by Petra Bank by borrowing the funds from the VISA member banks. After all, many of the banks' credit card customers had spent the funds in the first place at the Russian merchant outlets and the customers had presumably paid their VISA card bills to the banks. It was just that the intermediary, Petra Bank, was not there any longer.

Just to make sure that such a calamity would not happen again, we introduced a formal risk management program at VISA that forced banks with weak balance sheets and operating in risky environments to pose collateral against their potential exposures on their VISA credit cards and travelers' checks.

One of the first banks forced to pose such collateral was the infamous BCCI, the Bank of Credit and Commerce International. When I met with them in their London offices seeking to establish the collateral fund, they were not at all pleased and not very cooperative. But eventually they did post the collateral — and did so just in time as the U.S. government soon thereafter shut down BCCI. We had lucked out with our preemptive risk management program, which seemed to be working well!

The Fall of the Berlin Wall

About that time, I was scheduled to give a speech on behalf of VISA at the Stadtsparkasse Bremen on the northern coast of Germany. The Stadtsparkasse was one of the few VISA card issuers in Germany at that time. I gave my speech in front of several hundred invited guests on the evening of November 9, 1989.

When I got back to my hotel, I turned on the television set to relax a bit and to get ready to fall asleep. On the local German channel, I saw pictures of people climbing on the Berlin Wall and trying to tear it down. I watched the TV for a few moments and thought that I was watching a badly done movie. The action was pretty slow and the photography amateurish. I turned off the TV and went to sleep.

The next morning, the banner headlines of every newspaper proclaimed: "Berlin Wall Falls!"

I was stunned and amazed. Without recognizing it, I had been watching the actual live pictures of Berliners tearing down the wall in the middle of the night. What I thought was a bad movie, was actually a live broadcast of this historic event. I had not recognized it for what it was and had turned off the TV set.

I had missed witnessing this historic moment because I thought it was a badly produced movie! It just goes to show that reality is often a bit more unexciting and boring than the glittering fantasy of a fast-paced movie. Recognizing and appreciating the importance of a truly historic moment, even if you see it in person, is not always easy.

Changing the VISA Logo

In the fall of the same year, I bought myself a sailboat to cruise with the family on San Francisco Bay. I had sold my last boat when we moved to Washington and it was time to have my own boat again. I attended the annual local boat show and found a wonderful Erickson 34 for sale. The company building the boats had just gone bankrupt and there were three Erickson boats for sale at very attractive prices. It was like getting a new boat at a used-boat price. In honor of VISA, I named the boat *"Charge."*

I also ordered a fancy new spinnaker for the boat and planned to have the name VISA emblazed on the Blue-White-Gold spinnaker. It would look just like a VISA card and I thought it would be great advertising for the company as I sailed on San Francisco Bay. When I told our General Counsel Bennett Katz about my plans, he was not very agreeable. He argued that he would have to give me a regular license to the VISA trademark in order to keep the brand protected. And he would have to treat me like all other licensees and charge me a royalty for it. He claimed that he could not make an exception for me without potentially endangering the legal protection for the VISA logo. I understood and I ordered my spinnaker without the VISA lettering. Nevertheless, I bought the spinnaker emblazed with the Blue-White-Gold colors of VISA — something he could not do anything against. Too bad that VISA could not enjoy all that free publicity!

But soon thereafter, I got a bit of a comeuppance. Jean Jacques Desbons was the Executive Vice President for Marketing of VISA International and we had adjacent offices. Jean Jacques was an urbane and elegant Frenchman who had attended the famed French military's *School of Cavalry* at Saumur and had been a member of the elite *Cadre Noir* — the Black Corps. He had proudly served his country in Africa on horseback prior to becoming a banker.

Jean Jacques decided that the old Bank of America logo stripes needed some freshening up. Rather than being a crisp Blue-White-Gold, the gold in the old logo looked more like a somewhat dirty brown. Whenever Jean Jacques presented me with a new rendition

At my fiftieth birthday, my family presented me with a hand-made VISA card crafted out of leaded glass.

of the slightly revised color scheme, I would pull out a picture of my boat under full sail and compare the colors: "No, Jean Jacques, the gold has to be a bit more brilliant to match my sails!" I would tell him kiddingly. But for him, this was serious business. We would love to banter with each other — and eventually he got the colors right!

Later on, Jean Jacques became President and CEO of the London-based Europe, Middle East and Africa Division, where he excelled in leading the VISA organization. Unfortunately, he passed away all too early.

Tracking Down the Fraudsters

VISA's Security Department employed a group of investigators that would go after perpetrators of credit card and traveler's check fraud. The group consisted of several former FBI agents, who had plenty of experience in going after crooks. The group was headed by Bill Neumann, who had been the head of the FBI for all of Latin America. Bill had a nose that could sniff out criminal activity wherever it occurred. He and his team were most helpful in tracking down the bad boys that were trying to forge VISA cards and traveler's checks.

The former FBI agents even had nicknames for the various types of criminals who tried to defraud the VISA system. There were the "hit-and-run" culprits and the "wine-women-and-song" guys. The "hit-and-run" breed would steal or forge a credit card and then hit the road to get away from the initial scene of the crime. I remember our agents talking about one guy who apparently stole a card at a Holiday Inn in San Francisco. He then headed south to San Jose, where he stayed at another Holiday Inn. He ate and drank all he could consume at the hotel restaurant. The next night, he did the same in Merced and the following day again in Fresno. Our agents swiftly drove down to Bakersfield and camped the next evening in the bar of the local Holiday Inn and waited until he showed up. With the help of the local police, they booked the surprised fellow who thought that he was having the time of his life! Brand loyalty was his undoing.

The "wine-women-and-song" criminals constituted a more locally oriented breed. They would steal a credit card and then hit the neighborhood bar. There they would spend as much as they could on wine, women and song. Then they would charge it on their stolen VISA card. They had such a good time that they repeated the process night after night until one of our agents would swoop in and nail them on the spot.

Another incident involved a member bank of the VISA system that was at that time a very large issuer of VISA traveler's checks. The issuing bank would sell the traveler's checks to tourists and businessmen that had to make payments, but did not want to run the risk of losing cash. The holder of each VISA check would sign the instrument when he bought it and then counter-sign it again in the presence of the merchant when he cashed the check. The merchant would then return the check with the two matching signatures to the bank, thereby completing the payment circle. As a result of this transaction circle, the fully countersigned traveler's checks were returned to the bank that had issued them in the first place. Finally, the bank would destroy the now fully paid VISA check. That destruction process would cost money, of course.

One day, a gentleman showed up at the bank that issued the checks and told them that he owned a very efficient shredding machine. He offered to do the cumbersome destruction process for only a small nominal fee, and the issuing bank eagerly accepted. Soon, a truck showed up to collect the seemingly worthless checks — presumably to be shredded.

A few weeks later, the bank noticed that several of the checks that had already been paid earlier were presented again for payment. What was happening? Apparently, a whole trailer-load of the checks had been shipped to the Philippines, where a roomful of ladies skillfully erased the two signatures from the checks. The crooks would then sign their own name on the checks. They would take the checks to a merchant, or even a bank, and countersign the traveler's checks in the presence of the sales person or bank officer and get cash. And thus, the same check was paid twice until our FBI team put a stop to it.

Traveler's checks were also relatively easy to forge. Often, we would notice a large volume of forged traveler's checks emanating from a specific country — more often than not a place in Asia. One set of crooks would forge the VISA traveler's checks and then sell them to other crooks at a discount.

Whenever we detected such a pattern, we would send one of our crafty ex-FBI agents to the source with maybe $100,000 cash in his pocket. He would hang out in the "wrong" bars and pretty soon, he would have pinpointed the source of the forged checks. He would identify the suspect and trade him the printing block in return for the cash. Our agent would return with the printing block and the forged checks stopped coming — at least for a while.

Internal Havoc

Strange things continued to happen at VISA. At one time, our security people informed me that the dapper and elegant young man who was staffing our reception desk was actually running a male prostitution ring from our front desk. He figured that nobody would notice a few more long-distance calls and thus he set up shop right there in front of our noses while most of the clientele was in Las Vegas.

There was even one occasion when one of my direct reports came to me and told me that probably someone had surreptitiously broken into the office computer. So I asked our ex-FBI crew to see what they could do to find the alleged perpetrator of the computer break-in. With the help of hidden surveillance cameras that had been installed in the building for security reasons, they quickly pinpointed a person on the executive floor who had entered the building at the time of the computer break-in. But in the end, the camera could not see directly into the victimized office and observe the suspect doing his work. We could not obtain conclusive proof and so we dropped the matter. But we all started to look a bit more carefully over our shoulders and to lock up sensitive material.

Chuck Russell was not too worried. He proudly proclaimed that there was nothing of interest to anybody else in his office. He announced that if he should die unexpectedly, his successor would find a totally empty office with only his last flight plan in the drawer. And he was telling the truth.

Turmoil at the Top

As part of the new staffing plan separating VISA U.S.A. and VISA International, Jon Christoffersen was appointed President of VISA U.S.A about a year before I arrived. He succeeded Chuck Russell in that position. Russell remained as CEO of VISA U.S.A. as well as CEO and President of VISA International. Why make it simple when complexity is much better?

Jon Christoffersen was an experienced and affable banker who originally worked at Seattle's Rainier Bank. In 1988 Security Pacific Bank of Los Angeles took over Rainier Bank. Soon thereafter, Jon Christoffersen jumped ship and joined VISA as the President of VISA U.S.A.

Jon quickly sized up the situation at VISA and decided to return to regular banking when the opportunity presented itself. He joined First Nationwide Financial as President and Chief Operating Officer. Promptly, Chuck Russell returned to the helm at VISA U.S.A.

The VISA carousel kept turning not only in the U.S., but also in London where a whole succession of Presidents passed the baton from one to another. There was Joao Ribera de Fonseca, Jacques Kosciusko and eventually Jean Jacques Desbons — all in the few years while I was at VISA.

It was in this environment that Jon Christoffersen resigned as President of VISA U.S.A. and a search for his successor was started. Carl Pascarella, the President of the Asia Division, and I were the two leading candidates to succeed Jon. In spite of the fact that Chuck Russell let it be known that he wanted Carl to have the job, the VISA U.S.A. Board decided to offer me the position. This might not have been a good omen.

Thinking that I might be a bit more insulated and independent from the turmoil on the international side, I accepted the offer to be President of VISA U.S.A. at the beginning of 1991. That turned out to be a troublesome decision.

SAGE ADVICE:
It is Almost Impossible to Change the Culture of an Organization

25 At the Helm of VISA U.S.A.

Tee Off at Pebble Beach

VISA U.S.A. typically held the first Board meeting of the year at the famed Pebble Beach Lodge near Carmel on the magnificent California coast. It was scheduled on purpose on the weekend before the AT&T National Pro-Am Golf Tournament, which brought most of the country's best golfers to Pebble Beach.

Many of the directors were avid golfers and so the opportunity to meet at that renowned resort, while much of the country was covered with snow and ice, was an important perk. VISA was a member-bank owned association at that time and so most of the U.S. directors were not paid regular board stipends. Obviously, they were paid a salary from their own banks and their duty included representing their banks on the VISA Board. All the more important for them were the implicit benefits, like staying at a world-class resort and being able to play golf there. Of course, VISA also reimbursed their first class airfare to the meetings.

Will Nicholson was the Chairman of the VISA U.S.A. Board, where he represented Colorado National Bank. He was also an enthusiastic golfer. In his youth, he had been a member of the U.S. amateur golfing squad and later became the president of the U.S. Golf Association. Coming to Pebble Beach every year was an absolute requirement for him.

If the VISA staff wanted to make sure to get a quick vote on a perhaps controversial issue without much discussion, the staff would schedule that agenda item for about 11.45 AM — just before the golfers led by Nicholson would head off for the first tee promptly at noon. Nobody would dare to be late for that all-important golf appointment and miss his starting time.

There were some twenty directors on the VISA U.S.A. Board. Several of them represented the biggest member banks, like Bank of America, Citibank, Chase and Wells Fargo. The smaller banks formed constituencies that elected board members to represent these groups of banks. In addition, Chuck Russell and I served on the board by virtue of our offices.

Many of the board members represented banks that were fierce competitors in the market place and would have liked nothing more than to beat the heck out of the fellow sitting next to them. But on the VISA Board, they had to cooperate for the good of the association that tied them all together and on which they all depended for a good share of their profits. They had to unite to devise common rules and regulations, develop compatible systems, and even joint marketing campaigns.

At every meeting, the Board had to wrestle with the creative tension that the founder Dee Hock had tried to balance: the desire to compete against each other, and the need to cooperate. To drive home the point, he coined another motto for VISA: "The Will to Succeed and the Grace to Compromise." To make sure that nobody forgot the message, he gave each director a pair of golden cufflinks with the slogan inscribed in Latin: "*Studium ad prosperandum, voluntas in conveniendum.*" As a result, order generally prevailed when the directors were together in the boardroom; but as soon as they returned to their respective banks, competition and rivalry took over again.

Reorganizing VISA U.S.A.

The first thing I did after becoming President of VISA U.S.A. was to streamline the organization. In essence, I tried to create a bit more order. My prior perch at VISA International had given me good insights into the functioning of the domestic organization as well. True to form, several of the department heads had built up little fiefdoms within their own organizations to serve interests that were outside their own span of control. But these little beachheads gave them the opportunity to speak out on issues not truly within their purview.

I restructured the organization and moved these little enclaves to the departments where they truly belonged. Everyone was a bit unhappy about losing a few people to some other department, but those losses were counterbalanced by gaining new groups of people that actually fit in better within their own organization. After a bit of grumbling at the beginning, everybody seemed to be happy with the new, more focused organization. Some of the small turf battles ceased. We were off to a good organizational start!

The VISA Marketing Juggernaut

VISA U.S.A. had a first-class marketing team led by three outstanding experts in the field: Brad Morgan, the Executive Vice President for Marketing was the head of the department; John Bennett was in charge of brand management; and Jan Soderstrom ran advertising. What made this extraordinary group so special was that they worked together as a team and if one had a great idea, the others would help to execute it.

John Bennett had come to VISA only a few years before from American Express and developed the slogan "VISA — It's everywhere you want to be." It was designed to emphasize the broad acceptance of the VISA card at a large number of merchants. This broad merchant acceptance distinguished VISA from American Express, which was more narrowly focused on the travel and entertainment markets. At the same time, the American Express card was aimed at an upscale market segment and had a prestigious cachet associated with it. So, we expanded the slogan a bit and added the line: "…and they don't take American Express" to drive home the point that VISA was more widely accepted. Most of our TV ads concluded with this jab at our competitor. This accomplished the dual objectives of first associating ourselves with the upscale prestige of the American Express name and then slapping it down by placing the action in a store or restaurant where they did not take the American Express card. But eventually, our own research showed that some people only remembered those last two words, and so we dropped the reference to American Express. But the slogan "VISA — It's everywhere you want to be" stayed with the company throughout my tenure at VISA.

I gave several speeches to business school audiences about VISA's marketing strategy. During those talks, I always showed the very first commercial of the VISA campaign, which featured Rosalie's Fish Food Restaurant in Marblehead, Massachusetts. Rosalie's took only VISA cards. I would then follow it up with the most recent commercial, which all the students were familiar with because they saw it regularly on TV. The uniformity of design and consistency of message was truly remarkable and invariably the students thanked me with a round of standing applause. Well, it wasn't really me that they were applauding, but our outstanding marketing and brand management team that executed the campaign flawlessly.

Many years after I left, VISA dropped the campaign for a few years. But in 2014 the company resurrected the original slogan after dropping the single word "It's." The new campaign again positioned the VISA card as being "Everywhere you want to be." I am sure that VISA paid a handsome amount of money to the ad agency for the recommendation to drop the "It's." Nothing much changed over a quarter of a century — a true rarity in band management these days.

Sponsoring the Olympics

The marketing group also focused on important sports events, such as the Olympics, to drive home the message that VISA was everywhere you wanted to be. My family and I had the pleasure to be invited by NBC, another sponsor of the Olympics, to watch the Olympic games in Barcelona and Albertville from front row seats.

These were exciting events that our kids loved to go to. It was great to see VISA as the only card accepted at these venues and it helped to cement the brand image around the world.

VISA also sponsored other sporting events, such as the U.S. Open Tennis Championships and the Champions Cup — a ski event that featured former Olympic and World Champions. Stars like Franz Klammer, Anderl Molterer, and Tamara McKinney were frequently there. These celebrities were always very popular with the ski enthusiasts and they performed like the champs that they were. VISA got lots of exposure for relatively little money.

World Cup Champion Tamara McKinney and my family ready to race at the VISA Champions Cup.

Someone on the marketing team had the bright idea that I should be the "forerunner" for the Champions Cup event held on the ski slopes at Beaver Creek, Colorado. Even President Ford was there, as he owned a house right on the ski slopes. I was to be the first skier down the mountain, with all the pros following in my trails. I tried my best. I made the first gate, but lost my balance by the second gate and then crashed ignominiously into the third gate.

With President Ford at the VISA Champions Cup in Beaver Creek

I learned my lesson and left the downhill slalom races to the real pros!

Actually, I turned my duties over to Bruno Richter, a good friend of mine from Bank of America days, who was now President of VISA Germany. Bruno was a Bavarian who had grown up on skis. He had been a member of the Washington State University ski squad and later coached the UC Berkeley ski team. He could ski with the best of them and represented VISA much better on the slopes than me.

Getting the Debit Card Off the Ground

When I came to VISA, debit cards were still in their infancy. While several trial projects had been floated, no broad acceptance had been achieved. ATM cards had met with some success, but their usage was mainly restricted to getting cash from ATM terminals. But they could not be used at merchant outlets that took only credit cards.

What was the right combination of features to unlock this important market? Wes Tallman was an experienced banker who was in charge of developing the Debit Card for VISA U.S.A. He was determined and unflagging in his efforts.

When the signature-only Debit Card met with reluctance by some bankers because a signature was fairly easy to forge, he turned to PIN-protected cards and so on. After each new iteration of the concept, Wes would hit the road and visit the member banks to solicit their views on what might work better. Eventually, he found the right combination of features: the VISA Debit Card could be used with a signature at all the merchants that accepted the regular signature-based VISA Credit Cards. At the same time, the card could also be used at ATM machines or PIN-based terminals to obtain cash from a bank account or to pay for a purchase. To accomplish that, the VISA Debit Card also carried an electronic acceptance mark, such as the PLUS or the INTERLINK symbol, which signified that the card could be used over these PIN-based networks.

To solidify our position in the market place and to obtain the necessary technology, we bought both the PLUS and the INTERLINK systems. Together, these two crucial acquisitions enabled us not only to obtain all the necessary technology, but also to get a jump on the competition in the marketplace by cobranding all the INTERLINK and PLUS cards with the VISA logo and vice versa. This started VISA Debit Card on the march towards market dominance. It was all due to Wes Tallman's determination and persistence.

Some people did not like the term "Debit Card" all that much. They thought that the use of the card might put a person further into debt. Instead, the card just debited the checking account balances in a bank account. The transaction was essentially equivalent to writing a check, and so I tried to make a modest contribution by calling the card a "VISA Check Card." Some banks liked the idea and branded their account access card as a VISA Check Card. But others stuck to the term "Debit Card." Oh well — you cannot win them all!

Fighting MasterCard

Chuck Russell made it clear to me that fighting MasterCard was to be one of my top priorities. Every year, the American Bankers Association had a special conference on credit cards where the two presidents of the rival card associations gave dueling presentations.

It was on one of those prior ABA occasions that Pete Hart, the easygoing and affable President of MasterCard, had taken on Chuck Russell. Pete said with a big grin on his face that in some countries the name VISA was very well known as the brand of a condom. Nonplused, Chuck immediately retorted to the roar of the audience: "Well, that just goes to show you that VISA is everywhere you want to be!"

My first ABA Bank Card Convention was in Dallas and I got to meet Pete Hart for the first time. Pete was a gregarious and easygoing gentleman, who had played football for Harvard College. Refined and intellectual, Pete was the polar opposite of Chuck Russell.

An excursion to the Dallas Cowboys football arena was part of the convention entertainment. I got to walk with Pete over the famed turf of the Cowboy stadium, with him expertly tossing footballs to everyone who would want to catch one. Having grown up in Germany, I had kicked many soccer balls, but I had never tossed a football in my entire life. In spite of this handicap, the two of us took a liking to each other. We ambled across the football field while chatting about the economic and financial issues of the day.

Our competing keynote speeches to the bankers' audience on the following day were civilized and respectful to each other.

Affinity Cards and the Co-Branding Boom

VISA cards were issued initially only by banks and carried only the bank's logo. But some of the banks soon found it useful to issue "*affinity cards*" with the logos of college alumni associations, sports teams and other associations on the face of the card. Nobody objected to the alumni cards, which sported a bear for the

University of California and Tommy Trojan for USC. The affinity cards helped greatly with each bank's marketing efforts as the cards catered to often fiercely loyal audiences. Affinity cards became an easy sell for the banks and also raised some money for the alumni associations or sports teams that sponsored them. The program proved to be a highly successful marketing tool in an otherwise undifferentiated marketplace. Our VISA market share grew strongly and everyone was happy. It was all for the good.

The next step was that some banks extended the affinity programs to cover airlines as well. The cardholders could earn frequent flyer miles on the cards and got to fly for free. The airlines cemented their relationships with their customers, the banks made good money and the cardholders got to fly for free. Again, everybody was happy!

But pretty soon, another innovation occurred: large corporations, such as AT&T and General Motors, issued cards that carried their own logo prominently on the front of the card next to the trademark of the issuing bank. These became known as *"co-branded cards"* because they showed two corporate logos on the plastic. Furthermore, many of these co-branded cards gave generous incentives or rebates to the cardholders. For instance, GM offered a five percent credit (two percent above a certain limit) of all charges to apply to the purchase of a new GM vehicle. That could amount to hundreds or even thousands of dollars in rebates on a new GM car. The card obviously helped to sell GM cars by building up credit balances that could be used only for the purchase of a GM vehicle. In a similar vein, AT&T offered a "free for life" feature on its "Universal Cards" that attracted a record number of new customers.

To top it all off, the highly successful co-branded cards were all issued through MasterCard. At the behest of our banks, we at VISA had instituted a "moratorium" on co-branded cards. Hopefully, this would keep these large and powerful corporations out of the credit card business and preserve this turf exclusively for the banks. But it did not work. As a result of the moratorium, our banks could not sign up co-branding partners and VISA as well as the banks lost the business. Consequently, VISA lost some market share, but it was less than one single percentage point. Given the huge success and popularity of the co-branded cards, this was no great surprise. Yet, Chuck Russell was very upset and somehow he blamed me for the slight decline in market share. In my defense, I argued that I had inherited the moratorium, which had been put in place before I worked for VISA U.S.A., but he did not accept that excuse. Consequently, our relationship became a bit more tense.

As VISA and MasterCard were both fighting for market share, our banks eventually realized that they could have signed up many co-branding partners as well. They began to recognize that they lost business due to the self-imposed moratorium on co-branded cards. The strategy to exclude our competitors had backfired! Soon, the initial reluctance to permit the largest U.S. corporations into the credit card business was overcome and both associations allowed co-branded cards to be issued. The moratorium had ended!

Nordstrom, the department store, owned its own bank and issued its own store credit cards. For a decade, Nordstrom had battled with VISA in the courts over the interchange fees that VISA charged. These interchange fees in turn influenced the fees merchants had to pay to their banks. It had not been pretty. I saw this as an opportunity to put old animosities to rest by allowing the Nordstrom Bank to issue VISA cards. It was an innovative deal that was widely hailed as path breaking. The American Banker even honored me in its September 21, 1993 issue as a "Leader of the Bank Card Business" for the successful innovation.

We had managed to level the playing field and the road was free for VISA banks to be competitive in the market place again.

Legal Wranglings With Discover Card

Bennett Katz was the General Counsel for VISA and he could argue a legal position with the best of them. One thing you could count on was that Bennett would always present you with the best possible legal case for whatever position the corporation wanted to take. He was a master at it!

In my days at the helm of VISA U.S.A., the litigation between Sears, then the issuer of the Discover Card, and VISA was grabbing the headlines. Discover was a fairly successful card issuer, but they did not have the global reach of the VISA merchant network. So, they wanted to issue cards with a VISA logo such that their cardholders could use their cards wherever VISA was accepted. In other words, Discover also wanted to be "Everywhere You Want to Be" — as the VISA slogan advertised so aptly.

Just like Nordstrom's, Sears wanted to issue its own VISA card, but VISA considered Discover, along with American Express, a direct competitor and did not permit these two rival companies to issue VISA cards. Otherwise, pretty soon there would be only one credit card organization and that would certainly arouse the ire of the anti-monopoly watchdogs of the government. In an interview with the *United States Banker* magazine I cited this as a big concern. The magazine featured a drawing of me on a surfboard on the front page of the February 1992 issue and headlined the article: "*VISA's Big Worry: Becoming a Monopoly.*"

Discover had set out on a somewhat sneaky course to enter the VISA system. They themselves probably thought that it was a brilliant strategy. They purchased a small failing industrial bank in Utah that happened to issue a few VISA cards. They bought that bank from the governmental Resolution Trust Corporation, which was charged with "resolving" the many bank and S&L failures of the 1980s. Obviously, the RTC tried to minimize the losses that would otherwise have to be covered by the taxpayers. As part of the RTC legislation, any purchaser of a failing institution would be granted all the rights that the failing bank had. In this case, that presumably meant that Discover — as the purchaser of the Utah bank — was now permitted to issue VISA cards as well.

Discover kept pretty quiet about their purchase, but they had to obtain an official approval by VISA for the design of their credit cards. So, they mailed the proposed new card design to VISA

The cover page of United States Banker Magazine

headquarters, showing the return address simply as "SFSC." A diligent employee at VISA reviewed the application and noted that the number of cards that were supposed to be issued with the new card design was to increase from something like 4,000 cards to 40 million cards. The clerk thought that this must be a typographical error. Maybe they wanted to increase their issuance from 4,000 to 14,000 or 40,000 she thought — but 40 million cards would certainly be a stretch. It would make this small-time Utah bank one of the largest VISA issuers in the country. So she called the phone number given in the application and a friendly voice answered:

"Sears Financial Service Corporation." Our employee was surprised and told her boss that apparently Sears, the owner of the Discover Card, was on the line and evidently wanted to get into the VISA business. And that's the way the ball got rolling.

VISA turned down the request because of its By-Law strictures against competitors like Discover and American Express issuing cards through the VISA system. In response, Discover sued VISA to exercise their rights under the RTC purchase agreement. Obviously, Discover argued that they should be able to enjoy all the prior rights of the Utah industrial loan company, including the right to issue VISA cards. A lower court in Utah found in favor of Discover, and VISA appealed to the U.S. Appellate Court in Denver. That's where things stood when I became President and CEO of VISA and the question was what to do next about the complex situation.

We had a VISA U.S.A. board meeting at the end of May 1993 in Cannes at the French Riviera, when the issue of what to do next was discussed. There were three basic options and each option found its group of supporters on the VISA board. The first group of directors wanted to fight it out in the courts, in spite of the fact that the initial trial court had found in favor of Discover. They realized that it was not going to be an easy fight to overturn the lower court decision. But they wanted to protect the VISA turf and keep competitors out of the system that they had built. These were the "hawks" that did not want to let Discover issue VISA cards. The second group, the "doves," wanted to settle the case and let Discover issue VISA cards, thereby opening the door to a direct competitor. And then there was a third group that could not make up its mind and wanted to wait until something else happened prior to making a decision. These were the "chickens."

After an exhaustive discussion, we counted seven "hawks" in favor of fighting it out in the courts, another seven "doves" in favor of settling the issue and then there was the "chicken" wing comprised of five undecided directors that considered it premature to make a decision. So there we were — a truly divided Board of

Directors. Given the deadlock, the board authorized me to engage in discussions with Phil Purcell, the CEO of Sears and Discover, to see whether a compromise solution acceptable to all could be found. I would have to deal with this controversial issue upon my return to the United States from France.

President Bush Talks to VISA

But not all was controversial at the 1993 Annual Meeting in Cannes. As the meeting date approached, we had started to search for a prominent keynote speaker who might stimulate the attendees and offer true insights into what was going on in the world at that time.

President George H. W. Bush had just returned to private life and in the discussions about whom we should invite, I suggested that he might be the perfect person to give the speech. Everyone agreed. I still had some connection with him from my days in Washington and I was tasked with getting the former President signed up. He was willing and agreed to come to France for the occasion.

This was his very first speech to a private audience after leaving the White House and the U.S. security apparatus swung into full action. Obviously, he was booked in the Presidential Suite at the Carlton Intercontinental Hotel overlooking the Riviera. A full complement of Secret Service security personnel was ensconced on the same floor to protect him.

A few weeks before the meeting, I received a phone call from his speechwriter. He wanted to know what the most important issues in international payments were these days, so that President Bush might address them. I told the speechwriter that all the bank executives in attendance had probably heard enough of payments problems and issues. In turn, he wanted to know what I would recommend that President Bush should talk about. I thought about it for a moment and suggested: "Why don't you tell President Bush to pick the two or three most important problems of his presidency and tell the audience how he solved these issues?" The speechwriter thought that was a great idea and hung up.

When President Bush gave his speech, he did exactly what I had suggested. He talked about the key global problems he had faced during his Presidency and how he came to the decisions to resolve these issues.

The first issue President Bush addressed was the fall of the Berlin Wall. The Berlin Wall had came down and the old Soviet Union collapsed within in the same time frame. He told the spellbound audience that he was very concerned that the military in the old Soviet Union might be upset with President Gorbachev and that there might possibly be a military coup to restore the old Soviet Union. So President Bush decided to keep quiet about this obvious victory of the free world over communism. He never gloated or stated: "We Won." Instead, he offered help to the new Russian state to overcome their economic and financial problems and to establish a more democratic system.

He then spoke about the liberation of Kuwait and why he decided not to pursue Sadam Hussein's fleeing troops all the way to Baghdad. Instead, he restrained the troops to the liberation of Kuwait alone. The international audience was spellbound and gave President Bush a thundering round of standing applause.

During the ensuing lunch, my wife Emily — herself a life-long Democrat — sat next to President Bush, essentially serving as his hostess. For over an hour he entertained her with interesting anecdotes about his life. But the main topic of conversation was "Ranger," his English springer spaniel hunting dog that he loved so much. Emily was impressed by him as a human being and might have voted for him if he had run again!

After all the debate and the divisiveness at the board meeting, I began to feel good again. Inspired by President Bush, I thought that even very difficult situations could be mastered and solved successfully.

SAGE ADVICE:
Eventually, Free Market Forces Will Prevail

26 The End Game at VISA

When I returned to San Francisco, my first priority was to get the situation with Discover Card resolved. While Discover had won the first round of their suit against VISA in a Utah court, we had appealed the case to the U.S. Court of Appeals. That court appeal was still pending. I packed my bags and travelled to Sears's headquarters in Chicago to see whether we could settle the litigation to the satisfaction and benefit of both parties.

Negotiating With Phil Purcell

Philip Purcell was working at the Sears Roebuck Corporation when they acquired the Dean Witter brokerage and wealth management firm. For many years, Sears had issued a store charge card to its customers. In 1986, Purcell turned the Sears store charge card into the Discover Card to fully leverage its business potential. That is how Sears got into the regular credit card business. When I visited Purcell in Chicago, he was the President, Chairman and CEO of Dean Witter Discover and a highly experienced business negotiator. Clearly, it was going to be a tough conversation.

Purcell had invested considerable time and money in the planned issuance of VISA cards. Rumor had it that Discover readied some 40 million VISA card solicitations after the lower court had ruled in its favor. But because VISA had appealed the case, all these solicitation letters were immobilized. Discover could not mail them and with the passage of time, they became increasingly stale and worthless. Purcell wanted to be compensated for that and asked me for $100 million in cash as well as access to the global VISA system to settle the issue. $2.50 per card was probably a reasonable expenditure to get the mailing lists ready, print the cards and envelopes and get ready for business. I figured that they had probably spent close to $100 million to get the 40 million Discover cards ready for issue. Purcell certainly thought that his request was within reason.

But $100 million was also an exorbitantly high penalty for VISA to pay — and it was money that we did not have. I told him that VISA U.S.A. had only some $40 million in capital and he wanted more than twice that amount! No problem, he countered: "You can just get that money from your member banks — they make a multiple of that amount every single year in profits!"

I could not persuade Purcell to accept a more modest payment and his hard line stance was unacceptable to me. As far as I was concerned, this was not a winner take all situation. If he wanted our permission to issue VISA cards, we were not going to pay him a penalty on top of that. He argued, of course, that the trial court had declared Discover the winner and he did not want to compromise. I also thought that his unreasonable proposal would never fly with the VISA board and politely told him that we would probably see each other in the appellate court, where our lawyers expected us to prevail.

That's where things stood when I headed to Dallas for the next meeting of the VISA U.S.A. board in August of 1993.

Chuck Russell Disappears

A few weeks before the board meeting, Chuck Russell suddenly disappeared. For a week, nobody knew where he was. I recalled his favorite dictum that if he left, nobody would find any records in his office — except for his last flight plan. While I never was absolutely certain, I assumed that he took off in his little private plane and visited the key players on the U.S. Board — something he had done at crucial times before. There were no airline tickets to be bought and nobody would know. He would leave no tracks.

When Chuck returned, he pretty much gave me the cold shoulder. I sensed that something was up.

The Board Meets in Dallas

I was ready to enter the boardroom at the Four Seasons Hotel in Las Colinas near the Dallas-Fort Worth Airport for the August 1993 VISA U.S.A. board meeting. At that very moment, Chuck Russell intercepted me. He asked Victor Dahir, the company's CFO, and me to wait for a few moments outside. The board wanted to meet in executive session first, Chuck explained. So Vic and I settled down in the seating area just outside the main boardroom.

Ten minutes passed, then twenty, then half an hour. With the passage of time I became increasingly nervous that something unusual was in the works. An executive session had never lasted that long!

There had been frequent rumors that Chuck Russell might want to resign or that the board was unhappy with him because of the somewhat bumpy introduction of the new electronic payment system that the international systems group was responsible for. But nothing concrete ever happened.

After half an hour of waiting, I said to Vic: "I wonder whether Russell is leaving...?" Vic just looked at me. Then I got more apprehensive and said to him: "Or maybe they are plotting something against me..." Vic just shook his head: "No way!"

Finally, the boardroom doors opened and Chuck called us in. The board meeting began, the minutes for the previous meeting were approved and the meeting took its regular course. I gave my presentation regarding the Discover card negotiations. I told the board that Purcell was unyielding and that I recommended that we pursue the litigation in the appellate court. Everyone agreed. The vote was unanimous in favor of my recommendation. That was a load off my shoulders, although the outcome of that litigation was certainly not assured. The rest of the board meeting was fairly routine and uneventful.

After the board meeting concluded, Chuck Russell came to me and said that he wanted to see me in my room. I agreed.

Stabbed in the Back

When Russell entered my room upstairs, he was visibly nervous, fidgeting with his fingers. "The Board would like you to offer your resignation!" he opened up to my great surprise. "Why?" I enquired incredulously. "Ohh, it's just time for a change!" I pressed him for the real reason. After some evasion, he finally said: "A square peg just does not fit into a round hole!" I was astonished and flabbergasted, but that was all he could offer.

I was totally dumbfounded. I thought I had resolved the Discover Card issue to the full satisfaction of the board. At least no one had spoken up against my proposal to reject the $100 million demand by Purcell and to pursue the matter in the courts. The vote had been unanimous in favor of my recommendation.

But then I reflected on Chuck's secret trip and the executive session called by him and things became clearer to me. He wanted to get rid of me and he had succeeded.

There was not much to be done. He had been able to persuade the Board and that was that.

Russell called Linda Baker, our Public Relations Director, into the room and she had a press release ready for publication. The release stated that I had voluntarily resigned my position as President and CEO. Russell's initial favorite candidate, Carl Pascarella, was to be my successor.

"With Visa well ahead in the debit card race and the overall market leader in credit cards, now is the appropriate time for me to explore several new personal and professional opportunities," I was quoted as saying in the press release.

Russell added: "Bob has brought his breadth of experience in the areas of finance and economics to Visa. His contributions have been noteworthy, not only in the United States, but also in the international arena. We thank Bob for his dedication and efforts and will miss his involvement in the business." Hmm, if he felt like that, why did he want me to leave?

It had all been carefully pre-planned by Russell. He was still a pretty smooth back-room operator, I thought.

I packed my bags and caught the next flight back to San Francisco. When I got home, I was alone in our house. There was nobody to share my grief as my wife Emily had accompanied our daughter Kimberly to her first day of college at Princeton University. When I called them with the bad news, my daughter got very worried and asked: "Dad, do I now have to quit Princeton because we can no longer afford to pay for the tuition?" I assured her that we had enough money and that she should start her studies. While there was joy on the East Coast about her new beginnings at Princeton, my mood on the West Coast was not so happy about the abrupt end to my career at VISA!

The Press is Incredulous

The news hit the front pages of the financial services press on the next day. The *American Banker* headline on September 1, 1993 read: "Visa President Quits; Top-Level Rift Seen." The article stated that the bankcard industry had been caught by surprise and noted that I had been in line to succeed Chuck Russell for the top job at VISA International.

The article also quoted unnamed sources as saying: "Something went very wrong in the Heller-Russell relationship after the annual board meeting in Cannes, France.... Heller did not know it was coming. He walked into the boardroom and there it was."

Various theories were offered by the paper: that the board did not want to take an aggressive stance against MasterCard; that there had been a slight drop in market share last year due to AT&T issuing all its new co-branded cards under the MasterCard logo; and that the board was displeased with VISA's defense of the Discover card suit — which we eventually would win in the

AN BANKER

Inesday, September 1, 1995   158th year

lution Fear irting Stock Acquirers

By RICHARD LAYNE

estors are battering the prices of active and poten- ink acquirers this quarter. the past two months, the ; of banks that have done e transactions this year are average of 1.9%, according x-Pitt Kelton, an invest- banking firm. res of banks perceived as buyers are down an aver- 1.6% in the two months.

Others Gain

contrast, less likely ac- s and less plausible acqui- candidates are up 6% in ist two months. Fox-Pitt n said.

firm said merger activity icked up since June 30, ig investors to focus on the

Visa President Quits; Top-Level Rift Seen

By STEPHEN KLEEGE

H. Robert Heller abruptly an- nounced his resignation late Monday from the presidency of Visa U.S.A. Inc.

The news, which came out of a board meeting in Dallas, caught the bank card industry by surprise. It fueled talk of a fall- ing-out between Mr. Heller and Charles T. Russell, the president of Visa International.

Visa moved Carl Pascarella, president of Visa's Asia-Pacific region, into Mr. Heller's former post at the domestic Visa corpo- ration.

Mr. Heller, who held both in- ternational and domestic jobs since arriving at Visa in 1989 from the Federal Reserve Board of Governors, was in line to suc- ceed Mr. Russell. The latter is 63 but has given no indication of his retirement plans.

Chuck Gathard

H. Robert Heller
Was U.S. chief since '91

ship" after the annual board meeting in Cannes, France, in early summer, one source said. "Heller didn't know it was com- ing. He walked into the board- room and there it was."

Courtesy of *American Banker*

appellate court. But the paper also noted that we had achieved a 70 percent market share in the debit card business and that we built public awareness of the VISA brand to an all-time high. All strong positives!

The American Banker also pointed at the revolving door under Russell, where one executive followed another in short succession and noted "Mr. Russell has been less successful at establishing a succession among the regional presidents and corporate staff." That was certainly true, but it also was a considerable understatement of the problem.

The *Nilson Report*, a well-known card industry newsletter, came to my defense and argued that I was "hemmed in by a board of directors representing thousands of members and concerned about competing too hard against MasterCard." The newsletter correctly argued: ."..as a leader of an association, you have to restrain yourself from acting as you would as a head of a private company."

A Real Street Fighter Takes Over

A few weeks later, on October 7, the venerable *New York Times* wrote an article about Carl Pascarella, Chuck Russell's chosen successor at VISA U.S.A. Noting that Pascarella was the third person to hold the job in less than four years, the paper commented: "Some of the turnover may stem from the difficulties of the 63-year-old Charles T. Russell, the president of Visa International, the parent organization, to settle on a successor."

The Times article went into the reasons why Russell wanted to have Carl Pascarella on board now and quoted him as saying: "Carl is a real street fighter, an aggressive marketer with unbelievable energy. You will see lots of changes." The Times apparently could not believe what they had heard Russell say and highlighted the article with a prominent subheading that read: "The No. 1 credit card looks for inspiration from a 'street fighter'." The sarcasm of the Times said it all!

The Times also quoted Russell as giving me a little kick in my pants by saying: "If we've been remiss over the last two or three years, it has been because of a lack of focus. We've run off and chased rabbits." I was gratified that one of these little rabbits, the VISA Check or Debit Card, turned into a market-dominating success story.

In any case, upon reflection, it was good to be no longer surrounded by "real street fighters." That was neither my style nor my professional aspiration.

The End of Chuck Russell

A few weeks after the Dallas board meeting, Chuck Russell asked me to have lunch with him at the *Bankers Club* on top of the Bank of America's headquarter building in downtown San Francisco. We needed to talk about coming to an agreement on my "departure package" from VISA and to settle several open issues regarding my final compensation.

I had been a member of the exclusive Bankers Club when I worked for Bank of America and had continued my membership in the club while I was at VISA. I used the club frequently to entertain out-of-town visitors, who found it more convenient to meet in San Francisco rather than having to travel to the VISA offices on the Peninsula.

Chuck had a rather forlorn look on his face when he showed up at the club. During lunch, he told me with a sad face: "You do not know this, but the Board has asked for my resignation as well. I am to retire from the company by the end of the year!" I was thunderstruck and totally surprised. So, he had tried to get rid of me and the Board got rid of him as well! I felt that justice had prevailed.

Just a few weeks later, on October 28, 1993, the *Financial Times* headlined its story on Russell's departure: "Visa head dethroned by big card issuers."

His machinations against me had not paid off for him. He was out as well — something that he had not at all expected.

I was reminded of one of the favorite sayings of my grandmother: "*Wer anderen eine Grube gräbt, fällt selbst hinein!*" Which translates literally into: "If you dig a ditch to entrap others, you will fall into it yourself!" Or in plain English: "Harm set, harm get!" I thought it fit the situation perfectly!

A few years after Chuck Russell retired, he took a spin on one of his beloved Harley Davidson motorcycles. Unfortunately, he crashed and killed himself. That was the sad end of Chuck Russell.

The Legal Aftermath

Just as I had expected, VISA U.S.A. won its appeal against Discover in the higher court and the U.S. Supreme Court let the judgment of the appellate court stand. VISA had won! My recommendation that we should fight it out in the courts was vindicated.

But that was about the last victory for VISA in the courts. Discover started a new lawsuit against VISA and MasterCard on antitrust grounds, demanding $18 billion for blocking the banks from issuing its Discover cards. This was the exact reverse of the previous lawsuit that we had won. The original suit was about Discover being allowed to issue VISA cards. The new lawsuit was about the VISA and MasterCard member banks not being allowed to issue Discover cards. On the last day before the trial in 2008, the parties settled. VISA agreed to pay $1.9 billion and MasterCard $900 million to Discover Financial Services. Phil Purcell's successors at Discover collected more money from VISA than Purcell could have ever dreamed of!

But that was not all. In 2007, VISA settled a similar lawsuit brought by American Express for over $2 billion.

The U.S. retail merchants also sued VISA and MasterCard about "excessive" debit card fees. That case was settled with VISA ponying up $2 billion to the retailers and agreeing to reduce its future fees considerably.

In its first Annual Report after converting the privately held VISA association into a publicly owned stock company, the newly formed VISA Inc. took 20 pages to disclose all the then pending litigation. The report listed the already mentioned Discover suit, the American Express litigation, the Interchange litigation, a class action lawsuit by a Mr. Attridge, the Multidistrict or Animal Land Litigation, the Retailers Litigation, the Opt-Out Case, the Indirect Purchase Litigation, the Department of Justice Antitrust Case, the Settlement Service Litigation, the New Zealand Interchange Fee Litigation, the Currency Conversion class action suit, the Parke class action suit, the ATM Litigation, the District of Columbia

Litigation, the AAA Antiques Lawsuit, the Hill Country Customs Cycle suit, the Venezuela Interchange Proceedings, the Cryptography Research lawsuit, Vale Canjeable, Starpay, PrivaSys, as well as various other intellectual property lawsuits.

VISA was turning into a veritable cash machine for its competitors and customers!

If VISA had been a law firm, it would have been a very busy and profitable enterprise indeed. Many of these lawsuits were the result of VISA's hardball tactics in the marketplace and the attempt to build a monopolistic enterprise on behalf of its banks that could extract high profits — just like I had feared. In addition to the billions of dollars already paid out, VISA potentially was on the hook for many more billions of dollars.

The street fighters were out in full force! But the litigation expenses showed that this was indeed an expensive way to run a company.

SAGE ADVICE:
The Higher the Mountains, the Deeper the Valleys
  Free After President Richard Nixon

27 Fair Isaac, the Scoring King

A few weeks after I departed from VISA, I got a call from Carolyn Worth, a good friend of our family who was a partner at the consulting firm KPMG. She wanted to know whether I would be interested in a board position at Fair, Isaac and Company in San Rafael near our home. I told her that I would be delighted to explore the opportunity. She arranged for a meeting with Bill Fair, the co-founder of the company.

While most people have not heard of Fair Isaac, Fair Isaac knows a lot about most Americans. Fair Isaac develops the algorithms that produce the ubiquitous FICO credit scores that provide a relative risk measure that banks and other credit grantors use to evaluate the creditworthiness of their customers. The FICO score is a key determinant of whether a person will qualify for a mortgage, a credit card, a car loan or any other type of credit. Specialized scoring systems are also used to determine how much interest the customers are asked to pay for their loans and how much they can borrow.

Nowadays, FICO scores and analytical tools are found in virtually all industries where Big Data need to be analyzed: banking, insurance, health care, retail, telecom, utilities and many more. Additional scoring systems produced by the company are not only used for credit decisions, but also to detect fraud, to decide which customers to solicit, which marketing offers to send to whom and also for general customer account management. FICO scores are the most ubiquitous credit scores in the world, with over 100 billion sold until now. That amounts to more than seven scores for each person living on earth!

Meeting the Founder Bill Fair

Bill Fair met with me at a small Italian garden restaurant not far away from my home in Marin County. He was a perfect gentleman and a congenial host. Soft spoken and attentive, he was the exact opposite of some of the folks that I had worked with in recent years.

Bill Fair, whose background was in engineering, founded the company in 1956 together with Earl Isaac, an expert mathematician. Tenacious and driven by a mission to excel, he built the company into the most prominent credit scoring company in the world. The company patiently built its customer base by offering ever improving products that helped the client companies make better decisions through data analysis.

Many of the senior officers of Fair Isaac had been with the company for a very long time. The same was true for the Board of Directors. Bob Oliver, a dean at the College of Engineering at the University of California, Berkeley, was the link that connected many of them. Bob had served as the Chairman of the Operations Research Department and was an expert in complex prediction models. He loved to tackle intricate mathematical problems such as calculating the probability of a mid-air collision or a nuclear reactor blow-up.

Bob Oliver and Bill Fair had been friends for a long time and played tennis together on a regular basis. I am sure that their tennis matches were nothing but calculations of the likelihood of getting a second serve in or estimating the chance of a better score by rushing the net.

From his perch at the university, Bob Oliver fed a steady stream of outstanding operations research and computer science students to Bill Fair and his corporation. Larry Rosenberger and Bob Sanderson were among the best of them. Larry became the long-time Director of Research and eventually the President and

CEO, and Bob Sanderson served for many years as Chief Operating Officer of the company. Both of them were FICO lifers and never worked for any other corporation. The contrast to VISA, with its ever-churning executive suite staff was pretty revealing.

Bill Fair believed that if you treated your staff well, they would pay you back with loyalty and hard work. Everybody in the company was allowed to take a day off to work on an innovative pet project of his or her own choosing. And if the project turned out to be marketable, the originator would be put in charge of the new product. That's the way Fair Isaac grew innovative solutions as well as committed managers.

Most important of all, Bill Fair had inculcated the entire company with a very collegial atmosphere. Everyone respected all colleagues regardless of whether they were a senior executive or a junior staffer.

When Bill Fair offered me a position on the Board of Directors of Fair, Isaac and Company, I was happy to accept. But one board position did not suffice to pay all my bills.

Consulting Gigs

Ed Jensen, who had been Vice Chairman of U.S. Bancorp in Portland and served for several years as a VISA director, was selected to succeed Russell as President and CEO of VISA International. Soon thereafter, Ed offered me a job as a consultant to VISA. I was to assess the regulatory climate in the main countries that VISA was operating in and to ascertain what potential threats to the company's franchise might arise. I was to pay particular attention to the activities of the Bank for International Settlements in Basel, Switzerland. The central bankers and regulators of the key countries around the world met there on a regular basis and tried to come up with new rules that would make banks and the international payments system a safer place.

I quickly formed a new company and named it the "*International Payments Institute*" in the hope of maybe building it into a larger consulting enterprise. I enjoyed the new assignment at VISA as it got me back to my old area of expertise in supervision and regulation. It also allowed me to be active in the international arena again. The project gave me the use of an office at VISA headquarters and I was able to link up with some of my old friends there. Ed Jensen liked the final report that I delivered to him and I was gratified. Finally, VISA International had an experienced banker and congenial leader at the helm.

I branched out and looked for other consulting assignments. Together with Dick Griffith, a friend from my days at Bank of America, I started to consult for various other companies. Risk management was in its infancy in those days and together we teamed up with Risk Management Technologies, a company headquartered in Berkeley, to offer pioneering risk management software to financial institutions. David LaCross, another Bank of America alum, had founded RMT a few years earlier and he now was its President and CEO.

Often we worked in conjunction with Ernst & Young, the professional services and accounting firm, and offered comprehensive risk management solutions to their clients. We had several interesting assignments, but I did not find the uneven workflow very much to my liking. There would be long periods with little to do. On those occasions, we would swing into a marketing mode, trying to sign up new clients. Then we had to wait for a couple of weeks or even months to get a decision on our proposal. If we were successful, a period of intensive work effort would follow, where nothing ever happened fast enough. The clients wanted to have their projects finished as soon as possible. Once the assignment was completed, the cycle would repeat itself. We were again in marketing mode looking for the next project. What bothered me most was that we did not get to see the full results of our efforts after we turned the project over to the client. At that moment, it became the client company's responsibility to implement the project or to run the software that we had installed.

I learned that I did not like to parachute into a company on a consulting basis and then leave again after just a few months.

Instead, I preferred to work more steadily and be involved on a longer-term basis. I wanted to be able see the small seedlings that we had planted grow into adult trees and eventually reap the fruits of our labor. Obviously, that would involve a long-term relationship.

Nevertheless, one day the managers at Ernst & Young asked me whether I wanted to join the company on a permanent basis. Did I want to become a Principal or a Partner in the firm? While the offer was attractive, there was one major catch: the policies of Ernst & Young did not allow for their Partners and Principals to have any regular connections to other corporations. That included serving on the board of directors of another company. It was all in or out as far as Ernst & Young was concerned. It was decision time for me!

Joining Fair Isaac

I went to see Larry Rosenberger, who had become the President and CEO of Fair Isaac after Bill Fair stepped back from his day-to-day responsibilities while remaining as Chairman of the Board. If Bill Fair was the father of credit scoring, Larry was the architect of optimal decision-making systems that helped banks and other institutions run their account management processes in an efficient fashion.

For instance, if a credit card customer was close to his credit limit or even exceeded it, how should the bank react? Should the bank see this as a sign that the person was probably overextended and freeze his credit line or should the bank recognize this as an opportunity to offer a larger — and hopefully more profitable — credit line to the customer? Distinguishing between these two situations was not at all obvious and could easily take up an hour or more time for a credit analyst. Larry devised a software decision-making solution that came up with the answer to the problem in a fraction of a second — and in addition made a decision as to how large a credit line increase should be offered to the client. The software was an instant success in the credit card industry and was later applied successfully to many other problems in banking, insurance, health care and other fields. As a reward for his outstanding job as Director of Research, Larry was rewarded with the overall leadership role of the corporation as President and CEO.

When I told Larry that I might have to resign from the Fair Isaac board if I took the job with Ernst & Young, he countered: "Why don't you stay on our Board and join the Fair Isaac staff on a full-time basis?" I had not expected a job offer to result from my resignation forewarning, but I was certainly flattered. Fair Isaac offered many analytic challenges and provided a stimulating work environment with many Ph.D.'s on its staff. When I was at Bank of America, I had built a "Debt Service Capacity Index," that evaluated the capacity of a country to serve its external debt with the help of fairly sophisticated statistical techniques. The analysts at Fair Isaac applied similar methods to the analysis of consumer debt issues. While the scale of the problem was dramatically different, the analytic approach was pretty much the same.

The company that Bill Fair had molded was also a most congenial workplace. Consistently, the Fair Isaac Company scored at the top of the "Best Places to Work in the San Francisco Bay Area." Furthermore, it was located in San Rafael, just a short distance away from my home. Compared to VISA, my commute was cut in half. It took me only a very short time to think about the proposal and I happily accepted.

A German Venture

Larry put me in charge of joint ventures and my initial focus was the Informa Corporation in Germany. Fair Isaac had formed a joint venture with two German partners and the company's mission was to penetrate the German market for scoring solutions. Germany often presented an impenetrable wall to outsiders who tried to do business in the country. This was due to cultural as well as business reasons. As a German native, it was easier for me to overcome these often invisible barriers. Not only did I speak the language fluently, but I also liked the local beer and the bratwurst.

One of our partners, Schober Marketing, owned the largest privately owned database in Germany. As part of the database, Schober had taken a picture of every single house in Germany — long before Google was founded and essentially copied this idea. Schober knew where every German lived, what car he drove and whether the family owned a dog or a cat. The combination of Fair Isaac with its analytic tools and Schober with its huge database provided many interesting business opportunities.

For me, the Informa joint venture also gave a welcome opportunity to travel a few times a year to Germany and to reconnect with old friends there.

Buying Risk Management Technologies

Being in charge of joint ventures also allowed me to look at potential business partners for Fair Isaac. I had worked successfully with David LaCross at Risk Management Technologies and I thought that their product offerings provided the perfect complement to Fair Isaac's solutions.

While Fair Isaac's products focused on the risk presented by an individual loan, RMT offered an enterprise-wide evaluation of the risk inherent in a bank's entire loan portfolio. To calculate the relevant risk parameters, the RMT model used Monte Carlo Methods that computed the so-called "value-at-risk" in a portfolio. Its simulations used hundreds and even thousands of random events to estimate the probability of a loss and could state with 99 percent accuracy how large the loss inherent in the overall loan portfolio of a bank might be.

Clearly, this methodology could also be useful to calculate the intrinsic risk of a credit card portfolio. I thought that our banks would love to be able to calculate these portfolio risk parameters. Both the bank's Chief Financial Officer as well as the credit card portfolio manager should be vitally interested in these data.

When Dave LaCross told me that he was looking for capital to further expand his business, I suggested that he sell the company to Fair Isaac instead. Not only would he be able to have access to a much larger pool of capital, but the Fair Isaac marketing and sales department would also be able to open many new doors for RMT. It looked to both of us like a marriage made in heaven. On a paper napkin in a Thai restaurant in Berkeley, we sketched the outlines of a potential deal.

After fleshing out the suggested transaction, I took the proposal to Larry Rosenberger, the CEO of Fair Isaac. The two of us spent a lot of time looking at the pros and cons of the acquisition. Eventually, we took the project to the Board of Directors for approval. Both of us thought that the price demanded by Dave LaCross was pretty hefty, but one of the board members encouraged us by saying that in his experience, a good acquisition was worth paying for and that paying a bit too much would not make a huge difference in the end.

The Board approved the transaction unanimously. In the press release Larry Rosenberger commented: "RMT is also in the business of helping companies make better decisions through data. Our two companies are well matched with regard to business purpose, the clients we serve and corporate culture." I added: "Together we plan to pioneer new financial risk management techniques. Fair, Isaac's current offerings focus largely on individual credit and account management decisions, while RMT's technology is used by CFOs and other financial managers to tackle enterprise-wide risk management. Together we can create the first integrated risk management solutions that range from retail-level decision-making to overall corporate strategy."

The acquisition seemed like the perfect match for Fair Isaac. The *American Banker* agreed and cited our transaction as one of the "ten most innovative deals of the year" in 1997.

But soon, it became clear that the acquisition of RMT was running into major difficulties with its integration into the mother company. Fair Isaac prided itself in holding the managers responsible for the success of their own units. While the company had a powerful sales organization that touched almost every major bank in the United States at the retail or credit card manager level, the salespeople did not have many contacts at the CFO or CEO level. Instead, their contacts tended to be with the head of the credit card, auto loan or mortgage division. The domestic salespeople had ambitious sales targets to meet and for them calling on the CFO sometimes represented a distraction from their own sales goals and took them out of their comfort zone.

Some people inside Fair Isaac also sensed that the managers of the credit card divisions in the customer banks were not necessarily eager to afford the CFO a detailed independent view into their operations. The divisional chiefs preferred that all the information given to the boss would originate with them, so that they had complete control over the analysis provided. Hence, they were not necessarily our allies in selling the RMT product to their boss.

While Larry and I had hoped that the integration of RMT into the Fair Isaac mother company would be an easy task, in practice it proved to be a difficult objective to achieve. While we made some progress in selling RMT products on the international side, it was a bridge too far in the domestic arena. Eventually, the RMT effort fizzled and after a new CEO took over at Fair Isaac, he quickly killed the RMT project. He had not done the acquisition and thus was not held to account for its success or failure.

Changing of the Guard

While credit scoring was the original core competency of Fair Isaac, Larry Rosenberger had significantly broadened the product spectrum by adding the highly successful account management tools. But by 1999, almost all the company's revenue still came from products and services aimed at the retail level of financial services companies. The future growth potential in that market seemed to be limited, especially as compared to other markets that could benefit from Fair Isaac's data analysis expertise.

The question was: what next? What products would provide for the next doubling of Fair Isaac's revenues? Eventually, the Board of Directors thought that a new hand at the helm was needed. They also wanted a person who could expand the company's vision and shake up the somewhat laid-back culture of Fair Isaac.

The Board turned to Tom Grudnowski, a long-term Andersen consultant, who was personally known to some of the board members. Tom was a dynamic guy who plunged into his work with gusto.

Just a few days after he joined the company, I took him to the San Francisco Yacht Club, where I was a member. With us was Pete McCorkell, the company's general counsel, who was also an accomplished sailor. Tom was feeling his oats as a freshly baked CEO and as we entered the venerable yacht club he announced: "I am feeling great — I need to get laid tonight!" I thought: "Oh my, not another street fighter!"

As it turned out, Tom could be an enthusiastic leader. But after assembling a new team for a task that he considered important, he quickly lost interest again and then turned to another project. The old team was soon abandoned and the task forgotten. Perhaps it was his training and experience as a consultant that showed through. In that role, he had to assemble a new team for each assignment, focus on achieving results quickly and then turn to a new project. And he had to do that again and again. It was precisely what I had not liked during my short stint as a consultant myself and it was a corporate culture that I did not appreciate.

Quickly, the entire senior team at Fair Isaac beat a path to the exit doors. Some did not like the relentless pressure to book more sales. For others, it was a question of the integrity of the leadership — or lack thereof.

After a while, only Larry Rosenberger and I were left from the original management team. Larry, who was totally devoted to Fair Isaac, was asked to head up research and development, his old bailiwick and the very heart of the organization. He buckled down and kept his nose to the grindstone. Given the respect that he enjoyed among the employees and the customers, he was untouchable — even by the new CEO.

Eventually, I decided to follow the example of the other senior executives and looked for the exit doors. But many of the stock options that I had received when I joined the company had not yet vested. I did not want to walk away from the considerable value that was to be mine, if I would only stick around a bit longer.

Sensing that Grudnowski also preferred to see me leave, I approached him and said: "Tom, I am nearing retirement age, but I am not quite there yet. In Germany, there is a status called *Pre-Retirement* that is often granted to people in my position." He wanted to know what that entailed. I told him it meant that I would be on a reduced salary, but would keep my benefits, including my rights to the soon-to-be-vested stock options. In addition, I would mentor other people and work on special projects that he could assign to me. Tom's reaction was swift: "That sounds great to me! Don't call me — I'll call you!" That was just what I had hoped for and Tom never called.

Many years later, Tom Grudnowski had long ago sailed into the sunset, but Larry Rosenberger was still at the company. He was now a *Senior Research Fellow* — an honor accorded only to him in the company's entire history. At the fortieth anniversary celebration of him joining the company, someone asked him: "Who was the most difficult boss that you ever worked for?" Larry was a bit embarrassed, but he responded: "Tom!" The next question was: "And who was your best boss?" "Bill Fair" was his obvious answer that was drowned out by the applause of the entire staff assembled for the festive occasion.

SAGE ADVICE:
One Bad Apple Can Ruin an Entire Fine Company

28 Management and Leadership

Leadership in Action

I joined the International Monetary Fund in the early 1970s, just as the existing international monetary system was falling apart. Oil prices were soaring, inflation was out of control, payments imbalances were increasing and everyone was worried about the need to recycle the increasing volume of Petrodollars coursing through the world economy.

The United States was forced to abandon its gold peg. As a result, the system of fixed exchange rates, which had provided a framework for international financial stability since World War II, broke down.

The world financial system had lost its anchor, and exchange rates were fluctuating wildly. Many people worried that chaos in international financial markets might result.

Quite a few discussions by the Board of Directors of the IMF were concerned with the future of the international monetary system and the role of the organization itself. Given the seriousness of the situation, these board meetings were always very decorous and sober affairs. As a Division Chief of the organization, I was privileged to attend all meetings of the board.

In addition, various international working groups had been formed and they reported regularly to the board of the IMF on their results. Many ideas and concepts were proposed and again abandoned. While there was much debate, no firm concepts and proposals had yet crystallized. Instead, the situation was still very fluid and even highly unrealistic ideas were considered and debated.

Through it all, the Managing Director of the IMF, Johannes Witteveen, presided at these discussions. He was surrounded by some twenty Executive Directors representing the various constituencies from around the world. On many occasions I had the opportunity to sit there and listen as the Board debated various proposals, alternative exchange rate regimes and the role of the dollar as a key currency. The Board also deliberated about the creation of *Special Drawing Rights* by the IMF and whether these SDRs might, could, would, or should replace the dollar as the central reserve asset of the international monetary system.

The Executive Director of the United States would present one viewpoint and the French ED would counter with an opposing position. The Iranian director might worry about how to invest all the money flowing into the oil-rich Middle Eastern countries, while the Brazilian ED was concerned about too much money in the world economy further exacerbating his country's own inflation worries. And, inevitably, the African ED fretted about not having any money at all to pay for badly needed imports.

Short-term concerns about how to manage current account imbalances often were in conflict with the desire to build a new long-term framework for the international financial system. To me, the discussions represented an incredibly diverse and complex set of options and opinions, if not a total cacophony.

After everybody around the table had had an opportunity to speak, there usually was total silence. I wondered how the Managing Director, whose obligation it was to summarize the results of the discussions, might arrive at a coherent conclusion.

And then, Mr. Witteveen, the former Finance Minister of the Netherlands and now the leader of the IMF, went to work. He would thank the participants profusely for their valuable contributions to the debate and laud their interest in the complex subject matter. He praised them for the frank and open discussion.

Then, somewhat tentatively and with a quiet voice, he would intimate that he thought that the discussion provided common ground and that he sensed that a consensus had emerged.

Consensus? I asked myself. I had only heard a multitude of diverse and often conflicting viewpoints. There had been a lot of discord and precious little agreement. Few had agreed with the views of the other delegates.

But Mr. Witteveen saw things differently. He would quote the statement of one of the Executive Directors and then another. Then, he summarized the views of a third participant in the debate and added a nuance presented by someone else. He would carefully build upon one element from one speech and then add a different idea from another commentator. Eventually, he assembled a finely detailed summary and conclusion. Suddenly, the entire full picture emerged like a vision before the eyes of the audience. It was like assembling a beautiful mosaic out of a random pile of tiny and differently colored stones.

Then, he would triumphantly announce that the Board had found common ground and reached a consensus! Quickly, he asked the directors for their consent to what he had just outlined. Of course, everyone was pleased by the compliments that he had paid to them and happy about having some of their ideas praised in public. They contentedly agreed to the vision presented. No formal votes were taken, the staff was tasked with working out the details and the discussion was concluded. Session closed! Mission accomplished!

I was stunned. The Managing Director had turned what appeared to me as an expression of diverse and often contradictory viewpoints into a coherent vision that everybody could agree to.

What I had just witnessed — not just once, but time and time again — was a superb demonstration of leadership that I will never forget.

Management and Leadership

Both leadership and management skills are essential attributes of persons at the top of a corporation or a government entity. But clearly, they are not the same.

Leadership has been with us since time immemorial. While tribal leaders were often chosen from those most accomplished in battle, in other societies leaders were selected on the basis of ancestry, accomplishment, or political acumen. Some leaders inherited their positions. In a few primitive societies the "Big Man" was selected on the basis of weight — undoubtedly, a sign of success in a subsistence economy.

Some of the most successful and enduring organizational structures were developed in ancient Greece and Rome over 2,000 years ago and they have existed ever since. The Roman armies of Julius Caesar and Augustus were early examples of a tight command-and-control structure, with clearly defined authority flowing down through the organization. Loyalty was expected and the penalties for disobedience were swift, sure and severe. The Romans conquered much of the world known to them and they successfully used their command-and-control managerial structure to rule over many different peoples.

During the industrial revolution, this managerial structure was adapted to the new requirements of the industrial age. Command-and-control structures were used to direct large numbers of generally unskilled workers to perform repetitive tasks, such as assembling an automobile or a radio. The modern corporation with a chief executive at its helm was born. These private companies evolved into structures that would eventually span the entire globe.

In all organizations, leaders are expected to lead. Integrity, consistency, and decisiveness are among the most important traits that these leaders should possess in order to be successful — both inside and outside of the organization. It is also generally recognized that the most effective leaders are those that are able to articulate a vision that people can understand, respect and emulate. Creating such a visionary image makes it possible to lead others without tight control. The vision creates not only a passion about the commonly shared goals, but also obviates the need for micromanagement by enabling the followers to make consistent decisions within the framework of the overall vision. This is a very important point, because the overall grand vision not only guides the staff, but also will also energize the workers and inspire them at an emotional or even spiritual level.

We can all think of visionary leaders who caused their people to achieve lofty goals — and often against great odds. In the public arena, names like Caesar, Napoleon, George Washington, Abraham Lincoln, and Winston Churchill come to mind.

It is ironic that visionary leaders may also create such a strong dependency among their followers that the individuals cease to question the goals and often also the methods to achieve them. Thinking back in history, it is not too difficult to come up with examples of such leaders, whose grandiose, but ill-fated ideas led their followers to ultimate disaster and ruin, while causing the death of millions. Adolf Hitler, Emperor Hirohito, Mao and Stalin stand out among many others.

Nevertheless, it is clear that large groups of people have to be managed if they are to achieve a common purpose or a desirable goal. Without such management, individual members of the group may work at cross-purposes, wasting their time and effort and as a result accomplish little.

An inspired visionary will provide leadership, while a manager tends to be focused on the development of a detailed plan and its execution. Thus, a manager is often a process-oriented administrator, while the leader focuses on innovation rather than planning the specific actions to be taken.

Managers are good at execution, while leaders excel at inspiration.

A manager works on doing things right, while a leader focuses on doing the right things.

Leaders tend to take risks, while managers like to avoid risk.

Managers often tend to develop and rely on systems. They

install new technology and control mechanisms on which they can rely to get things done and to keep processes on track.

True leaders will focus on finding the right people to get their goals accomplished. They will inspire trust in their people. Indeed, they will often refer to them as their colleagues, while managers think of them as employees or staff that they need to control.

Leaders are originators, while managers tend to be imitators and institute "best practices" management models that are designed to emulate what others have already developed. While there clearly is room for learning from the experience of others, just following the fellow in front of you will never get you to lead the parade. Indeed, some managers are so averse to innovation that they refer to leading companies as being on the "bleeding edge," something to be avoided at all costs.

Leaders show originality, while managers will copy and adapt. If a good leader does his job correctly, others will follow him voluntarily and will often ignore the entire managerial structure between the leader and themselves.

The Peter Principle at Work

In many top-down management structures it is difficult to groom future leaders. The key reason why it is difficult to groom effective leaders is that the managerial talents required to rise in the organization are fundamentally different from those of a true leader. The famous *"Peter Principle"* postulates that in any bureaucracy, people will rise to the level of their own incompetence. This is certainly not an effective way to select a visionary leader!

Many organizations try to overcome these natural difficulties through the creation of a formal mentoring or leadership training program. But even here we find that this training function is often outsourced to universities or other institutions known for their leadership-training programs. It may require super-human idealism to train your own successor when you still want to remain at the helm for a few years. The degree of unselfishness required to devote much effort to such an intensive mentoring effort is not found in many people — especially in leaders who may envision themselves as totally unique and as irreplaceable.

Modern Leadership Structures

International organizations generally have to rely on their sovereign member countries to implement the vision of the organization. These countries are independent sovereigns not under direct control of the leadership of the organization. It is particularly difficult to find effective leaders for international organizations who have the talent to be consensus builders for the organization as a whole.

Interestingly enough, this general management problem is also becoming more and more relevant to the modern corporation. When one looks across the corporate landscape, one recognizes more and more organizations that rely on a cooperative, consensus-driven leadership structure. What has changed in the world to bring about this change in organizational structure? I believe it is the emergence of the knowledge worker as well as the development of decentralized information systems that have brought about this development.

Modern CEOs can no longer just tell their employees which screw they have to tighten or which component they have to install. Instead, they have to rely upon the independent and self-directed actions of a multitude of knowledge workers to accomplish the corporate objectives. Examples of such important, and largely independent, knowledge workers can be found in many different industries: there is the molecular biologist, who works on the development of the next life-saving drug; there is the independently working engineer, who may bring about the latest revolution in nano-technology; and there is the foreign exchange or bond trader who instantly adjusts the bank's portfolio position in reaction to breaking news. Then there is the auditor, lawyer or consultant working rather independently in a large professional organization that provides just a loose structure for groups of autonomous professionals. Examples for these totally empowered knowledge workers who make significant independent decisions in the pursuit of the overall vision can be found in virtually all modern industries.

But the modern world is also subject to a great deal of uncertainty and risk. Therefore, a good leader has to operate in a way that allows him and his team to survive if events do not turn out as anticipated. In banking organizations, this may involve the use of sophisticated risk-management techniques that limit risks or the implementation of modern portfolio managing techniques that hedge one set of possible outcomes through countervailing measures. Proper risk management is clearly part of running a safe and sound financial institution.

Many of today's industrial and commercial leaders can be found in small innovative and entrepreneurial companies. Many of these start-up companies are not known for their management training programs or indeed for their operational excellence. While large established corporations are generally good at execution, these small entrepreneurial companies excel at innovation.

To be a leader of a modern organization, the leader must never be uncertain of his goals, but he must also be nimble and flexible enough to change. Even the old Romans knew that. *Numquam incertus — Semper apertus* was the Roman exhortation to its leaders. Never uncertain — always open!

The captain of a ship that is trying to reach a distant destination knows that he has to be willing to constantly adjust to changing circumstances. He has to continuously correct the ship's course to take account of changing wind, currents and unforeseen obstacles in order to reach the ultimate destination. His eyes firmly fixed on the horizon, the captain and the crew together aim for their ultimate objective, following the vision that guides the entire team.

True Leadership Qualities

That brings me back to my initial comments about Mr. Witteveen and the leadership he exercised at the IMF many years ago. In a way, he was anticipating the leadership principles that are now common place in modern knowledge-based corporations, where the leaders set out the broad vision but not detailed objectives. He did so because he knew that as a leader of an international organization that comprised many sovereign member states, he could not command them to do anything. Instead, he had to be a collegial leader of his board and a seeker of consensus. He knew that he could lead by enunciating a vision of what he wanted to accomplish. But he had to rely on the organization's sovereign member states to attain the vision and the goals.

In a way, that is the true measure of an inspired and inspiring leader: Having the ability to lead, so that others will follow out of their own free will.

SAGE ADVICE:
True Leaders Lead by Inspiring Others to Follow

29 Boards and Governance

A s a teenager back in Germany, I sometimes wondered what my future life would be like and how long I would live. In those days, a 60-year old man was considered quite old and I thought that it would be a considerable accomplishment to reach that ripe old age. Also, it would mean experiencing the beginning of a new Millennium in the year 2000.

As that moment was actually approaching, I was still quite healthy and certainly not yet ready to call it quits on this earth. I celebrated the Millennium with my wife Emily and several friends at the San Francisco Yacht Club. We drank champagne and watched the spectacular fireworks go off over the San Francisco skyline next to the Golden Gate Bridge. As a 16-year old, I had only hoped that I would live long enough to experience that moment, but I certainly had no idea that I would be able to enjoy it in this amazing setting.

I had just left Fair Isaac, and the question for me was what I should do next.

Becoming a Full Time Director

In my professional career I had garnered just about every possible title. I had a doctor's degree, been a Professor, a Chairman, a Chief, a Director, a President, a CEO and a Governor. In Germany, where it is customary to address a person with *all* his titles, it would have taken quite a while to greet me. Others might say that I never had a steady job.

I had greatly enjoyed my time as a board member of VISA U.S.A. and the Fair Isaac Corporation. While I was at VISA, I also served as a Trustee and a Member of the Executive Committee of the U.S. Council on International Business and eventually became the Vice Chairman of the Commission on Financial Services of the International Chamber of Commerce in Paris. The other attendees at these meetings were prominent international businessmen and as a result, the discussions were always very spirited. This most interesting experience had the side benefit of bringing me to Paris about twice a year.

In addition, I had served on more than a dozen boards running academic and not-for-profit institutions. On the civic front, I had been a Trustee of the World Affairs Council of Northern California and the Institute for International Education in San Francisco. The latter institution was nice enough to honor me with its 75th Anniversary Distinguished Service Award.

All that had been interesting and provided me with lots of stimulating contacts and friends. Why not make a career out of it?

Being on a board would give me a leadership position in the company and I could use my financial, economic and general business expertise to make these companies run better and, hopefully, more profitably. I would not be involved in running the day-to-day business, but be able to focus more on setting the strategic direction and to assist the managers with any problems that they might encounter. I loved problem solving. All that was very attractive to me.

So I set out to join a variety of different boards. Some of them were boards of public corporations, such as Bank of Marin and Sonic Automotive, which owns one of the largest car dealership groups in the country. Others were private company boards, such as Eton, which sold portable emergency radios and Cavallino, a strategic consulting and capital firm. There were advisory boards, such as Financial Technology Ventures and Main Capital

Management. I also occupied leadership positions at not-for-profit organizations, such as serving as the chairman of the board of Marin General Hospital and being on the advisory board of the Tiburon Rhomberg Center of San Francisco State University, which does research on the eco-system of the Bay. And then there was The San Francisco Yacht Club.

Sometimes, I felt a bit like Noah from the Biblical Ark. But instead of two animals from each species, I had two of every type of organization: two public and two private companies; two advisory boards and two not-for profits; but only one club — because it was twice as much work as any of the others!

From BMW to Sonic Automotive

Soon after I left the Federal Reserve Board and started working for VISA, I received a call from BMW. They wanted to know whether I might be interested in joining the newly formed BMW Advisory Board for North America. The company wanted to explore the possibility of locating a manufacturing plant in North America and needed an expert who knew about the U.S. economy, but was also fluent in German. I qualified.

There were two other U.S.-based members and the rest of the Board was composed of the top leadership of the BMW Group in Germany: Eberhard von Kuenheim, the President and CEO of BMW led the distinguished group. Helmut Panke, the Head of Strategic Planning, and Bernd Pischetsrieder, the chief of Production, also attended regularly. Both of them were to become future CEOs of the BMW Group. In addition, Wolfgang Reitzle, the head of Product Development attended frequently. Reitzle later on became President of the Ford Premier Automotive Group, which included Jaguar, Land Rover and Volvo. The matriarch of the Quandt family, Johanna Quandt, frequently showed up for our meetings as well. The Quandt family owned almost 50 percent of the BMW Group and Mrs. Quandt was purported to be the richest women in Germany. She was the sister-in-law of Harald Quandt, with whom I had taken glider plane flying lessons in Germany when I was still in high school. Given the importance of the project, the BMW Advisory Board was a distinguished group, indeed.

We would meet alternatingly in Germany and the U.S. and during board discussions everybody spoke in the language that he was most confortable with. The discussions were truly bilingual. On our trips to Germany, we would frequently visit the various BMW factories in Bavaria and I learned a lot about automobile design and production.

At first we debated the question where in the world the new plant that BMW was planning to build should be located. Other European countries as well as Latin America were seriously considered. But eventually, the importance of the American market and the need to protect the company from the large currency swings between the German Mark and the U.S. Dollar won the argument in favor of the United States.

Next came the question where in the United States the plant should be situated. After an initial screening of dozens of potential locations, three favorites emerged: near Boston in Massachusetts, Omaha in Nebraska and Spartanburg in South Carolina. All had excellent airports as well as railroad spurs adjacent to the potential factory sites. This was an absolute requirement for any large-scale manufacturing facility that also had to import heavy components, such as automobile engines, from Germany. Herr von Kuenheim, as everybody reverentially called him, liked the Boston location very much. For him, Boston was the most cultured American city and he enjoyed its almost European ambiance. It was also the location closest to Germany and had direct Lufthansa flight connections. The rest of us pointed out that Massachusetts had not only very high labor costs, but was also highly unionized. Nebraska and South Carolina competed fiercely for the plant by each offering very attractive tax benefits. In the end, the existence of many BMW suppliers near Spartanburg in South Carolina and the relatively short and convenient rail connection to the harbor of Charleston carried the day.

We all flew to Spartanburg, donned hard hats and helped to shovel the first blades of earth for the new plant. Not much later, the gleaming new plant was finished with its highly robotized, but flexible production lines. BMW donated several brand new sedans to the South Carolina State Highway Patrol, and they proudly escorted us in a huge car parade to the plant opening on November 15, 1994.

Mission accomplished!

Much to my own chagrin, now that the gleaming new production facilities of BMW in the U.S. were operational, they determined that there was no further need for a U.S. Advisory Board. They knew how to run the factory by themselves. In short order, the U.S. board was unceremoniously abolished. For me, it had been a tremendous opportunity to learn about the car business.

A few years later, a good friend and neighbor of mine, Tom Price, invited me to join the board of First American Automotive, a new car dealership group that he had assembled in California. My BMW experience stood me in good stead at this new enterprise, which was scheduled to go public at the dawn of the new Millennium.

As luck would have it, the so-called dot-com stock market crash occurred just when FAA wanted to go public. The crash effectively closed the market to all new companies and Tom Price had to look for an alternative. He found that in a merger with Sonic Automotive, a car dealership group headquartered in Charlotte, NC that had gone public just a few years earlier.

Sonic Automotive had been founded by Bruton Smith, who was also the Chairman and CEO of Speedway Motorsports, the famed operator of NASCAR car racing tracks. An indefatigable entrepreneur, Bruton Smith is not only a billionaire, but also the only octogenarian who is chairman and CEO of not one, but two companies listed on the New York Stock Exchange.

As part of the acquisition of First American by Sonic, Tom Price and I were invited to join the board of directors of Sonic. That board already included Bill Benton, the former Global Vice President of Marketing for Ford and Bill Belk, scion of the East

Coast department store chain that carries the family name. Later on, Bob Rewey, the former President of Lincoln Mercury, joined the board along with Vic Doolan, the former President of BMW of North America and Volvo of North America. Tom Capo, a former Treasurer of Daimler Chrysler also served on the board for several years. All together, it was a quite distinguished board that brimmed with automotive expertise. In that illustrious company, I was grateful for the know-how I had acquired as a result of my BMW experience.

While Sonic thrived, things did not always go smoothly. The company had a long string of uninterrupted profits, when the devastating recession of 2008 hit. Both General Motors and Chrysler spiraled into bankruptcy and had to be rescued by the government. Fortunately, Sonic's more than 100 dealerships were focused on luxury and import brands, which survived the economic downturn better than the domestic car companies. We had the most BMW dealerships of any franchise dealer group and were also well represented with Mercedes dealerships and other popular brands, like Honda and Toyota.

Nevertheless, when a corporate bond issue of over $100 million was due for refinancing in May of 2009 and the financial markets were essentially closed, things got very tough indeed. Where to get the money? As chairman of the Audit Committee, I had a seat at the center of the storm. Banks were not willing to lend us any new money to help us manage through the liquidity crisis and our bonds were selling in the public market for 35 cents on the dollar. The value of the company's stock on the New York Stock Exchange plunged to less than one dollar. Times were tough.

But David Cosper, our steadfast CFO, and the rest of the management team pulled the company through the liquidity crisis. Eventually, as the financial storms passed, the company's stock recovered as well. Anybody who bought the stock at the depth of the crisis multiplied his money by a factor of twenty-five as the company's stock climbed from $1.00 to over $25.00 over the next few years! Sonic was back like a Phoenix out of the ashes!

For me it was a lesson to always have plenty of liquidity at hand and to never to stretch a company's balance sheet so much that the company cannot weather any external misfortunes that it might have to confront.

Now Sonic is prospering again and is transforming the entire car retail industry though path-breaking innovations that will eventually change the entire car-buying experience.

SAGE ADVICE:
Always Have Plenty of Liquidity

Two Different Bank Boards

At one point, I was asked to join the board of a small local bank, Tamalpais Bank. The bank was named after the mountain dominating Marin County. At my first board meeting, a very senior officer reviewed many of the crucial ratios that need to be carefully controlled if a bank wants to prosper and be safe and sound. I noticed that one of the critical financial ratios was substantially above the limit established by the board as bank policy. When I asked him what he planned to do to rectify the situation, his answer was that the FDIC, one of the bank's supervisory agencies, did not measure the ratio properly. But even if one were to grant his point, the ratio was still considerably above the limit established by the board. He thought that there was nothing to worry about and that this would increase the lending capacity and the profitability of the bank.

It goes without saying that any management should follow the direction set by the board and stick to the policies and rules established. As a former bank regulator myself, I was dismayed. I had witnessed first hand that such disregard for control procedures often bodes ill for the future of an institution as management puts short-term performance over long-run stability. Not wanting to be associated with such sloppy management, I decided that it was best not to get further involved with the institution and resigned from the board right after that first meeting.

Now it was the turn of the bank's senior management to be upset. They thought that if I were to announce my resignation, the bank's reputation would suffer and the stock price might plunge. I told them that I would resign very quietly. We drafted a press release that stated that I had found the workload much more demanding than anticipated and that I resigned mainly for that reason. That was certainly true, as changing the bank's lending culture would have required a superhuman and time-consuming effort.

Soon after leaving the board of Tamalpais Bank, I was invited to join the board of directors of the Bank of Marin, another local bank. Many of the original founders of the bank were still on the board and the management ran it in a very prudent fashion under the boards active guidance and supervision.

A few years later, the banking crisis of 2008 resulted in widespread credit difficulties and concomitant failures of many American banks. Tamalpais Bank was ill prepared for that financial turbulence because it had made too many bad loans. The FDIC intervened and the bank was taken over by another, much larger and well-capitalized bank. I was glad that I got off that board in the nick of time.

In contrast, Bank of Marin barely suffered any credit losses during the recession because all loans were underwritten in a very conservative fashion. Like a resilient ship in a stormy sea, the bank continued to thrive in spite of the financial turmoil surrounding it. It was all due to the prudent policies followed by the bank's board and management.

SAGE ADVICE:
Sometimes It Is Necessary to Act As Quickly as Possible

Marin General Hospital — Beware of Good Intentions

At the beginning of the Millennium, I received a phone call from Marin General Hospital inquiring whether I would be willing to serve as the chairman of their new capital campaign. The hospital badly needed expensive new capital equipment, including an MRI machine, and wanted to start a $5 million capital campaign.

My wife Emily had served on the hospital's Volunteer Board and worked there also part-time. I also knew many of the doctors at the hospital. Of course, I was very interested in having a fine hospital in our neighborhood as well. Given that we lived in an earthquake-prone region, you never knew whether you would be able to reach the world-class medical facilities in San Francisco in case that the Golden Gate Bridge was closed or had collapsed.

When the hospital asked whether I was willing to head up their capital campaign, I gladly accepted. That honorary position also gave me an ex-officio seat on the Marin General Hospital Board of Directors. In the end, our capital campaign raised some $6.5 million — a full 30 percent more than the $5 million target. We felt that we had done a good job. Soon thereafter, I was asked to join the Board of Directors as a regular Board member — an invitation that I was happy to accept.

The hospital had a somewhat unusual organizational structure, as the building itself was owned by a public entity: the Marin Healthcare District. In turn, the Healthcare District had leased the building to the not-for-profit Sutter Health system at a time when the freestanding Marin General Hospital ran into severe financial difficulties in the mid-1980s. It was clear that a freestanding hospital would have a hard time making ends meet, and the hospital had accumulated a significant amount of debt. Thus, the association with Sutter Health was a way to keep the hospital alive.

Sutter turned the financial situation of the hospital around and paid off the MGH debt, which had been accumulated in the earlier years. All the two-dozen hospitals within the Sutter Health system functioned under a common corporate umbrella, which provided for central cash management and a consolidated capital budget.

Sutter, in turn, made the appropriate investment decisions for the entire system, but it gave considerable latitude to each hospital and its Board of Directors in running the day-to-day affairs of each hospital.

There was always a small vocal minority among Marin residents that wanted to exercise public control over the hospital and that had never agreed with the original 1985 lease arrangement. They wanted a government-controlled hospital and did not want "their" hospital to be run by a private not-for-profit organization. At first, they fought lengthy court battles to break the lease, but they were unsuccessful in the courts. However, their constant agitation resulted in continuing acrimony about the way the hospital was run.

After a devastating earthquake in Los Angeles, the State of California had passed a law that required all hospitals to be retrofitted for enhanced earthquake safety by 2013 at the latest. The Marin General lease to Sutter expired only two years later in 2015. Sutter offered to build an entirely new $400 million hospital building in accordance with the law. There was to be no cost to the local community and the taxpayers, but Sutter wanted a new long-term lease so that the costs of the building could be amortized over a reasonable period of time. But the local agitators were not swayed by that offer. Instead, they said: Build us a new building by 2013 as the law requires and then get out when the lease expires in 2015. Clearly, it was unacceptable for Sutter to build a new hospital and then to vacate it only two years later.

The opponents of Sutter continued to agitate for an early termination of the lease and eventually Sutter acquiesced. Lengthy negotiations resulted in a voluminous early-termination agreement of the lease and Sutter vacated the premises in 2010 — the very same year that I happened to serve as Chairman of the MGH Board.

With Sutter on the way out, and having turned down the Sutter offer to build a brand-new hospital, the Healthcare District now had the obligation to build a new hospital to meet the state's earthquake standards. But where should they get the money?

When the Healthcare District realized that Sutter had swept some $120 million in funds into the central treasury in full compliance with the terms of the lease, the District decided to sue for the return of these funds. The Healthcare District also argued that I, as Chairman of the Board, had allowed the funds to be moved to Sutter. They further claimed that I was personally responsible for this transfer of funds, which had taken place in strict compliance with the lease agreement and with full approval of the entire board. So, the Healthcare District Board sued me personally for $120 million. Never mind that virtually all the money had been transferred prior to me being chairman.

I was flattered that they thought that I had enough money to personally pay the $120 million. Of course, Sutter had indemnified the entire Board and we had a substantial insurance policy covering any potential liability of the directors as well. Nevertheless, it was not an altogether comfortable position to be in.

In addition, there were various items in the lease-termination agreements that were disputed, and so the Healthcare District decided to sue on those issues as well. For instance, the termination agreement provided that Sutter should pay for a new computer system for the hospital — but who should pay for training the nurses and the staff on the new system? Should it be the District who received this new equipment for free or Sutter, which had agreed to pay for the new computers? There were also questions regarding who was responsible for the accumulated nurses' pensions and other issues.

The Healthcare District sued Sutter Health in the Superior Court of Marin County, as they wanted a local jury to adjudicate their case — in spite of the fact that the lease provided for arbitration in case of any disputes. Immediately, the Superior Court judge threw out the suit and told the parties to resolve their issues in arbitration as agreed upon.

The first thing the arbitrator did was to rule that I had always acted in good faith and in accordance with California law. Consequently, there was no triable issue of fact against me. She dismissed the case against me before the trial even started and I felt vindicated.

The last thing the arbitrator did at the end of the lengthy proceedings was to declare me as a "prevailing party." She ruled that the Healthcare District should reimburse me for the $800,000 in lawyer's expenses that I had incurred and that Sutter had advanced on my behalf. Now I felt doubly vindicated!

The arbitrator also ruled that Sutter had been correct and entitled to sweep the $120 million in net income into the central Sutter Treasury in accordance with the terms of the lease. As far as all the contested issues were concerned, she ruled that of the total of $224 million claimed by the Healthcare District, Sutter owed a paltry $21.6 million to the District — less than 10 cents on the dollar!

But always talented in the public affairs arena, the District trumpeted this as a major victory as they got $21.6 million that they did not have before. Never mind the hundreds of millions in false claims that were denied to them. Both Sutter and I felt vindicated in our stewardship of the hospital.

When the Healthcare District regained control of the hospital, they decided to lease the building again to a new not-for-profit board that they themselves appointed — in essence admitting to the fact that the publicly elected Healthcare District Board was incapable of running the hospital itself.

SAGE ADVICE:
No Good Deed Goes Unpunished

Why Clubs Are Different

Clubs constitute a most important institution in any society because they provide for the voluntary association of like-minded individuals. Their governance structure is by necessity different from that of a regular corporation. In a sense, clubs are upside-down organizations where the ultimate power resides in the membership, which means all the members of the club. I was privileged to serve on the Board of Directors and later as a flag officer of the venerable San Francisco Yacht Club. As I rose to the pinnacle of the club leadership and became a "*Commodore*," there were innumerable occasions when other club members sidled up to me at the bar and started out with: "As a Member of this Club, I find that...!" And then followed a complaint that the soup was not hot enough, the dues were too high, the children in the clubhouse were too noisy or something else that irked the member at that moment. Obviously, as a member of the club, the person felt that this complaint should be addressed immediately to his or her full satisfaction.

In almost every club there are also various factions that are interested in different aspects of the association. In a sense, most clubs provide a big umbrella for several different interest groups. For instance, in virtually every yacht club there is a group that is interested in racing, while some are more fascinated by cruising. Other members, typically parents with children, are engrossed in youth activities and training, while many of the older folks are more interested in having good dining facilities available. And then, there is always the bar crowd that enjoys discussing and second-guessing every decision taken by the board. That group is affectionately referred to as the *Barnacles*.

When I became the Commodore of the San Francisco Yacht Club, I thought that all these diverse interests should be represented on the board and so I worked hard to persuade the nominating committee to have members from all these constituencies represented on the board. As it turned out, each board member faithfully represented the views of his or her constituency — but what was best for the Club as a whole was sometimes neglected. The meetings lasted sometimes until midnight. Even the smallest difference of opinion could lead to endless debates and as one prescient sage once told me: "The arguments were so vicious because so little was at stake!"

Our wise and experienced General Manager, Steve DePetro, set me straight: appoint members with good general judgment to the board. Then, assign them to the various committees to represent the board's view and have them bring back the Committee member's viewpoint to the board for a general discussion. He was right. That model leads to a much more harmonious and consistent decision making process that takes into account the views of all members and does not result in the confrontational airing of particularistic viewpoints.

SAGE ADVICE:
Have Each Board Member Represent the Interests Of the Entire Organization and Not Just the Views of One Constituency

Board Competence and Diversity

The principle that all board members should have a broad-based institutional knowledge and expertise in the business of the organization applies to all types of organizations.

Several years ago, considerable controversy surrounded the board of directors of the Hewlett Packard Corporation. Some of the long-standing board members were accustomed to a competency-based board. The original board was largely composed of friends and colleagues of the founders Bill Hewlett and David Packard. Like them, many of the board members were engineers. Together with a few venture capitalists, like Tom Perkins, they liked to discuss the strategic direction of the company, what new promising products might be produced and what innovative technologies the company might adopt.

Over the ensuing years, several outside directors were brought in that brought more diverse backgrounds to the table. Board discussions changed from new innovations and products to focusing on governance issues and on serving various constituencies. The new board members insisted on dotting all the "i's" and crossing the "t's." All that is well chronicled in several books and a multitude of magazine articles.

From my experience, it is absolutely necessary for board members to have considerable expertise in the relevant industry. Just being an intelligent person does not constitute a sufficient qualification for board membership. Actually, it is counterproductive for a person to be on the board of a company in an industry where he or she does not have any domain expertise. Sooner or later, there will be a need to participate in a strategic decision for the company and if the person does not understand what is involved, either the company is ill-served or the board member will find himself out of place — or both. Just being of a different gender, ethnicity or residing in a certain geographic location does not mean that one can contribute positively to a substantive discussion.

As John McCoy, who used to serve as the CEO of one of the nations largest banks, aptly put it: "At the end of the day, a bank board member still has to be able to read a balance sheet."

That does not mean that the nominating committee should not strive to have a broad representation of different perspectives on the board, but all board members should have a considerable amount of subject expertise that will positively contribute to the success of the corporation. The shareholders, employees and customers of the company all depend on good and competent judgment being exercised in the boardroom.

SAGE ADVICE:
A Highly Competent Board is the Best Board

Board Size and Effectiveness

When I was in charge of the Financial Studies Division at the International Monetary Fund, one of my favorite assignments was to run the IMF's seminar series. I had a free hand to invite whomever I wanted to come to the IMF and to give an economics lecture to the staff. The barometer of success was drawing a large audience and instigating a spirited discussion afterwards. I asked many eminent economists and Nobel Prize winners to come to Washington and to speak. In some ways, the IMF was like a large university with many outstanding economists on its own staff. As a consequence, virtually all the prominent speakers that I invited accepted the invitation.

A side benefit was that prior to the lecture, I was privileged to host a luncheon for our distinguished guest. I had the freedom to invite whomever I wanted to the lunch. In most cases, the Managing Director of the IMF attended these luncheons personally and a spirited discussion on whatever ailed the world economy at that time ensued.

These luncheons typically ranged from five to twelve guests and I quickly noticed that if there were fewer than seven people in attendance, there was just one discussion around the table. As soon as there were more than seven, the discussion would break into two or even three small groups with each conversation quickly focusing on a different topic. Seven seemed to be the magic number where the break from one to several conversations occurred.

I found that also to be true later in life as I sat around many board tables. If you have seven or less participants, there will be one focused discussion. If there are more than seven board members, the discussion will swing from one topic to the next without all persons who want to speak on the issue being able to weigh in.

The difference between small and large boards is also very much apparent at the Federal Reserve. When the seven-member Board of Governors meets, there is typically one focused discussion among the board members around the table. The Chairman usually does not play a significant role in structuring the discussion and the informal dialogue flows freely among the seven Board members.

In contrast, at the Federal Open Market Committee, where the twelve Federal Reserve Bank Presidents join the seven Governors, the group around the table swells to some nineteen persons. With many people simultaneously trying to speak, the Secretary of the Board will keep a list of the people who raise their hand, indicating that they want to have the floor. Then, the Chairperson will call on the next person on the Secretary's list and give permission to speak. I observed that the FOMC deliberations were much more formalistic and structured than the more informal and spontaneous deliberations by the smaller Board of Governors. In my days at the Fed, the "Rule of Seven" was generally proven to be accurate.

At the other extreme, I experienced a small, private corporation, Eton. I have been a member of the Eton Board for more than a quarter of a century. The company produces mainly specialty radios and in addition to Esmail Hozour, the President and CEO of the company, there are just three other members of the Board of Directors. The CEO brings virtually all issues of importance to his board and we discuss them freely and in an unstructured way. Everybody contributes his ideas and nobody has to wait to be given permission to speak. The discussion moves rapidly and fluidly from topic to topic, helping the CEO solve the issues on which he wants input. The tiny four-member Eton Board is most efficient in addressing all relevant issues and it is very enjoyable as well.

SAGE ADVICE:
If You Want an Effective and Engaged Board: Keep it Small

Private and Public Governance

Corporations are complex organizations that are essential to the functioning of a modern society. They allow the citizenry to organize themselves for various special purposes, be they for profit or not-for-profit. Shareholders, owners or members of these organizations typically elect boards of directors to govern these organizations.

What distinguishes these private organizations from government is that all persons living in a certain area or jurisdiction are automatically subject to the governmental edicts. Instead, in a private corporation, it is up to the individual to join up voluntarily to be a member of the group.

Governments have the absolute power to establish laws and to enforce them. They also have the authority to tax and throw those unwilling or unable to pay the tax into jail. The only alternative for a citizen to paying the taxes imposed is to renounce his or her citizenship and to move abroad.

In contrast, private corporations have only limited power over their shareholders or members, who can always resign from the organization by simply selling their shares or dropping their membership. Private organizations have to rely upon the willingness of the shareholders or members to invest in the corporation or to voluntarily pay their dues. Furthermore, their customers can always walk away. Corporations cannot coerce any person and throw anybody in jail — as the government can.

For me, having spent my early childhood under a dictatorship, the distinction between public coercion and a private voluntary association is most important. From that experience, I have concluded that whatever can be done by the private sectors, should be done by the private sector and not by the government.

SAGE ADVICE:
Whatever Can Be Done by the Private Sector
Should Be Done in the Private Sector

PART VI

Reflections on Life

What were the stations of a full life well lived?

I spent my childhood in wartime Germany, where bombs rained down almost any day and where people were hiding in cellars and caves.

Then, I came to America to attend college, but stayed for a lifetime.

Next, I taught at a prestigious university and then started a fulfilling career spanning business and government.

Eventually, there were positions of leadership in government and at private corporations.

Along the way, I learned many important lessons and there was much to be cherished.

And at the end, it is time to say thanks to a welcoming country and many good friends and family!

30 Living the American Dream

The Mountain of Life

I have often thought about the journey of life as similar to climbing a mountain. A small child will play in the soft and gentle meadows, pick flowers and discover the little animals that live there as well. Older children will find themselves in a well-ordered school environment, where they learn basic skills that they can use later on. But everything is carefully controlled under the supervision of adult teachers and is similar to life in a corral. Every now and then, the young children are permitted to explore the neighborhood and they come to learn that there is a much larger world out there. At times, they romp around freely and explore increasingly steep and rising hills. Sometimes, they will stray from the safe path and get into trouble. Hopefully, this will become a learning experience. They will also acquire new tools and skills that will come in handy later on.

Then, the more serious part of the journey begins. From one job experience to another, the climb becomes ever more challenging and steep. Some people will make the ascent in a group or as part of a team, where one carries the food and others transport the equipment. In such teams, a few may set out as scouts and others will stay behind as support troops. A few will attempt the climb by themselves as solo practitioners that are convinced that they can achieve all that they aspire to alone.

Next comes the steepest and most dangerous part of the ascent. Some people decide that they have accomplished enough and slow down. They have attained what they want to accomplish. Others stumble or get hurt and cannot proceed. They are out of breath or have lost their will to succeed. Friends as well as competitors fall behind.

Eventually, the climber arrives on the mountain peak and everyone else is situated below him or her. Nobody is speaking to him any longer because he is up there alone on the summit and the others are below. It is lonely up there at the top. Most people do not get to spend much time up there, at the pinnacle of success.

Then comes the descent, which is perhaps the most dangerous part of the journey. It is easy to stumble and to fall down the mountain.

Only a few people will try to scale another peak. Those who make it to the top twice are very rare individuals indeed.

Finally, at the end of the journey, one arrives back in the gentle meadows where a new generation of little children is at play. Some older people will enjoy taking care of the children in the fields and teach them everything they know. Others will form groups of like-minded friends and enjoy talking with each other about what it was like up there on the mountain. Still others will sit around in the meadow and write stories about their life and hope that someone will read them.

Thus is life.

The Good...

If you would tell me that I would have to do it all over again, I would gladly do it. I enjoyed all the jobs that I ever had and would be pleased to do them again. Teaching at UCLA was a wonderful and enriching experience and I learned much from my colleagues and students alike. The time at the University of Hawaii was mostly fun in the sun. The work at the International Monetary Fund broadened my horizons and I met some of the brightest and most successful leaders in the entire world. My position at Bank of

America was challenging and every day brought new questions to solve. On the Federal Reserve Board, I was able to influence the economic future of the entire nation and helped to shape the future of the American banking system. VISA was a wild and exciting ride and Fair Isaac offered many intellectual and analytical challenges that affected the financial life of almost every American. And finally, on the various boards, I could apply a lifetime of learning to the issues faced by the various companies and organizations.

...and the Bad

Yes, there were many negatives as well. I gave a talk to my colleagues soon after I arrived at Bank of America. The purpose of the talk was to introduce myself. I started out by saying that I was born in war-time Germany — and soon thereafter Germany lost the war; I attended Parsons College — and the college lost its accreditation and went out of business; I came to the University of California at Berkeley — and the student riots broke out; I moved to UCLA — and the city and the campus were engulfed in race turmoil; I joined the International Monetary Fund — and the entire international monetary system collapsed. I finished my self-introduction by wistfully saying: "And now I am at Bank of America!" Everybody laughed. But they did not laugh for long, as only a few years later Bank of America itself almost failed.

Learning From Your Experiences

Everything in life depends on how you look at it. For every mountain, there is a valley. But if I look more closely at the successes and mishaps that I experienced in my lifetime, it is apparent that I was lucky enough to always dance through the raindrops.

During World War II, millions of people on all sides of the conflict suffered severe losses, lost their limbs or even paid with their life. I survived securely in my family's cellar and the cave until the Americans came and liberated us. Studying at Parsons College allowed me to attain a foothold on the educational ladder in the

United States. I was barely fluent in English and if I had gone to an elite college, I might never have made it and returned disappointed to Germany. Experiencing the riots in Berkeley and Los Angeles allowed me to gain perspectives and insights that I would have never had gotten otherwise. These experiences helped to form my world-view that the individual is what matters most and that groupthink can often lead to disaster.

The collapse of the Bretton Woods international monetary order allowed me to witness the development of a more flexible, albeit still imperfect, global monetary system. And the various banking crises that I experienced both at Bank of America and at the Federal Reserve helped me to understand what it takes to build and construct a safe and sound banking system. And then, there was VISA and its chaordic organization. I learned what corporate culture is all about and how important it is inculcate an organization with the right values.

Those were all lessons for life.

What if I Had Not Come to America?

This brings me to maybe the most important question of all: what if I had not left Germany and become an American?

If there had been no World War II, I would probably have stayed in Germany and lived an orderly, neat and tidy life. But if the Nazis had won the war, I would have undoubtedly been told to join the Hitler Youth and then been drafted into the German army. Most likely, I would have been sent to occupy another country, where I would have been despised and loathed. Clearly, it would have been impossible for Germany to occupy almost all of Europe in perpetuity. Eventually, the suppressed people would have rebelled and the revenge would have been brutal. There is a good chance that it all would have ended in a huge catastrophe for many others and me.

If I had stayed in Germany instead of coming to America, I probably would have become an economic journalist as I intended to be when I graduated from high school. I would have made a modest living and spent most of my career at one newspaper, as is customary in Germany. It would have been a contented life and an unspectacular career recording and reporting what others had done.

Educational and Professional Opportunities

After Germany lost the war, I saw the Americans as the victors — and everyone likes a winner. Even small children do so. So I set out to come to America as a young adult. At first, I only wanted to follow my girlfriend and to see the country for one year, to see what the nation and its people were like. But when I saw the additional educational opportunities in front of me, I decided to stay longer. I wanted to obtain the additional learning and earn the advanced degrees.

After completing my education, the challenging and rewarding professional opportunities enticed me to stay in America. To become a professor at the age of twenty-five would have been impossible in Germany. Subsequently, I moved from one opportunity to another as they presented themselves. Each step up the ladder called for some courage and risk taking. It represented another leap into the unknown. But with greater achievements also came greater rewards — both financially and professionally.

Clearly, the financial rewards were not the only incentive that drove my decisions. Several times during my career I accepted a lower compensation to take on a more challenging and intellectually rewarding position. But over the long run, that additional experience also opened up new gates to greater opportunities in the future.

Throughout life, I tried to keep on teaching and learning. Some of these learning opportunities included formal courses offered by employers or educational institutions. Other learning consisted of reading and studying at home. I would also count teaching and lecturing among the learning experiences because not only did I have to prepare for these talks by studying new material, but the audiences with their challenging questions and comments would in turn educate me about alternative viewpoints and interpretations that I had not thought of before. The best way to learn is to teach!

Payback Time

I was fortunate to be able to enjoy a well-rewarded and satisfying professional career in America. I believe that it is entirely appropriate to also give back to the community and to society at large. I am not speaking only about the taxes that I paid more or less willingly, but more importantly about the time I spent on many boards of not-for-profit and educational institutions. Serving on boards of institutions such as the World Affairs Council and the Institute of International Education was truly gratifying. I also found serving as the Chair of the Board of Directors of Marin General Hospital very rewarding — in spite of the turbulent times that the hospital went through during my years on the board. Having the owner of the hospital building sue me afterwards for many millions of dollars did not make the actual experience any less satisfying. When the judge threw out the entire suit against me and declared me as the prevailing party, this only reinforced my view in the ultimate justice of the American system.

Living the American Dream

I was able to live the American Dream throughout my life. Over the years, our family owned many comfortable houses in spectacular settings: on top of the Brentwood Hills overlooking the entire Los Angeles Basin; on the slopes of Koko Head in Hawaii with a spectacular view of Diamond Head; in the leafy suburbs of Washington DC; and on the slopes of Mount Tiburon with a view of the Golden Gate and the San Francisco Bay. Now I am looking over the Belvedere Lagoon at the ever-changing panorama of Mount Tamalpais in marvelous Marin County. What could be better?

A Supporting Family

My mother always protected and nourished me when I was a small child. Unfortunately, she passed away all too early. After that, my grandmother Oma Lisa and my two aunts Mia and Li took my mother's place. To them I am forever grateful.

After I came to America, I made many friends that helped me along the way. They are too numerous to mention.

Among all of them, my faithful companion and wife Emily stands out. She and I have been married for well over 40 years and it is still a joy to be with her. She willingly and, I hope, happily played a supporting role, while she could have had a career of her own. Together, we moved about a dozen times from one end of the country to the other. We raised our two delightful and successful children, Kimberly and Christopher. They now have children of

The view from our house in Belvedere

their own and lead fulfilling professional lives. And so humanity moves on.

Thanks to America

We all choose our own path in life. Fortunately, a friendly and welcoming country provided me with much support and opportunity to thrive. This made it a lot easier to accomplish the things that I set out to achieve. There were no obstacles in my way. Instead, there were many individuals that reached out with a helping hand, encouragement and good advice.

For me, America is truly the land of unlimited opportunities! And for that I am very grateful.

CONCLUSION:
America is Still the Land of Unlimited Opportunities

About the Author

Robert Heller was born in Cologne, Germany shortly after the beginning of World War II. After an early education in Germany, he came to America in 1960 to study at the now defunct Parsons College in Iowa, the University of Minnesota and the University of California at Berkeley. He earned his Ph.D. degree in economics at Berkeley in 1965.

In the same year, he began his teaching career at UCLA and subsequently served as chairman of the Economics Department of the University of Hawaii.

In 1974, he became the Chief of the Financial Studies Division of the International Monetary Fund in Washington DC. Four years later, he joined Bank of America in San Francisco as a Senior Vice President and Director of International Economic Research.

President Reagan appointed him in 1986 as a Governor of the Federal Reserve Board in Washington DC. He served as the Administrative Governor and as Chairman of the Committee for Bank Supervision and Regulation.

He returned to the private sector in 1989, first as Executive Vice President at VISA International and then as President and CEO of VISA U.S.A. Afterwards, he was a Director and Executive Vice President of the Fair Isaac Corporation.

He has served as a director of numerous public and private corporations, not-for-profit associations, educational organizations and international institutions.

A prolific writer, he is the author of four books that have been translated into several languages and hundreds of articles in the popular and scientific press. He is a frequent guest on CNBC and has appeared on all major television networks.

He and his family live in the San Francisco Bay area.

CPSIA information can be obtained
at www.ICGtesting.com
Printed in the USA
FSOW03n0636060915
10604FS